Over 350 Lean and Luscious Recipes

From

THE COOKING
CARDIOLOGIST

Recipes To Help Lower Your Cholesterol,
Reduce Risk of Heart Disease, Control Weight,
Increase Vitality and Longevity

For information contact: Advanced Research Press, Inc.,
150 Motor Pkwy., Suite 210, Hauppauge, New York 11788.

SECOND EDITION

Library of Congress Catalog-in-Publication Data

Richard E. Collins

The Cooking Cardiologist

1. Cooking   2. Health   3. Cardiology

1. Title

ISBN 1-889462-05-5

Printed in the United States of America

Published by: **Advanced Research Press**

Publisher/President: Steve Blechman

Managing Director (Books): Roy A. Ulin

Art Director: Rob Wilner (DotCom)

Cover Design: Sam Powell

Editor: Fran Luxa

Copy Editor: Carol Goldberg

Graphics: Les Hays Studio

Photographer: Pat Drickey

Food Stylist: Cari Rennie

Nutrition Consultant: Shelly Oestmann, R.D.

Printed by: R.R. Donnelley & Sons

DEDICATION

To my wife Donna and my three daughters, Heather, Kelly and Robyn, who have put up with my cooking. They have tasted many a recipe and rejected a few. I appreciate their tolerance as I messed up the kitchen. I tried to clean up my own mess, realizing that no man has ever been shot while doing the dishes! And to my dog, Ozzie, who has never rejected any of my cooking.

Thanks to Fran Luxa, who helped with The Cooking Cardiologist cookbook. With Fran's encouragement and inspiration this book has actually come into existence.

ACKNOWLEDGMENTS

There are many people I would like to thank: Shelly Oestmann, Cardiac Nutritionist, Alegent Health, Omaha, NE, all of my family, patients, friends, colleagues, Dr. Dean Ornish, Jean-Marc Fullsack, Les Hays Studio, Designers, Omaha, NE, Pat Drickey, Photographer, Omaha, NE, Cari Rennie, Food Stylist, Omaha, NE and special manufacturing representatives.

ABOUT THE AUTHOR

Richard E. Collins, M.D., was instrumental in the formation of the Alegent Health Heart Institute in Omaha, Nebraska, and served as its medical director from 1993 to 1997. He is currently director of the Alegent Heart Disease Reversal and Wellness Program and a leading researcher involved in reversal of heart disease through changes in lifestyle and diet. He has worked extensively with world-renowned experts in this field, including Dr. Dean Ornish.

A native of Nebraska and a graduate of the University of Nebraska College of Medicine, Dr. Collins completed his Internship at Immanuel Medical Center in Omaha. He also holds a Master of Science degree in Biomedical Engineering from Drexel University in Philadelphia. In the Navy, Dr. Collins served as physician to the United States Congress. He completed Internal Medicine and a Cardiology Fellowship at the Mayo Clinic in Rochester, Minnesota.

Dr. Collins is a Fellow of the American College of Chest Physicians and the American College of Cardiology. He maintains memberships in leading professional organizations including the Nebraska affiliate of the American Heart Association, where he has served as president; the American Medical Association; and the National Association of Physician Broadcasters. He also serves on the speaker's bureaus of several major pharmaceutical companies.

While Dr. Collins commitment to lifestyle modification as a means of reversing and/or preventing heart disease is very well known, his creativity in the kitchen is legendary. He has devoted countless hours to the development of culinary delights using only ingredients known to promote good health. His delicious, heart-healthy recipes have established him as a popular chef at health fairs, cooking demonstrations and conventions coast to coast, as well as a frequent guest on radio and television shows.

With an outgoing personality and an infectious enthusiasm for lifestyle modification, it's no surprise the author's own philosophy is to "look on the light side' of life. As such, he has conducted many programs on humor and its positive role in heart health.

Dr. Collins is active in the Omaha community where he resides with his wife and three daughters.

TABLE OF CONTENTS

RECIPE ICONS

 Prevention Diet

 Low-Fat Vegetarian Diet (Ornish Diet)

 Totally Vegetarian (Vegan)

IMPORTANT

This cookbook is not a substitute for nutritional counseling or physician advice. Nor is it a promotion for any product. Please consult your physician in regard to recommendations before beginning any lifestyle program.

Dr. Richard Collins is a cardiologist for the next millennium.

I first met Dr. Collins in 1993. At that time, he was the Chief of Cardiology at Immanuel Hospital in Omaha (now Alegent Health Heart Institute), the first hospital site for the Ornish program. To say he is extraordinary would be insufficient; unique may be more accurate, for he embodies the best of state-of-the-art high-tech interventional cardiology as well as the ancient art of cooking. He is as at home in a kitchen as in a cardiac catheterization laboratory.

For Dr. Collins, both cooking and angioplasty are powerful tools for service and healing. Yet they are also quite different. During angioplasty, the patient is a passive recipient of care. Balloons are inflated inside coronary arteries, wire mesh stents are inserted, and the patient just lies there. In this book, Dr. Collins empowers you with information that may enable you to save your life or the life of someone you love.

It may be difficult to believe that a spatula may be as powerful a tool for healing as a stent, but the scientific data shows that it often can be. Since 1977, my colleagues and I have conducted a series of scientific studies demonstrating that the progression of even severe coronary heart disease often can begin to reverse when people make comprehensive changes in diet and lifestyle. We have published our findings in the most well-respected peer reviewed journals, including the *Journal of the American Medical Association*, *The Lancet*, the *American Journal of Cardiology*, *The New England Journal of Medicine, Circulation*, and others.

While diet is important, the other parts of the program include moderate exercise, stress management techniques (stretching, breathing, meditation, and relaxation techniques), group support, and stopping smoking. All of these interact.

In our research, we found that within a few weeks after making comprehensive lifestyle changes, the patients in our research reported a 91 percent average reduction in the frequency of angina. Most of the patients became essentially pain-free, including those who had been unable to work or engage in daily activities due to severe chest pain. Within a month, we measured increased blood flow to the heart and improvements in the heart's ability to pump. Within a year, even severely blocked coronary arteries began to improve in 82% of the patients.

When I began the Lifestyle Heart Trial, I believed that the younger patients with milder disease would be more likely to show regression, but I was wrong. Instead, the primary determinant of change in their coronary artery disease was neither age nor disease severity but adherence to the recommended changes in diet and lifestyle. No matter how old they were, on average, the more people changed, the better they became. Indeed, the oldest patient in our study showed more reversal than anyone. This is a very hopeful message, since the risks of bypass surgery and angioplasty increase with age, but the benefits of comprehensive lifestyle changes may occur at any age.

With support from the National Heart, Lung, and Blood Institute of the National Institutes of Health, my colleagues and I extended our study from one year to five years. We found that most of the study participants were able to maintain comprehensive lifestyle changes for five years. On average, they demonstrated even more reversal of heart disease after five years than after one year. In contrast, the patients in the comparison group who made only the moderate lifestyle changes recommended by most physicians (i.e., a 30% fat diet) worsened after one year and their coronary arteries became even more clogged after five years. These findings add important scientific evidence and credibility to our program. Also, we found that the incidence of cardiac events (e.g., heart attacks, strokes, bypass surgery, and angioplasty) was 2.5 times lower in the group that made comprehensive lifestyle changes after five years.

The next question was: how practical is this lifestyle program?

Beginning in 1993, my colleagues and I at the non-profit Preventive Medicine Research Institute established the Multicenter Lifestyle Demonstration Project. It was designed to determine (a) if we could train other teams of health professionals in diverse regions of the country to motivate their patients to follow our program of comprehensive lifestyle changes: (b) if this lifestyle program may be an equivalently safe and medically effective but more cost-effective alternative to bypass surgery and angioplasty inselected patients with severe but stable coronary artery disease: and (c) the resulting cost savings. In other words, can patients avoid bypass surgery and angioplasty by making comprehensive lifestyle changes at lower cost without increasing cardiac morbidity and mortality?

The first site of this demonstration project was directed by Dr. Collins in Omaha. Later, we trained additional sites around the country. We found that almost 80% of patients who were eligible for bypass surgery or angioplasty were able to avoid it by changing diet and lifestyle. Mutual of Omaha calculated an average savings of $29,529 per patient. These patients reported reductions in angina comparable to what can be achieved with bypass surgery or angioplasty. Because of these findings, many insurance companies are now reimbursing the cost of our program at the hospitals and other sites we have trained.

None of this would have been possible without Dr. Richard Collins' pioneering vision and efforts at the beginning as an interventional cardiologist. Now, he has gone a step further by making patient education his full-time commitment. In *The Cooking Cardiologist,* he shows how changing diet not only can be a powerful way of healing your heart, it can be fun, easy, and tasty as well. He speaks from the heart, he cooks for the heart, he serves through his heart.

Dean Ornish, M.D.
Founder, President, and Director
Preventive Medicine Research Institute
Clinical Professor of Medicine
School of Medicine, University of California, San Francisco
January 1999

BEWARE THE SAUTE PAN!

We are living in America as if we have just finished a Thanksgiving Day dinner. FATigued. And it isn't due to the turkey. It has to do with the type of fuel we are burning in our bodies. We are consuming too many calories with an over abundance of fat and simple sugars. We are yo-yoing insulin and fat. This metabolic roller coaster plays havoc with our general energy level. For several hours after a heavy caloric meal laced with fat, blood sugar rises, insulin responds and our arteries begin to be stunned by a fatty tide (turbid fat in the blood stream). All of these fats—canola oil, olive oil, soy oil, hydrogenated oil, transfatty acids, shortening, butter, vegetable oil, palm oil, coconut oil, bacon grease and lard—can cause this fat tide. Oil by any other name is just fat. These fats raise cholesterol production in the body. True, fats containing different ratios of saturation have different effects, but they all raise total fat levels. All create this fat tide within minutes to hours of ingestion. It is this lipid front that passes into the bloodstream that numbs the endothelium (the inside lining of the arteries) and prevents the artery from expanding (dilating). Recent investigation has shown that arteries cannot expand as well after a heavy fatty meal. This effect seems to be blocked by the addition of supplemental anti-oxidants.

Ask any cardiologist. More people die after a high calorie, high fat meal than while holding on to a snow shovel. Stress, lack of exercise and excess fat are the top three killers in America. In fact, the original description of sudden death, or heart attack in the 1800's, was acute indigestion or "over-consumption."

Aggressive control of fat and cholesterol has been shown to reduce the incidence of angina (chest pain) within weeks of cutting fats to less than 10% of calories or starting an aggressive lipid management with medications. Cholesterol control can reduce adverse clinical events—death and second heart attacks—more so than shrinking plaques. This process is called plaque stabilization. While more research is needed, preliminary findings appear to confirm that cholesterol and fats do more than cause plaques to form; they also interfere with arterial function.

So how do the French get by with so little heart disease, yet eat, drink and be merry? Why does the mediterranean diet seem to protect those people against heart disease? Some investigators say that it is the red wine. Others suggest it is lifestyle, less stress, ethnic qualities, hereditary gene protection or just not accurately reporting the cardiovascular death rate. In any event, this French paradox does seem to exist. My wife and I traveled extensively in France, especially to smaller villages. It was clear that while the French reputation for superb cuisine is justified, their portions are smaller, dairy consumption is less (hard to believe, but true) and cooking techniques more proven. They poach, bake, broil and steam. In America we are aggressive with cooktop browning, frying, grilling and oil sautéing. The difference between American and European cooking is that we use oil for cooking while Mediterraneans use oil for flavoring. Too much oil makes us lazy in the kitchen and sleepy in the living room. When cooking with abundant oil, one does not need to be attentive to cooktop temperature. We cook at higher temperatures to get the job done faster. The latest American trend is to deep fat fry the Thanksgiving turkey. A twenty-pounder can be cooked in 45 minutes! French frying (actually we should call it more American than French) allows us to get our fast food order "hot and now." Deep fat frying adds fat as well as holding the fat in the food. They same is true for grilling or sautéing with oil, fat and butter.

In looking at trends in America, the Food Marketing Institute (FMI) reported in *Trends in the United States:Consumer Attitudes and the Supermarket 1997,* that the amount of fat as a percent of calories has dropped in the U.S.A., but the total amount of fat consumed in our average diet has not. That is because we are consuming more calories and processed foods. We are at an all time high. Just look at the size of our grocery isles and the number of products available. Processed foods have more hidden fats and simple sugar. Especially abundant are transfatty acids (the solid fat that is more dangerous). Studies suggest that we are getting fatter in America not because of "fat phobia" (the trend had started before the influx of fat-free items), but because we are eating more calorie dense foods, foods that add calories before filling you up.

All calories do count, including sugar and carbohydrates, but fat calories add up faster. One tablespoon of oil contains 14 grams of fat; that's 126 calories. One cup of oil has over 2,000 calories. It doesn't matter if it is vegetable, canola or olive oil. The total amount of fat is the same in all.

BEWARE THE AMERICAN GRILL

In America, just ask for grilled vegetables in any restaurant, and you'll get vegetables smothered with a coat of oil, blackened with grill marks. It is a macho thing! The perception is, if it lacks grill marks, it just isn't grilled right. You can't even taste the delicate flavor of the vegetables anymore. I've seen chefs take the skin off chicken and grill it with a coat of oil. What's the difference? Maybe a change in the saturated to unsaturated fat content. Either way, it's all fat. You will notice right away that the cooking techniques in this recipe book are more genteel, use no oil and require lower heat.

The outdoor American grill is the most dangerous cooking apparatus in America.

High heat with high fat and rich animal proteins increase the risk of carcinogens. The grill makes the perfect setting. Research has shown that blackened food on the grill is extremely carcinogenic. A study released in 1996 suggests using a 7-ingredient marinade to lower the risk of carcinogens. (See recipe, page 173, *Healthy Meat Marinade*) Findings confirm that lowering the cooktop temperature and avoiding blackening foods extensively reduces these carcinogens.

The next time you are outdoors and see a heavy smoke bomb coming from your neighbor's grill, you'll know that family is on at least a 40% fat plan. Where there is smoke there is FAT. **BEWARE. Grill smoke is heavy in airborne carcinogens.** Do not be downwind. Research indicates chefs and cooks often die of respiratory ailments and cancer of the lung.

Here are a few suggestions to avoid FATigue and reduce the risk of "cooktop demise".
- Oil holds flavors on the palate. When reducing the amount of oil or cooking fat-free, use extra herbs and spices. Use fresh herbs and spices to turn up the flavor.

- Be gentle. No-oil cooking requires lower heat and more attention. Restaurants use lots of oil so the chef does not have to be so watchful.

- Fat-free foods have lower moisture. A trick to get fat-free cheese to melt is to hydrate it well before melting. Marinate it in cold water, vegetable or mushroom broth for five minutes.

- Get to know your food items. Certain vegetables have natural oils – the pectin in apples (a faux oil), onions, and even banana peels can be used to coat a non-stick pan in place of spray oil.

- Sauté onions or mushrooms in small amounts of frozen concentrated apple juice to caramelize.

- Sauté vegetables in vegetable broth instead of oil.

- When steaming vegetables use distilled water instead of tap water. You will be surprised how avoiding chlorine improves the taste of vegetables.

- Add one tablespoon of rice vinegar to water when steaming vegetables. They will keep their color and have a richer flavor. For additional flavor, add fresh herbs to the steamer.

- When grilling alternate meat products such as soy burgers or sausage, use vegetable broth to keep the product moist while grilling.

- When using nuts or seeds in salads, dry roast them first to enhance the flavor. A little goes a long way.

- Use earthen bakeware with lids and just a trace of oil for roasted root vegetables.

- When poaching fish, use a small amount of dry vermouth. It will cut down on the fishy taste.

- When baking tofu sticks, place on wire rack to brown both sides evenly.

- When baking a pizza, pre-sauté vegetables on the grill to cut down on baking time. Use a pizza stone to prevent burning the crust.

- Always have a good vegetable broth handy. Frozen or fresh broth will make a big difference in starting a new recipe. See section on vegetable broth, page 68.

- Cook rice, grains and beans in broth. The flavor will be spectacular.

- Thicken sauces with vegetable purees. Strained baby prunes will thicken any rich mushroom sauce.

- Make alternate cream sauces with soy milk and fat free powdered buttermilk, or use Butter Buds®.

- Cook with fresh and spicy condiments, flavored mustards, sweet chutneys and ready-to-go salsas.

- When sautéing, remember just about anything will work. Hydration is the key. You can use wine, beer, natural non-carbonated spring water or frozen apple juice concentrate. I have even heard of using Coca Cola®.

- Oil sprays are handy, but use them sparingly. Flavor sprays are available. You can make your own with spices, oil and a handy spray bottle.

Keep your favorite family recipes, even though they may not be healthy. There is no need to go to another cookbook. You can simplify the recipe by substituting low-fat ingredients, cutting down on the oil and using other protein sources to alter the dish and make it extremely healthy. See tables on tricks and protein substitution.

COOKING MINDFULLY

Most of the time people eat without attention or awareness. Look at the people in a fast food restaurant. The only time they look at their food is to give it direction. This lack of attentiveness may be the reason that obesity is one of America's major health problems. We love our food too little. If we were to spend time enjoying every bite, savoring flavors and eating with awareness, we would end up eating less. Cooking with awareness creates less deprivation. Food then becomes more satisfying.

During a live radio interview, I had to convince a radio announcer that soy burgers can taste just as good as any hamburger in America. I told him that it's done by being attentive to cooking and flavoring. He really did not believe that a soy burger had flavor, so I cooked a soy burger on the set and also brought a burger from Burger King®. The "big burger" was wrapped in its usual King wrapper. Unknown to the radio announcer, I had substituted a soy pattie for the Burger King hamburger. He tasted both, but said good-bye to my soy burger, and commented that he preferred a "real" burger from Burger King®. That's right, he chose his burger by association! The bun, onion and the exact pickle-mustard ratio were familiar tastes, and the packaging was what he expected, but it was a soy burger.

We really think that we are attentive to eating, when we really are not.

Visual presentation is an important aspect of food.

Great chefs are not only superior cooks, they are artists painting with utensils. Chefs create a picture with food: color, aroma, texture and taste in that order. "Plating" a dish is as important as cooking it. Institutionalized cooking often lacks presentation. Buffet dining is even more of a challenge to keep eye appeal and rev up tastes. Government soy burgers of the '70s were forced on our school children, who were barely able to keep them down. Why? Cooking techniques in the schools did not change. The same handling and cooking techniques for hamburger were used for these pre-cooked vegetable products. By the time these "burgers" reached the kids, they were overcooked, tough, dry and lacked eye appeal.

Cooking with visual awareness can happen in your kitchen and only takes a few extra minutes. Have a variety of plates, square, oval or oblong, antique plates, art deco dishes of the '70s; or don't use any! Fit the plate to the food. Serve your next burger on wood planks or miniature metal racks. You can even use the fruit or vegetable in its own container. The best onion soup I tasted was served in a large, hollowed out onion that had been roasted.

You will be eating healthier and enjoying it more if you cook with awareness and are mindful of the food. You can change your perception of food by implementing these visual changes, making eating fun for the entire family.

STOCK UP

Show me great chefs and chances are you will never see their secrets to making basic stock broth. Behind every great recipe is a great basic stock, whether it is beef, chicken or vegetable. In fact, except in strictly vegetarian restaurants, most "vegetarian dishes" start with a chicken stock. This is okay for most, but not when you are looking for other protein options. **In this cookbook, having a great vegetable stock is the key.** In making a vegetable stock, the goal is to draw rich flavor from the vegetables.

Carefully prepare stock vegetables as you would for eating. Wash, scrape, pare, peel, separate and discard bruised or brown portions. No need to peel the covering of many vegetables because that is where most of the flavor is located. This includes onion skin. When the skin is left on the onion, it will give a rich color to the stock. Be sure to cleanse the vegetables thoroughly to remove chemicals, oxidants, pollutants, etc. Treat them as though you are taking them for a luxurious Saturday night bath. The better the vegetables look, the better the broth. Making a vegetable stock of foods leftover in the refrigerator at the end of the week is really not a good idea. You will not have consistent results with your recipes.

To make the flavors of the vegetables pop, blend, mince or chop just before cooking. Even roasted vegetables are excellent for use in your stock. Use fresh when possible and organic if available and watch your balance of the vegetables. Avoid the cauliflower class: broccoli, artichokes, cabbage, white turnips, Brussels sprouts and potatoes. These are too starchy and earthy. Your stock needs upper earth foods such as celery, the stalks and the nobs. Avoid the green celery tops since they can be bitter (the yellowish leaves are better). The outer leaves of vegetables contain more nutrients. When using tomatoes, hold back the seeds. Parsley is essential, along with those onions. The 7-vegetable broth is my favorite. It has a careful balance of sweetness. (See index).

I cannot say enough about the most important ingredient, water. I would avoid tap water when boiling or steaming vegetables. It is too harsh in chemicals, pH and chlorine. Use natural, non-carbonated, bottled spring water or potable distilled water for your stock.

After boiling and straining, add sugar and lemon juice. Caramelized sugar will make it even more colorful. Reduce the broth and chill it immediately. A handy technique is freezing the broth in small easily accessible containers. I like to freeze the broth in ice cube trays with fresh herbs for use when a recipe calls for dill, thyme, tarragon, or whatever you prefer. You will be ready with your flavored stock.

Another helpful trick when you use your stock is to place the broth in a closed airtight squirt bottle. Use it for rehydrating fat-free cheese and keeping your plant proteins moist. You will always have fresh stock ready for sautéing and keep your cooktop from excessively drying out foods when grilling. The trick to get non-fat cheese to melt is to marinate it in vegetable broth 5-10 minutes before using. Because non-fat means just that, there is no oil to work with the heat. Adding moisture to non-fat cheese allows the cheese to melt. You'll have cheese oozing over the edges of any food.

The vegetable stock is ideal for rehydrating TSP, textured soy protein. TSP often has an earthy soy flavor. Use vegetable broth in the immediate few minutes of reconstituting the protein. Add the flavors of the dish to the rehydrating liquid. I prefer never to use hot tap water.

Note the recipe for barbecue beef using alternative protein TSP. Hydrate the product with BBQ sauce, and for richer flavor, rehydrate with mushroom broth. If you are not a vegetarian or if you are not on the Ornish plan, TSP could be reconstituted with fat-free chicken or beef stock.

We have used a broth source known as Chicken Not®, listed in the reference index under Dixie, U.S.A. There are also vegetable broths available in cans, one by Swanson®. You can spice this up a bit by adding a touch of ginger and soy sauce to give it an oriental flavor. There are also powders on the market that can be reconstituted with water. They are not ideal, but good in a pinch when needing a vegetable stock in a hurry.

ALTERNATIVE CUISINE

The objective of this cookbook is not to make a totally vegetarian America, but we do need to think in terms of alternative protein sources and to attempt to reduce our animal protein consumption. An American consumes about 85% of protein from animal sources. Other countries are down to 50% of total protein calories. In a few subcultures, vegetarians outlive non-vegetarians by 7-8 years. And yet, being a vegetarian is not always healthy. In fact, some

Food Guide For Vegetarian Meal Planning*

Fats, Oils and Sweets
use sparingly

Dairy Group**
0-3 servings daily

Dry Beans, Nuts, Seeds, Eggs, and Meat Substitutes Group
2-3 servings daily

Vegetable Group
3-5 servings daily

Fruit Group
2-4 servings daily

Bread, Cereal, Rice, and Pasta Group
6-11 servings daily

*For serving sizes, see the ADA Web site www.eatright.org
**Vegetarians who choose not to use milk products need to select other food sources rich in calcium.
Source: American Dietetic Association

Figure 1

vegetarian recipes are heavy in saturated fats. For a healthy review of food options, see figure 1, *Food Guide for Vegetarian Meal Planning*.

The key here is on what you would like to accomplish: To improve energy, cut back on fat and change your protein base to more vegetarian. To drop weight, cut down on fat, simple sugars and carbohydrates. To prevent heart disease, back off on cholesterol foods and fats. To reverse heart disease, make the big leap with fat restriction to less than 10% of calories and avoid eating anything with a mother.

Tigers, lions, dogs or cats can feed on fat, lard, and meat until "the cows come home" yet they do not develop heart disease. Humans on this diet increase their risk of heart disease. A study done in the '60s compared various diets producing arteriosclerosis (hardening of the arteries). In that study, rabbits were fed casein protein (animal protein) and another group of rabbits were given soy protein. The fat content remained the same. After months on varied diets, the arteries were examined by autopsy. It was discovered that the rabbits who ate the plant proteins did not develop heart disease, and yet the fat content of both diets was the same. In all the early animal atherosclerotic studies, the key was the addition of cholesterol with the fat. And where does cholesterol come from? Any animal source! One could argue that maybe we humans are in a separate class, neither a herbivore nor a carnivore. Perhaps we should be "alternavores," using other food options and plant proteins.

Europeans and Far Eastern individuals visiting America are appalled at the size of our portions, especially the amount of animal sources on our plates. Someday research may very well find that it is the overabundance of the protein sources and not the fat that is killing Americans. We have among the highest incidence of osteoporosis, renal failure and heart disease in the world. Statistics state that our fat consumption is decreasing, but our incidence of these diseases is increasing. Animal proteins coupled with low phosphorus intake can cause calcium loss through the kidneys. Animal proteins, because of the types of amino acids (protein building blocks), are much harder for the kidneys to handle. High protein animal diets put an extra load on the kidneys. These diets create an acid blood and ketosis. Appetite falls and weight can drop. In the long haul, they are diets with only short-term goals. On the other hand, research has shown that diabetics who change to plant proteins, namely soy, do improve their renal function.

Tofu intake has been equated with lower risk of colon cancer. Soy may reduce the risk of breast cancer as well. See the section on alternative proteins.

It may be what is NOT in plant proteins that may be protective. Soy is low in methionine (an amino acid, a building block of protein). Methionine converts to homocysteine. Animal proteins are rich in homocysteine. The higher the homocysteine level in the body, the greater the risk of stroke and heart disease. Folate and vitamin B6, vitamins rich in plants, reduce homocysteine levels and allow homocysteine to convert back to methionine which is not toxic to the arteries. Mom was right, eat your vegetables!

ALTERNATIVE PROTEINS

The soybean is among the oldest recorded food in the history of the human race. Known as glycine max, it is the most versatile legume. Far Eastern countries have been chopping, mashing, curdling, fermenting, and liquefying these beans since the existence of the Roman Empire. A farmer today can produce 33% more protein from an acre of soybeans than from any other crop. Its protein efficiency is the highest of any plant and the FDA now recognizes this plant as a complete protein. Soy contains all the essential amino acids (building blocks of proteins).

New research is telling us that adding soy to our diets can harden bones, reduce the chance of heart disease and lower the risk of cancer. The FDA is developing new labeling guidelines for food products with soy adding that it reduces these risks. Americans as a group are heading for the water supplying the "fountain of youth": anti-aging creams, pills, vitamins, herbs, minerals, and alternative therapies. We are anxious to learn the secrets of avoiding disabling disease. Soy: is it the miracle food for generations?

From an epidemiological point of view, analysis of cultures and lifestyles demonstrates the value of a plant diet. Adding soy to the diet as a protein source stands out very strongly in other cultures and societies. At the Second International Symposium on the Role of Soy and Preventing and Treating Chronic Disease held in Brussels in 1997, studies confirmed soy's importance in reducing osteoporosis, a disabling disease of aging women, and even men. As we grow older, bone density lessens, and in some unfortunate women, accelerates. Most soy food products have a number of biologic substrates including isoflavones, which are known to produce estrogen-like activity. Genistein and daidzein are two of the isoflavones found in abundance in soy foods. Research presented at this symposium confirms a significant increase in bone mineral content and bone density with the addition of soy protein containing at least 56 mg of isoflavones, or approximately 40 grams of soy protein. This amount is easily obtained in two servings of soy a day, or in a soy shake (see recipe).

The soy shake coupled with flax seed powder can have an even more dramatic effect on reducing cholesterol levels. (See recipe for Super Smoothie).

In a study published in the August, 1995 *New England Journal of Medicine*, participants with high cholesterol were able to reduce their cholesterol by at least 10% when they substituted soy for animal protein. Participants typically ate several servings of soy products a day.

The good news is that soy helps to lower the bad guy cholesterol (LDL) and raise the good guy (HDL). These changes are even more prominent when the cholesterol level is high.

Several studies have recently confirmed that the isoflavones appeared to lower the cholesterol. Soy shakes without these isoflavones failed to lower cholesterol.

Our recipe book is loaded with cholesterol-lowering smoothies. They are a great way to start the day with protein, fruit, and fluids. All are quick and easy to prepare. They are made rich with these isoflavones by using a product from Twin Laboratories known as Vege Fuel® which is available unflavored, or in chocolate and strawberry banana flavors. This isolated soy protein by Supro® mixes well and is lactose and fat free. Two scoops can provide 30 grams of protein! Several of our recipes have included Vege Fuel® as a protein additive, boosting the total protein yet keeping the fat content under control. This is good news, as an Italian study confirmed that the addition of soy can keep cholesterol from rising, even when extra cholesterol and fat were added to the diet. This suggests a protective effect and is important to those who hate "exclusion diets" just to lower cholesterol.

Not all soy derivatives have the same amounts of isoflavones. In general, the more processed the soybean, the less the amount of usable soy in the food product. Soy oil and soy sauce lack any nutritional benefit. Mature soybeans have the most isoflavones and soy concentrate has the least. Be sure to check the type of soy derivative and serving portions. Refer to Figure 2. The usual serving size for roasted soybeans is 1/2 cup; for soy flour, 1/4 cup; TSP, 1/4 cup; soymilk, 1 cup and tempeh or tofu, about 4 oz. The number of isoflavones can vary greatly with the serving size. Soyprotein concentrate lacks sufficient isoflavones. Soy concentrate is the usual form of soy found in soy burgers. The healthiest soy is in the most natural state of the bean.

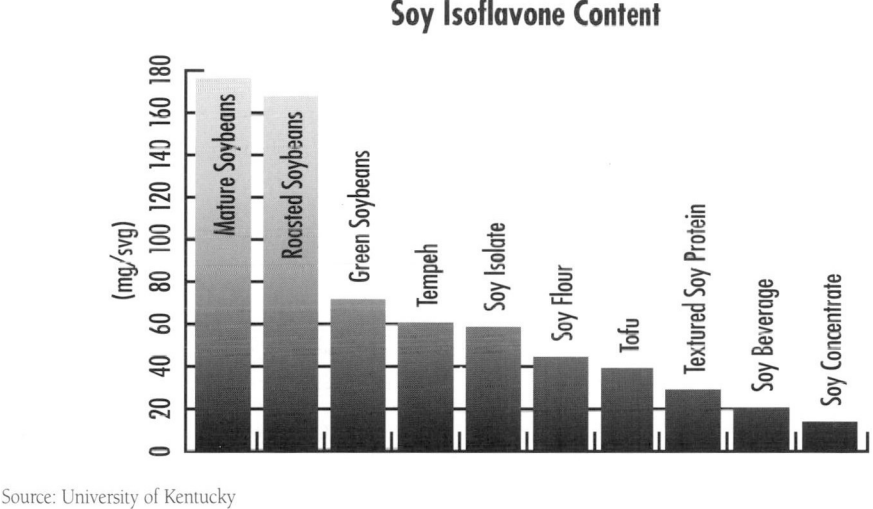

Source: University of Kentucky

Figure 2

The effect of reducing cancer appears even more exciting. A recent publication has shown a significant reduction in colon polyps with the intake of tofu. The greater the amount of daily tofu consumption was equated with the lesser number of polyps. Polyps are known to be pre-cancerous for colon cancer. The mechanism of protection may be related to proteinase inhibitors, calcium or the isoflavones.

In addition, studies are underway to confirm soy's role in reducing the risks of prostate and breast cancer. Dr. Dean Ornish is currently conducting a study on men with prostate cancer. The participants are enrolled into a life-style change program with one component being a strict vegetarian diet with an abundance of soy protein. Several other studies are in progress at The National Cancer Institute, the University of California and the University of Texas.

In the Mayo Clinic Health Letter published in May 1997, the conclusion was that there is evidence that adding soy to your diet makes good nutritional sense. It is a healthful diet addition. Soy has been shown to lessen menopausal symptoms, improve renal function in diabetic men and even lessen headaches (migraines).

So, is it a cure-all? Definitely not. However, a plant protein diet coupled with proper lifestyle changes can have a dramatic effect on impacting chronic disease and reversing heart disease. Recent dietary studies have shown that additional plant proteins, vegetables, fruit and calcium, coupled with a low-fat diet can have as much of a significant effect in lowering blood pressure as medication.

Well okay, you agree that a diet rich in soy is healthy, but how is it done? You cannot grill those soybeans, but there are healthy ingredients, including soy products, that can be incorporated into recipes for great tasting healthy meals. And you do not have to give up what you like to eat, just simply change your recipe. You can cook Italian, Mexican, Oriental, and even traditional meals American style. Hot dogs are available made from tofu, and soy burgers are an excellent meat alternative, nothing like the soyburgers we experienced in the '70s.

You Can Have Great Taste With Soy Products

The following is a list of soy foods available and hints for making delicious dishes.

Whole soybeans: Dry soybeans belong to the legume family. They have the property of being a bean and a nut. Soybeans are harvested when they are fully mature and dry. Whole soybeans are available in natural food stores.

Preparation: Dry soybeans expand when cooked. One cup of dry soybeans becomes two cups of cooked beans. Wash and drain. Soaking dry soybeans shortens the cooking time and improves the flavor, texture and appearance. In a large pot add six cups of water for two cups of dry beans. Let the soybeans stand at room temperature for about 6-8 hours, or overnight. It is not necessary to refrigerate the beans during the process. Drain, rinse and cook beans.

Cooking: Put the soaked beans into a large pot, add six cups of fresh water for each pound of beans. Do not add salt at this time as it delays the softening of the beans. Bring the water and beans to a boil allowing the steam to escape. Reduce the heat to simmer and cook the beans for about three hours until tender.

Soy beans are also available canned and cooked. My recommendation is to use the black soy bean from Eden Foods®. Grown organically, these beans are rich in protein and low in fat. They are excellent for making a black bean burger (see recipe section).

Green vegetable soybeans are harvested just prior to maturity. They are similar in size and color to lima beans and slightly smooth to the touch. They come in pods or separated out of the pods. These beans possess a firm, crisp texture. Green soybeans are most often found in the frozen food section of Asian markets or natural food stores.

Soy milk: Soy milk is the rich creamy fluid of whole soybeans. The beans are mashed and the fluid extracted. It has a unique nutty flavor and rich nutrition. Soy milk is used in a variety of ways.

Soy milk is sold in supermarkets, health food stores and specialty food shops. It is most commonly found in aseptic (non-refrigerated) quart and 8-oz containers, but is also sold refrigerated in plastic quart and half-gallon containers.

Unopened, aseptically packaged soy milk can be stored at room temperature for several months. Once it is opened, soy milk must be refrigerated, and will stay fresh for about five days.

Soy milk is available as a plain, unflavored beverage or in a variety of flavors including chocolate, vanilla, and almond. With the growing interest in lower fat products, a number of light soy milks with reduced fat content are appearing on the market. Plain, unfortified soy milk is an excellent source of high quality protein, B vitamins and iron. Some brands of soy milk are fortified with vitamins and minerals and are good sources of calcium, vitamin D and vitamin B12. Soy milk is free of the milk sugar lactose and is a good choice for persons who are lactose intolerant. Soy milk can be use in almost any way that cow's milk is used. It is ideal in refreshing drinks, over cereal and even used in cream sauces that are cholesterol free and low in saturated fats (see recipes). Use soy milk in pancake and waffle mixes and create your own delicious experience.

Tofu: Tofu, also known as soybean curd, is a soft, cheese-like food make by curdling fresh, hot soy milk with a coagulant. It is analogous to cottage cheese. Traditionally the curdling agent used to make tofu is nagari, a compound found in natural ocean water, or calcium sulfate, a naturally occurring mineral. These curds are generally pressed into a solid block. When used in a variety of recipes, tofu acts like a sponge and has a miraculous ability to soak up any flavor added to it. Crumble it into a pot of spicy chili sauce and it tastes like chili. Blend it with cocoa and sweetener and it becomes chocolate pudding.

Three main types of tofu are available in our grocery stores. Firm tofu is dense and solid and holds up well in stir fry dishes, soups, on the grill, or anywhere you want the tofu to maintain its shape. Firm tofu is also higher in protein, fat and calcium than any other forms of tofu. Many forms are already flavored with smoke, Italian, or Mexican spices. Soft tofu is a good choice for recipes that call for blended tofu or in oriental soups. Silken tofu is made by a different process that results in a creamy, custard-like product. Silken tofu works well in pureed or blended dishes. You will find that the tofu used in the recipes in this book are silken, firm and extra firm. This is due to availability of the product, since it is aseptically packaged and has a long shelf life. Once opened, it should be stored covered with water that is changed daily. It will last 3-4 days in the refrigerator.

Tofu tips: Tofu also freezes well, firming the consistency when thawed. Prior frozen tofu is chewier than regular tofu and will absorb flavors readily. Another tip in changing tofu to a more cheesy-like substance is to use the tofu press (see tools for cooking).

Tofu is rich in a high quality protein. It is a good source of B vitamins and iron. While 50% of the calories in tofu come from fat, a 4-ounce serving of tofu contains just 6 grams of fat. It is low in saturated fat, high in 3-omega fatty acids and contains, of course, no cholesterol. For most Americans, tofu is not ready for prime time dinner, yet it is a great protein substitute and can easily be cloaked into a main dish. It is not good naked, and for that reason stir fry has given tofu a bad rap. You are suddenly confronted with a mass of white substance with virtually no taste. You'll find no stir fry recipe for tofu in this cookbook.

The trick is to add the flavors and spices to tofu when it's processed into the recipe. Its protein base attaches to flavors like a magnet. Crumble half tofu with blue cheese and you will reduce the fat but extend the flavor of the blue cheese for use in any recipe.

Tofu is most commonly sold in aseptic packages, water-filled tubes and vacuum packs. Tofu is usually found in the produce section of the grocery store. Unless it is aseptically packaged, tofu should be kept cold. Once a tofu package is opened, leftover tofu should be covered with fresh water for storage in the refrigerator. Do not store tofu beyond a week. Tofu can be frozen up to 5 months.

Just released is pasta made from tofu. It boosts the protein content up to 12 grams per serving and yet retains all of the properties of pasta. In fact, the aftertaste of soy is gone and the pasta has a lesser tendency to become glutinous. It is the pasta for the next millennium. See the reference index and suppliers for availability.

Textured Soy Protein (TSP): TSP, commonly referred to as TVP® (which is a registered trade mark of Archer Daniels Midland), is produced from soy flour after the soy bean oil has been extracted, then cooked under pressure, extruded and dried. TSP comes in several forms, granules, flakes or chunks. TSP has no cholesterol and no fat. It is an excellent source of protein and fiber. It is high in potassium, a good source of essential amino acids and also contributes calcium and magnesium to your diet. It is very low in sodium. To rehydrate the granules, pour about 7/8 cup of boiling water or liquid of your choice over one cup of textured soy protein. Stir and let stand for 5-10 minutes. For chunks or flakes, pour one cup boiling water over one cup of chunks or flakes, stir and set stand 10-15 minutes. If using in casseroles or soups, pre-simmering is not necessary. If using for stovetop dishes, add another cup of liquid, bringing the TSP liquid to boil, lower heat and simmer 15-20 minutes until fork tender, but not mushy. Broths or stocks can be used in place of water and provide textured soy protein with an excellent taste.

There are several tips in using TSP. Remember it can be used as a meat extender. Most people will not notice the difference if you replace 1/4 of ground beef in meat loafs and burgers, with rehydrated TSP. You can replace the ground meat entirely in recipes such as chili, tacos or sloppy joes.

TSP has a long shelf life. Stored in a tightly closed container at room temperature, it will keep for months. Once it has been rehydrated, however, store the TSP in the refrigerator and use it within a few days.

There are hundreds of products that fit into the category of meat alternatives. They can be flavored to taste like beef, pork, chicken, or even tuna fish. They can be made into products such as hot dogs, deli meats, burgers, sausages, and "bacon" strips. The majority of recipes in the book use one brand. This again is due to availability of the product in most supermarkets. Meat alternatives are sold as frozen, canned or dried. More and more meat alternatives are now available in regular grocery stores as well as in health food stores. With so many different meat alternatives available, nutritional value in these foods vary considerably. Most of the time they are lower in fat than the foods they replace. Most meat alternatives made from soybeans are excellent sources of protein, iron and B vitamins, and are sometimes fortified with other nutrients.

Soy flour: Soy flour is made from roasted soybeans that have been ground into fine powder rich in high quality protein and other nutrients. Soy flour also adds a pleasant texture and flavor to a variety of products. Two kinds of soy flour are available. Natural, full fat soy flour contains the natural oils found in the soybean. Defatted soy flour has the oils removed during processing. Both kinds of soy flour will give a protein boost to recipes.

Tips on using soy flour: Soy flour will thicken sauces and gravies. Toasting soy flour before use enhances its nutty flavor. Simply put the soy flour in a dry skillet and cook it over moderate heat, stirring occasionally.

Full fat soy flour contains all the natural oils in soybeans. Cooking techniques for breads: You can replace up to 1/8 of the flour in yeast breads, and 1/4 of the flour in quick breads, with soy flour. Be sure to stir well before measuring. Also in cooking bread, you can replace some of the milk with soy milk. The addition of both soy flour and soy milk does bring out more of a soy flavor.

Soy increases the chance of your breads browning faster. You should bake the bread at a slightly lower temperature to avoid excessive browning. Remember, soy will not cause the bread dough to rise, and therefore it cannot totally replace whole wheat grains.

A FINAL NOTE ON SOY

You will notice in the cookbook that many of the soy foods mentioned in recipes indicate the manufacturer. We do not endorse any one particular manufacturer. We have included the actual brand to make it easier for you to know exactly what to use when the recipe calls for a soy alternative. These products are some of the better ones we've found. They are nationally available through most full-service grocery stores. If you cannot find the products, just ask your grocer. See also the index for suppliers. For more information, contact 1-800-TALK-SOY (1-800-825-5769) for a listing of soyfood providers.

NOTES ON THE RIGHT TOOLS

My grandfather was a carpenter. As a young lad I loved to go to his basement workshop and watch him work. One day he turned to me and said, **"If you ever want to do the job right, have the right tools."** Good advice! Ask any chef, and he or she will have favorites along with securely guarded knives and pans. These recipes require a few good tools.

A high quality non-stick sauté pan. I prefer two types, a small 10" and a larger 16" pan. The 10" pan has higher sides to flip a large quantity of cooking ingredients. Williams Sonoma has a good selection of sauté pans. The sauce pan has a rounded side. I prefer square sides.

A non-stick grill pan with ridges is a must. It lifts the food product off the pan and creates great grill marks and reduces the chance of "burning" when oil is not used. It is perfect for burgers and for grilling vegetables on the cooktop.

Wire racks for use in roasting tofu sticks.

A non-stick baking pan or sheet.

A stone pizza plate or a round ventilated pizza pan for cooking pizza.

A wide blade Japanese-style cutting tool for chopping vegetables. I prefer not only the chef knife, but also a cleaver-type chopper.

A good quality food processor.

A multi-speed blender for smoothies.

A clay roasting dish for roasting vegetables.

A tofu press, a handy gadget for tofu. It helps to remove the water content of tofu, making it firmer and crumbly and converting it to "soy cheese." It is available from Unique Utensils, PO Box 3112, Littleton, CO, 8016. It is known as the "tofu squeeze".

SO WHAT'S COOKING?

While I cannot tailor make a cookbook for everyone, I can show you basic recipes and techniques to fit your diet plan. That is why we have labeled recipes for specific dietary options.

Just look for the following key indicators on each recipe.

 PREVENTION DIET: Cholesterol < 100 mg./day
Calories from FAT: <20%

 LOW-FAT VEGETARIAN DIET (Ornish Diet):
Cholesterol <10 mg./day
Calories from FAT <10%
No added oils or fats added to products
No animal products, except for egg whites and
non-fat dairy products

 TOTALLY VEGETARIAN (vegan):
No animal products
For dairy products, use soy products

These recipes can be easily altered by using plant protein cheeses (soy cheese, vegetarian mayonnaise, soy sour cream, etc.) to make them vegan and low-fat. Many of the vegan recipes or prevention recipes can be converted to Ornish standards by substituting or omitting certain food products. See Appendixes A and B on Plant Protein Substitution and Cooking Options.

Have a Long and Delicious Life
Richard Collins, M.D.

APPETIZERS/BEVERAGES

Easy Oven Baked Tofu Sticks, page 23

EASY OVEN BAKED TOFU STICKS

Serving Size: 6

Amount	Measure	Ingredient – Preparation Method
2	packages	MORI-NU® Lite SILKEN TOFU, FIRM – drained
1/2	cup	cracker crumbs – crushed fine
2	tablespoons	cornmeal
1 1/2	tablespoons	seasoning of choice, creole, cajun, lemon pepper, etc.
1/2	teaspoon	chili powder
1/2	teaspoon	salt

Drain two blocks of tofu and wrap in paper towels for 15 minutes.

In shallow bowl, mix together cracker crumbs, cornmeal, seasoning, chili powder and salt. Set aside. Lightly oil large wire cake or cookie cooling rack. Remove paper towels from tofu; cut each block into 12 sticks about 3 inches long and 3/4 inch thick. Dredge each stick in crumb mixture; place on wire rack. Place rack in 375 degree oven for 35 to 40 minutes, until crisp and brown. Serve warm drizzled with sauce or with sauce on the side for dipping. Makes 6 servings of 4 sticks each.

Comment: use sauce of your choice, goes well with fat-free red sauces or fat-free ranch salad dressing.

For a real time saver, you can purchase potato shake mixes and use in place of the cracker crumbs, cornmeal and seasonings.

Nutritional analysis: Calories 38.2, Fat 1, Cholesterol 0, Carbohydrate 2.3, Protein 5, Sodium 184.

ANGEL EGGS

Serving Size: 6

Amount	Measure	Ingredient – Preparation Method
3	medium	potatoes – boiled
6		eggs – boiled
1/2	cup	KRAFT® Miracle Whip Nonfat Dressing
1	tablespoon	mustard
1	teaspoon	Dijon mustard
1	teaspoon	sweet pickle juice
		paprika

Peel and boil potatoes until done. Mash potatoes to a very fine consistency, when cool add nonfat Miracle Whip, mustards and pickle juice, mix well. Set aside.

Peel boiled eggs. Cut in half, (DISCARD YOLKS) and fill with potato mixture. Sprinkle with paprika.

Comment: delightful "deviled" eggs turned into ANGELS.

Nutritional analysis: Calories 82, Fat 0.2, Cholesterol 0, Carbohydrate 14, Protein 4.8, Sodium 248.

BLACK BEAN DIP

Amount	Measure	Ingredient – Preparation Method
2	cups	black beans, drained
4	teaspoons	tomato paste
3	tablespoons	water
1	clove	garlic, minced
2	teaspoons	lime juice
1/2	teaspoon	ground cumin
2		green onions, chopped fine
3	tablespoons	mild green chilies, chopped

In a food processor or blender, place the black beans, tomato paste, water, garlic, lime juice and cumin. Process until mixture forms a smooth paste. Transfer to a medium size serving bowl and stir in the green onions and green chilies. Cover and chill in refrigerator 2-3 hours before serving. Makes 2 cups.

Nutritional analysis based on 2 tablespoons: Calories 32, Fat 0, Cholesterol 0, Carbohydrate 6, Protein 2, Sodium 12.

BLACK SOY BEAN HUMMUS

Serving Size: 4

Amount	Measure	Ingredient – Preparation Method
1	clove	garlic, plus 1 teaspoon powdered garlic, minced
1	15 ounce	can, EDENSOY® Organic Black Soy Beans, drained
1		small yellow onion
2	tablespoons	lemon juice
1 1/2	tablespoons	soy sauce, low sodium
1	teaspoon	balsamic vinegar
2	teaspoons	Cajun seasoning
3		green onions, chopped

Pierce top of unpeeled onion with fork in 2-3 places. Place in a small microwave dish. Microwave on high 2-3 minutes. Remove from microwave, peel and chop. Place the onion with all the remaining ingredients in a food processor, process until smooth. Before serving fold in green onions or use as a garnish. Serve with fat-free chips.

Nutritional analysis: Calories 90, Fat 1.5, Cholesterol 0, Carbohydrate 22, Protein 9, Sodium 358.

CAPONATA HORS D' OEUVRES

Amount	Measure	Ingredient – Preparation Method
2	cups	peeled, diced eggplant
¾	cup	onion, finely chopped
½	cup	celery, finely chopped
½	cup	green pepper, finely chopped
3	tablespoons	tomato paste
1	teaspoon	crushed fresh garlic
½	teaspoon	crushed red pepper
24	slices	french bread, sliced 1/2 inch thick
1	cup	nonfat mozzarella cheese, shredded

Combine all the ingredients except for the bread and cheese in a medium size saucepan. Cover and cook over low heat, stirring occasionally, for 45 minutes, or until the vegetables are tender and the mixture is thick. Add a few tablespoons of water only if necessary to prevent mixture from scorching. Remove the pan from the heat and set aside. Arrange the bread slices on a baking sheet, and bake in a 400 degree oven for 5 minutes, or until lightly browned. Spread each slice with a tablespoon of the eggplant mixture, top each slice with small amount of shredded cheese. Return the hors d' oeuvres to the oven, and bake for 6 to 7 minutes, or until cheese is melted. Arrange on a serving platter and serve hot.

Nutritional analysis per slice: Calories 34, Fat 0, Cholesterol 2, Protein 2.5, Sodium 122.

CHEESY – STUFFED NEW POTATOES

Serving Size: 4

Amount	Measure	Ingredient – Preparation Method
8	small	new potatoes
¾	cup	nonfat cottage cheese
2	tablespoons	dry, Ranch Style fat-free dressing mix
2	tablespoons	minced parsley
2	tablespoons	minced chives
1	teaspoon	dill weed
		pepper to taste
8	small	dill or parsley sprigs

Place potatoes in a medium size saucepan, cover with water. Bring to a boil over moderately high heat, cover and simmer potatoes until tender. Drain and set aside. Meanwhile, place cottage cheese in a food processor or blender and whirl until smooth. Transfer to a small bowl and stir in the dry dressing mix, parsley, chives, dill weed and pepper. When potatoes are cool enough to handle, slice about 1/4 inch off the top of each. With a small spoon or melon baller, remove 1 to 2 scoops of potato, be careful not to break the skin. Fill the potatoes with the cheese mixture and garnish with dill or parsley sprigs.

Nutritional analysis: Calories 68, Fat 0, Cholesterol 0, Carbohydrate 12, Protein 4, Sodium 70.

CHILI CHEESE DIP

Serving Size: 8

Amount	Measure	Ingredient – Preparation Method
16	ounces	American or cheddar – grated, fat-free
1	can	Hormel Vegetarian Chili
1/2	cup	chunky salsa, hot, medium or mild, your choice

Place cheese in a crockpot. Add chili and salsa, cover and heat on low. Stir occasionally until cheese has melted. Serve with your favorite chips or fresh veggies.

Nutritional analysis: Calories 27.2, Fat 0, Cholesterol 0, Carbohydrate 4.9, Protein 2.0, Sodium 128.

CREAMY SPINACH DIP

Serving Size: 12

Amount	Measure	Ingredient – Preparation Method
1	10 oz. pkg.	chopped spinach – thawed and drained
1 1/2	cups	sour cream, fat-free
1	cup	KRAFT® Miracle Whip Nonfat Dressing
1	package	Knorr Vegetable Soup Mix
1	8 ounce	waterchestnuts, canned – drained
1	bunch	green onions – chopped fine

Drain spinach until very dry. In medium bowl, stir together spinach, sour cream, Miracle Whip, soup mix, chestnuts (which have been finely chopped) and green onions. Cover; refrigerate for 4 hours or overnight. Stir before serving. Serve with cocktail bread, crackers or fresh vegetable dippers.

Nutritional analysis: Calories 45.5, Fat 0, Cholesterol 0, Carbohydrate 8.4, Protein 2.3, Sodium 226, Potassium 55, Calcium 12.

CROCKPOT TACO DIP

Serving Size: 8

Amount	Measure	Ingredient – Preparation Method
1 1/2	cups	TVP Granules
1	package	taco seasoning mix
2	tablespoons	beef flavor granules
1	envelope	Butter Buds®
1 1/2	cups	water – hot
16	ounces	American or cheddar – grated, fat-free
1	4 ounce can	green chilies

Place TVP granules in medium size crockpot, add taco seasoning, beef granule and Butter Buds to TVP. Pour hot water over this mixture, mixing well. Add green chilies and cheese. Heat on low for

1-2 hours, stirring occasionally. Serve with low fat Dorito Chips. Makes about 4 cups.

Nutritional analysis: Calories 200, Fat 0.5, Cholesterol 8, Carbohydrate 21.7, Protein 39.3, Sodium 961.

CURRIED MOCK MEATBALLS

Amount	Measure	Ingredient – Preparation Method
1	pound	MORNINGSTAR FARMS® Ground Meatless – thawed
1	cup	quick-cooking oatmeal
1/2	cup	Egg Beaters® (egg substitute)
1		onion, finely chopped
1	tablespoon	curry powder
1	teaspoon	ground ginger
		pepper to taste

SAUCE

Amount	Measure	Ingredient
1/2	cup	honey
1/2	cup	Dijon mustard
2	tablespoons	lemon juice
1/4	cup	water
		curry powder to taste

Combine the meatball ingredients in a medium-sized bowl, mixing thoroughly. Spray a large baking sheet with nonstick cooking spray. Shape the meatball mixture into 50 (1 inch) balls. Place the meatballs on the baking sheet and bake in a 350 degree oven for about 25 to 30 minutes. Transfer the meatball to a chafing dish to keep warm. Combine the sauce ingredients in a saucepan, simmer over medium-low heat just until hot. Pour the sauce over the meatballs, tossing gently to mix, and serve.

Nutritional analysis (per meatball): Calories 24, Fat 0, Cholesterol 0, Protein 2.5.

DEVILED CRAB DIP

Amount	Measure	Ingredient – Preparation Method
1 1/2	cups	nonfat sour cream
2	tablespoons	spicy brown mustard
2	cups	imitation crab – finely chopped
1/2	cup	green onions – finely chopped
		paprika, for garnish

Combine the sour cream and mustard in a medium sized bowl. Fold in the chopped crab and onions. Transfer the dip to a serving dish, cover and chill for several hours. Prior to serving, sprinkle with paprika. Serve with small chucks of sourdough bread or crackers.

Nutritional analysis per tablespoon: Calories 14, Fat 0, Cholesterol 0, Protein 1.5, Sodium 30.

DILL DIP

Serving Size: 12

Amount	Measure	Ingredient – Preparation Method
1	10 ½ ounce	MORI-NU® Lite SILKEN TOFU, FIRM
⅛	cup	lemon juice
½	teaspoon	salt
½	teaspoon	sugar
2	teaspoons	dillweed
½	teaspoon	onion powder
½	teaspoon	garlic powder
1	teaspoon	Beau Monde Seasoning

Place all the ingredients in a blender or food processor. Blend until smooth. Spoon the dip into serving bowl. Cover and refrigerate until serving time.

Helpful Hint: Can be made ahead of time and stored in refrigerator for best flavor.

Nutritional analysis: Calories 12, Fat 0.1, Cholesterol 0, Carbohydrate 0.6, Protein 0.5, Sodium 95.

FRUIT DIP

Serving Size: 6

Amount	Measure	Ingredient – Preparation Method
1	8 ounce	cream cheese fat-free
1	7 ounce jar	marshmallow cream
1	tablespoon	orange rind – grated
¼	teaspoon	ginger

Combine all ingredients, mixing well. Serve with fresh fruit.

Nutritional analysis: Calories 102.8, Fat 0.1, Cholesterol 0, Carbohydrate 26.6, Protein 0.6, Sodium 15.

GREENIE BEANIE DIP

Serving Size: 1

Amount	Measure	Ingredient – Preparation Method
2	cups	green picked soybeans, steamed
3	tablespoons	nonfat, plain yogurt
2	medium	ripe tomatoes, peeled, seeded and chopped
¼	cup	fresh coriander or parsley, minced
½	teaspoon	ground coriander
½	small	red onion, chopped fine
4	teaspoons	lime juice
1	clove	garlic, minced
1	small	jalapeno pepper, seeded and chopped fine

Place the cooled soybeans in a large bowl and mash until almost smooth, leave a few lumps for texture. Mix in the remaining ingredients. Makes 2 1/4 cups.

Nutritional analysis based on 1 tablespoon: Calories 9, Fat 1, Cholesterol 0, Carbohydrate 1, Protein 0, Sodium 2.

This makes an excellent first course served on shredded lettuce for 4 people.

HEATHER'S HUMMUS

Serving Size: 8

Amount	Measure	Ingredient – Preparation Method
1	large	carrot, peeled
2	15 ounce	cans organic garbanzo beans, drained, reserve some of the liquid
1		clove garlic
2	teaspoons	honey
1	tablespoon	lemon juice
3	tablespoons	fat-free ranch salad dressing

Cut peeled carrot in chunks, place in food processor. Process until finely grated. Add all other ingredients. Process until smooth. Add small amount of reserved bean juice if necessary. Serve with your favorite fat-free crackers.

Nutritional analysis: Calories 115, Fat 1.4, Cholesterol 0, Carbohydrate 14, Protein 5.

HOT ARTICHOKE AND PARMESAN CHEESE DIP

Serving Size: 12

Amount	Measure	Ingredient – Preparation Method
1	13.5 ounce	artichoke hearts – canned
3	slices	Italian bread
4	tablespoons	reserved brine from artichokes
1/4	cup	KRAFT® Miracle Whip Nonfat Dressing
1/2	cup	parmesan cheese – grated, fat-free

Drain artichokes, reserving 4 tablespoon of brine. Combine all ingredients in a food processor. Process about 1 minute to make a smooth paste. Spoon into a sprayed 1-1/2 quart baking dish. Bake 20 to 25 minutes in a 350 degree oven. If desired, broil 2 minutes to lightly brown. Allow to rest 10 minutes before serving with your favorite low fat crackers or vegetables.

Nutritional analysis: Calories 44, Fat 1.3, Cholesterol 3, Carbohydrate 5.6, Protein 2.3, Sodium 149.

HOT COCKTAIL LINKS

Serving Size: 5

Amount	Measure	Ingredient – Preparation Method
1	package	fat-free vegetarian hot dogs – thawed
1	cup	fat-free barbecue sauce

Cut each link in 3 pieces. Place in small crockpot, pour barbecue sauce over links. Cook until heated thoroughly. Place in small chafing dish to serve.

HOT AND SPICY HORSERADISH/ MUSTARD SPREAD

Serving Size: 12

Amount	Measure	Ingredient – Preparation Method
2	cloves	garlic — chopped
3	tablespoons	horseradish
1	8 ounce	MORI-NU® Lite SILKEN TOFU, FIRM
2	teaspoons	mustard
1 1/2	teaspoons	lemon juice
1	teaspoon	soy sauce, low sodium
2	teaspoons	apple cider vinegar
		salt to taste
		2-4 tablespoons water

In a food processor or blender, blend chopped garlic and horseradish well. Add remaining ingredients, except water, and blend again, scape down sides of processor, as necessary. Add water slowly, as needed, until mixture reaches a creamy, spreadable consistency. Serve with pretzels as a dip or serve over a hot baked potato. Wonderful.

Makes 1 1/2 cups.

Nutritional analysis: Calories 11, Fat 0, Cholesterol 0, Carbohydrate 0.8, Protein 0.5, Sodium 33.

LAYERED TACO DIP

Serving Size: 14

Amount	Measure	Ingredient – Preparation Method
1	cup	sour cream, fat-free
1/2	cup	KRAFT® Miracle Whip Nonfat Dressing
1	package	taco seasoning mix
1	16 ounce	fat-free refried beans – canned
2	bunches	green onions – diced
3	medium	tomatoes – chopped/drained
1	large	avocado – peeled and chopped
2	cups	nonfat cheddar cheese, shredded

Combine sour cream, Miracle whip and taco seasoning, mix well. To assemble spread refried beans on large serving plate evenly. Top with sour cream mixture. Sprinkle on onions, tomatoes and avocado in layers. Cover with shredded cheese. Serve chilled.

Nutritional analysis: Calories 118, Fat 2.4, Cholesterol 4, Carbohydrate 11.2, Protein 12, Sodium 540.

MOCK PATE

Serving Size: 14

Amount	Measure	Ingredient – Preparation Method
1 ½	cups	textured vegetable protein, granules
¾	cup	vegetable broth – heated
3	tablespoons	vermouth
½	teaspoon	garlic salt
1	tablespoon	Beau Monde seasoning
4	ounces	cream cheese, fat-free
2	tablespoons	sour cream, fat-free
2	tablespoons	dry ranch style salad dressing mix, fat-free
1 ½	teaspoons	onion powder

Rehydrate textured vegetable protein with hot oriental broth, add vermouth, garlic salt and Beau Monde seasoning. Set aside for 15 to 30 minutes. Mix together well, cream cheese, sour cream, dry salad dressing mix and onion powder. Add to textured vegetable protein mixture when cool. Place in refrigerator 4 to 6 hours before serving.

Nutritional analysis: Calories 98.6, Fat 0.2, Cholesterol 1, Carbohydrate 9.6, Protein 14.6, Sodium 132.

Comment: garnish with capers or small cocktail onions.

MOCKAMOLE

Serving Size: 14

Amount	Measure	Ingredient – Preparation Method
2	cups	green picked soybeans – steamed
1	teaspoon	lemon juice
½	cup	tomatoes – peeled and chopped
4	tablespoons	canned jalapeno chilies – chopped
2	tablespoons	onion – diced
2	teaspoons	horseradish sauce
2	teaspoons	parsley flakes
1	clove	garlic – minced
		salt and pepper to taste

Mash green soybeans. Blend with the rest of the ingredients and serve with low fat tortilla chips.

Nutritional analysis: Calories 50, Fat 4.6, Cholesterol 0, Carbohydrate 2.6, Protein 0.7.

OH SO TASTY! FRUIT DIP

Serving Size: 16

Amount	Measure	Ingredient – Preparation Method
1	package	french vanilla instant pudding mix
1	cup	skim milk
1	cup	sour cream, fat-free

Combine instant pudding mix with milk. Whip until thick. Fold in sour cream. Refrigerate until ready to serve. Serve with your favorite sliced fruits.

ONION GARLIC "BUTTER"

Amount	Measure	Ingredient – Preparation Method
2		onions
1	whole	garlic bulb – cloves divided and peeled

Cut top off unpeeled onion, press 1/2 of the garlic cloves into each onion. Place in microwave baking dish, microwave on high 5-7 minutes. Remove, peel onion and place in food processor and process until pureed.

PARTY CHEESE BALL

Serving Size: 16

Amount	Measure	Ingredient – Preparation Method
2	8 ounce	cream cheese fat-free – softened
2	cups	nonfat cheddar cheese, shredded
2	tablespoons	pimento – chopped
2	tablespoons	green pepper – chopped
2	tablespoons	onion – diced fine
2	teaspoons	Worcestershire sauce
1	teaspoon	lemon juice
		ground red pepper and salt to taste
4	tablespoons	roasted soy nuts, diced fine

Combine cream cheese and cheddar cheese, mixing at medium speed with electric mixer until well blended. Add all remaining ingredients, except soy nuts, mix well. Chill. Shape into ball, garnish with soy nuts. Chill until ready to serve.

Nutritional analysis: Calories 65, Fat 1.1, Cholesterol 4, Carbohydrate 2.6, Protein 9.8.

PINEAPPLE CHEESE LOG

Serving Size: 10

Amount	Measure	Ingredient – Preparation Method
1	8 ounce	cream cheese fat-free
1	4 ounce can	pineapple – crushed, drained
2	tablespoons	green pepper – chopped fine
1	tablespoon	onion – chopped fine
1	teaspoon	seasoning salt
		parsley, fresh – chopped fine

Mix together cream cheese and well drained pineapple, stir in green pepper, onion and seasoning salt. Refrigerate until thoroughly chilled. Shape into a log. Roll in chopped parsley. Chill overnight. Serve with reduced fat crackers.

Nutritional analysis: Calories 96.2, Fat 0.7, Cholesterol 3, Carbohydrate 20.8, Protein 3.8, Sodium 165, Potassium 179, Calcium 12.

PINEAPPLE SALSA

Serving Size: 6

Amount	Measure	Ingredient – Preparation Method
1	cup	fresh pineapple, diced
1		small jalapeno chile pepper, seeded, minced
1	clove	garlic, minced
3	tablespoons	onion, minced
1	tablespoon	fresh cilantro, chopped
2	teaspoons	grated lime zest
1	teaspoon	lemon juice

In medium size glass bowl, mix all ingredients. Cover and refrigerate until ready to use. Salsa keeps well refrigerated up to 3 days.

Nutritional analysis per 1/4 cup: Calories 23, Fat 0, Cholesterol 0, Carbohydrate 6, Sodium 40.

ROASTED GARLIC DIP

Amount	Measure	Ingredient – Preparation Method
1	large	bulb (entire head) garlic
1	cup	no-fat ricotta cheese
		black pepper to taste

Preheat the oven to 375 degrees. Wrap the garlic in aluminum foil, set on the middle oven rack, roast for 1 hour. Remove the garlic from the oven and cool until easy to handle. Separate the garlic into cloves. Working over a food processor or blender, pinch each garlic clove until the roasted flesh slips out. Add the ricotta cheese and pepper. Process for about 20 seconds until smooth. Transfer to serving bowl. Excellent dip for veggies. Makes 1 1/4 cup.

Nutritional analysis based on 1 tablespoon: Calories 21, Fat 0, Cholesterol 0, Carbohydrate 1, Protein 2, Sodium 16.

SALMON BALL

Serving Size: 6

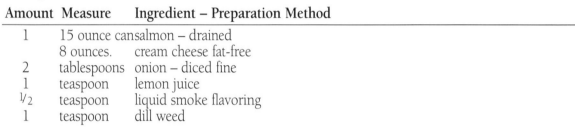

Amount	Measure	Ingredient – Preparation Method
1	15 ounce can	salmon – drained
	8 ounces.	cream cheese fat-free
2	tablespoons	onion – diced fine
1	teaspoon	lemon juice
1/2	teaspoon	liquid smoke flavoring
1	teaspoon	dill weed

Drain salmon, remove bones and skin. Blend all ingredients together, mixing well. Shape into a ball. Garnish with small amount of parsley flakes or fresh parsley. Refrigerate for 2 - 3 hours before serving. Serve with crackers or small slices toasted french bread.

Nutritional analysis: Calories 17.4, Fat 0.5, Cholesterol 7, Carbohydrate 0.2, Protein 2.9, Sodium 23, Potassium 51, Calcium 3.

SALMON MOUSSE

Serving Size: 12

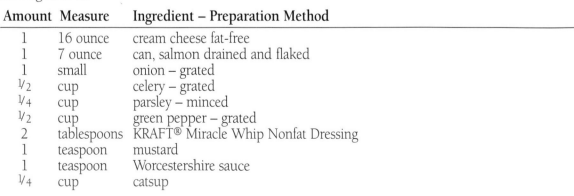

Amount	Measure	Ingredient – Preparation Method
1	16 ounce	cream cheese fat-free
1	7 ounce	can, salmon drained and flaked
1	small	onion – grated
1/2	cup	celery – grated
1/4	cup	parsley – minced
1/2	cup	green pepper – grated
2	tablespoons	KRAFT® Miracle Whip Nonfat Dressing
1	teaspoon	mustard
1	teaspoon	Worcestershire sauce
1/4	cup	catsup

Mix all ingredients together, chill in refrigerator for 4 to 6 hours before serving. Serve with assorted reduced fat crackers.

Nutritional analysis: Calories 50.1, Fat 0.1, Cholesterol 6, Carbohydrate 6.2, Protein 6.1, Sodium 411, Potassium 115, Calcium 29.

SHRIMP AND MUSHROOM SQUARES ♥

Amount	Measure	Ingredient – Preparation Method
CRUST		
1 ½	cups	cooked brown rice
1		egg white
FILLING		
1	cup	sliced fresh mushrooms
2	tablespoons	dry white wine
1	cup	frozen cooked whole salad shrimp, thawed, or 1 cup diced cooked shrimp
1	cup	cottage cheese, fat-free
1	cup	nonfat mozzarella cheese, shredded
¾	cup	diced green onions
1	cup	Egg Beaters® (egg substitute)
1	teaspoon	minced fresh garlic
		salt and pepper to taste
2	tablespoons	grated parmesan cheese

To make the crust, combine the cooked brown rice and egg white in a small bowl, stir until well mixed. Coat an 8 x 12 inch pan with cooking spray, pat the mixture into an even layer on the bottom of the pan. Set aside.

To make the filling, place the mushrooms and wine in a nonstick skillet, and sauté over medium-high heat until the mushrooms are tender and the liquid has evaporated. Remove the skillet from the heat, and add the remaining filling ingredients except for the parmesan cheese. Mix well. Pour the filling over the rice crust, spreading evenly. Sprinkle with the Parmesan and bake in a 375 degree oven for 40 to 45 minutes, or until the filling is set. A knife inserted in the center should come out clean. After removing from oven, let set for 10 minutes. Cut into squares, transfer to a serving platter. Makes 16 appetizers.

Nutritional analysis: Calories 40, Fat 0.2, Cholesterol 12, Protein 7.6, Sodium 150.

SIMPLE FRUIT DIP

Serving Size: 8

Amount	Measure	Ingredient – Preparation Method
1	8 ounce	cream cheese fat-free
1/4	cup	sugar
1/4	cup	brown sugar
1	teaspoon	vanilla

Mix all ingredients together well with electric mixer and chill. Great served with slices of green Granny Smith apples or strawberries.

Nutritional analysis: Calories 45, Fat 0, Cholesterol 0, Protein 0.5.

SMOKE'N CANNON BALLS (STUFFED TOFU BALLS)

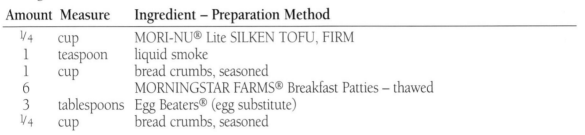

Serving Size: 12

Amount	Measure	Ingredient – Preparation Method
1/4	cup	MORI-NU® Lite SILKEN TOFU, FIRM
1	teaspoon	liquid smoke
1	cup	bread crumbs, seasoned
6		MORNINGSTAR FARMS® Breakfast Patties – thawed
3	tablespoons	Egg Beaters® (egg substitute)
1/4	cup	bread crumbs, seasoned

In food processor place tofu and liquid smoke, process until creamy, remove and pour into mixing bowl. Add 1 cup bread crumbs, stir until well blended. Set aside. Crumble patties, add egg substitute and 1/4 cup bread crumbs. Mix well. Shape into 24 small meatballs, (about 1 teaspoon each). Take about a teaspoon of the tofu, bread crumb mixture and place in palm of hand, flatten out to a thin shell like thickness. Place a meat ball in middle and form tofu mixture around meatball. Place all of the balls on a well sprayed cookie sheet. Place in a 400 degree oven and bake 10-15 minutes until lightly browned, remove from oven, insert each with a decorated toothpick. Serve with your favorite fat-free salsa, ranch or cheese sauce. Dynamite!

Nutritional analysis: Calories 85.4, Fat 1.9, Cholesterol 0, Carbohydrate 144, Protein 6.1, Sodium 473, Potassium 39, Calcium 15.

SOUTHWEST TOFU DRESSING/DIP

Serving Size: 12

Amount	Measure	Ingredient – Preparation Method
¼	cup	tofu lite firm
4	tablespoons	catsup
1	tablespoon	honey
1	teaspoon	chill powder
1	tablespoon	cilantro
3	tablespoons	California Sun-Dry Tomato Spread, fat-free

Combine all ingredients in food processor. Process for a few seconds at a time, using pulsing motion in order to blend all ingredients, scrape down sides of processor as necessary. Chill several hours before serving. Store any remaining dressing in covered container in refrigerator.

Serve as salad dressing or as a dip with veggies, crackers, polents, etc.

Nutritional analysis: Calories 34, Fat 0.5, Cholesterol 0, Carbohydrate 1.5, Protein 0.5, Sodium 255.

SPICY HOT MOCK HAMBURGER CHEESE DIP

Serving Size: 20

Amount	Measure	Ingredient – Preparation Method
1	pound	MORNINGSTAR FARMS® Ground Meatless – thawed
16	ounces.	fat-free refried beans
1	medium	onion – diced fine
1	teaspoon	garlic salt
1	tablespoon	Worcestershire sauce
1	cup	Pace Thick and Chunky Salsa
32	ounces	American or cheddar – grated, fat-free
1	tablespoon	chili powder

Place all ingredients in a slow cooker, cover and heat on low until cheese has melted. Mix well and serve with low fat tortilla chips.

Nutritional analysis: Calories 113, Fat 0, Cholesterol 6, Carbohydrate 10.3, Protein 18, Sodium 849.

SPINACH MOCK MEATBALLS

Amount	Measure	Ingredient – Preparation Method
1	16 ounce	MORNINGSTAR FARMS® Ground Meatless – thawed
1	teaspoon	Italian seasoning
1	teaspoon	whole fennel seeds
1	teaspoon	fresh garlic, crushed
1/2	teaspoon	crushed red pepper
		salt to taste
1	10 ounce	package frozen chopped spinach, thawed and squeezed very dry
1 1/2	cups	cooked brown rice
1	cup	finely chopped onion
1/3	cup	nonfat parmesan cheese
2		egg whites
1 1/2	cups	fat-free marinara sauce

Combine the ground meatless with the herbs and spices in a medium-sized bowl, mixing thoroughly. Set aside for 15 minutes. Add the remaining ingredients, (except for the marinara sauce). Mix thoroughly. Spray a baking sheet with nonstick cooking spray. Shape the ground meatless-spinach mixture into 32 1 inch balls. Place on baking sheet. Bake in a 350 degree oven for about 25 minutes. Heat the marinara sauce in a small saucepan. Transfer the balls to a serving platter and serve hot, accompanied by the sauce.

Nutritional analysis per appetizer: Calories 20, Fat 0, Cholesterol 0, Protein 2.5, Sodium 50.

SPINACH-MUSHROOM FORMAGGINI

Serving Size: 10

Amount	Measure	Ingredient – Preparation Method
1 1/2	cups	tofu lite firm
1 1/2	cups	ricotta cheese fat-free
1	teaspoon	garlic powder
1/2	cup	spinach, canned – drained, well
1	cup	artichoke hearts – drained, sliced
1	2.5 ounce	mushroom caps – drained, sliced
1	cup	nonfat mozzarella cheese, shredded
1/2	cup	parmesan cheese, shredded, fat-free

Place tofu in food processor with 2-3 artichokes. Process until smooth. Pour into medium size bowl. Add ricotta cheese, garlic powder, spinach, artichoke hearts, mushrooms and mozzarella cheese. Garnish with grated parmesan cheese before baking. Place in a casserole dish and bake 15 to 20 minutes. Serve with toast points. Small slices of French bread, brushed with fat-free Italian dressing. Place under broiler until browned. Dip may be frozen.

Nutritional analysis: Calories 80, Fat 1.5, Cholesterol 4, Carbohydrate 5, Protein 7, Sodium 470.

STUFFED GIMME LEAN SAUSAGE MUSHROOMS ♥

Serving Size: 12

Amount	Measure	Ingredient – Preparation Method
24	medium	mushroom caps
4	teaspoon	Campbell's Healthy Request Chicken Broth
1	cup	onion – diced
1	14 ounce	gimme lean sausage
1/4	cup	Worcestershire sauce
4	teaspoons	garlic powder
2	teaspoons	lemon pepper
1	teaspoon	poultry seasoning
3/4	cup	ricotta cheese fat-free
1/2	cup	grated parmesan cheese fat-free

Gently wash mushrooms and trim the tough ends from stems. Remove stems from the caps. Chop stems finely.

Heat chicken broth in a large sauce pan; add chopped onions and chopped mushroom stems. Sauté this mixture in 4 tablespoons chicken broth about 5 minutes. Add all other ingredients, except parmesan cheese. Cook over medium heat, stirring often, 5 to 8 minutes.

Stuff this mixture into mushroom caps and sprinkle with parmesan cheese.

Place the mushrooms on a cookie sheet. Bake for 8 to 10 minutes in 425 degree oven.

Nutritional analysis including mushrooms: Calories 125, Fat 0.4, Cholesterol 0, Carbohydrate 15, Protein 66, Sodium 660, Potassium 330, Calcium 17.

SWEDISH MEATBALLS

Serving Size: 10

Amount	Measure	Ingredient – Preparation Method
1	14 ounce	Gimme Lean Sausage®
1	14 ounce	Gimme Lean Beef®
¾	cup	bread crumbs
1	teaspoon	poultry seasoning
¼	cup	Egg Beaters® 99% egg substitute
		chopped onion to taste
		salt and pepper to taste
2	cans	SWANSON Vegetable Broth
¼	cup	flour
2	tablespoons	ketchup
1	cup	sour cream, fat-free

Meatballs: mix together Gimme Lean products with bread crumbs, poultry seasoning, egg beaters, chopped onion, salt and pepper. Roll into tiny balls. Brown in sprayed teflon skillet.

Sauce: heat vegetable broth and thicken with 1/4 cup flour. Add ketchup and cook for approximately 2 minutes. Remove from heat and add sour cream. Pour over meat balls. Heat on low prior to serving.

Nutritional analysis: Calories 169, Fat 0.7, Cholesterol 6, Carbohydrate 18, Protein 16, Sodium 630, Potassium 38, Calcium 12.

TACO DIP

Serving Size: 12

Amount	Measure	Ingredient – Preparation Method
1	8 ounce	cream cheese fat-free
1	5 ounce	tofu lite firm
1	envelope	taco seasoning mix
1	bottle	taco sauce
1	large	sweet onion – chopped fine
1	large	green pepper – chopped fine
2	cups	lettuce – shredded
2	cups	tomatoes – diced
2	cups	Grated Healthy Choice, Fat-Free Pizza Cheese

Place tofu in food processor and process until creamy, remove and place in bowl; blend in cream cheese and taco seasoning. Spread on large serving plate. Top with taco sauce. Layer the ingredients as listed on top of the taco sauce. Serve with nacho chips.

Nutritional analysis: Calories 84.3, Fat 0, Cholesterol 0, Carbohydrate 6.1, Protein 8, Sodium 176, Potassium 104, Calcium 14.

WEST INDIES CRAB APPETIZER

Serving Size: 4

Amount	Measure	Ingredient – Preparation Method
8	ounces	imitation crab – shredded
1	medium	onion – diced
1/3	cup	seasoned rice vinegar
1/3	cup	ice water
1	tablespoon	WONDERSLIM® Fat/Egg Substitute
		coarse ground pepper to taste

Combine all ingredients in medium bowl, cover and refrigerate 24 hours before serving. Serve with crackers of your choice.

Nutritional analysis: Calories 62, Fat 0, Cholesterol 6, Carbohydrate 9.4, Protein 6, Sodium 451, Potassium 61, Calcium 18.

Comment: real crab meat can be used in place of the imitation crab, but this increases the cholesterol to 50 mg.

WHITE BEAN DIP

Amount	Measure	Ingredient – Preparation Method
2	cups	great northern beans – drained
1/2	cup	nonfat, plain yogurt
3	cloves	garlic, minced
2	teaspoons	lime juice
1/2	teaspoon	ground cumin
3	tablespoons	mild green chilies, chopped

In a food processor or blender, place the beans, yogurt, garlic, lime juice, garlic and cumin. Process the mixture to form a smooth paste. Transfer to a medium size serving bowl and stir in the green chilies. Chill in the refrigerator 2-3 hours before serving. Makes 2 cups.

Nutritional analysis based on 2 tablespoons: Calories 32, Fat 0, Cholesterol 0, Carbohydrate 6, Protein 2, Sodium 12.

BLUEBERRY BANANA SHAKE

Serving Size: 4

Amount	Measure	Ingredient – Preparation Method
2	cups	nonfat vanilla frozen yogurt
1	cup	EDENSOY® Organic Soy Beverage – Vanilla
1	cup	blueberries
1		banana

Place all ingredients in a blender, and blend at high speed until smooth.

Nutritional analysis: Calories 168, Fat 0, Cholesterol 1, Carbohydrate 33, Protein 6, Sodium 98.

Comment: powdered soy protein supplements may be added to the shake, to increase the protein grams by 10 to 20 additional grams.

CHOCOLATE DELIGHT SMOOTHIE

Serving Size: 1

Amount	Measure	Ingredient – Preparation Method
1	cup	EDENSOY® Organic Soy Beverage Vanilla
1	scoop	VEGE FUEL® (TWINLAB® protein powder)
2	tablespoons	Hersheys Fat-Free Chocolate Sauce
1	medium	banana – sliced

Place all ingredients in a blender and blend until smooth. Great way to start the day!

Nutritional analysis: Calories 350, Fat 4, Cholesterol 0, Carbohydrate 66, Protein 17.2, Sodium 245, Potassium 908.

CRANBERRY SMOOTHIE

Serving Size: 1

Amount	Measure	Ingredient – Preparation Method
1	cup	cranberry juice
1		banana – sliced
6		frozen strawberries
2	scoops	VEGE FUEL® (TWINLAB® protein powder)

Place all ingredients in blender, blend about 2 minutes. Pour in glass and serve.

Nutritional analysis: Calories 388, Fat 1.6, Cholesterol 0, Protein 30, Sodium 15, Potassium 1981, Calcium 140.

CREAMY STRAWBERRY SMOOTHIE

Serving Size: 4

Amount	Measure	Ingredient – Preparation Method
1	package	MORI-NU® Lite SILKEN TOFU, FIRM
1	10 ounce box	strawberries, frozen – thawed
1	medium	banana – sliced
1	cup	orange juice
1	tablespoon	honey

Place all ingredients in blender and blend until smooth.

Nutritional analysis: Calories 163.6, Fat 0.4, Cholesterol 0, Carbohydrate 31, Protein 9, Sodium 7, Potassium 299.

EGGLESS NOG

Serving Size: 10

Amount	Measure	Ingredient – Preparation Method
1	quart	skim milk
1	cup	fat-free egg substitute
1/4	cup	sugar
1/2	cup	instant vanilla pudding mix
		2-3 teaspoons vanilla extract
1/2	teaspoon	ground nutmeg

Place all the ingredients in a blender, blend until smooth. Chill for several hours. Shake or stir eggnog well before serving.

Nutritional analysis: Calories 102, Fat 0.3, Cholesterol 4, Protein 5, Sodium 211.

GOOD NIGHT SMOOTHIE

Serving Size: 1

Amount	Measure	Ingredient – Preparation Method
1	package	Goodnight Kisses™ Hot Cocoa Mix
1/2	scoop	VEGE FUEL® (TWINLAB® protein powder)
1	cup	hot water
1/8	teaspoon	peppermint extract

Place all ingredients in a blender. (Do not place lid tightly on blender, as steam from hot water needs to escape.) Blend until smooth. Serve immediately.

Nutritional analysis: Calories 150, Fat 4.5, Cholesterol 0, Carbohydrate 27, Protein 17.

HOT APPLE CIDER

Serving Size: 1

Amount	Measure	Ingredient – Preparation Method
2	cups	water
3	sticks	cinnamon
1	tablespoon	whole cloves
1/2	teaspoon	whole allspice
2	quarts	unsweetened apple juice

Place the water and spices in a large pot, bring to a boil over high heat. Reduce the heat to low, simmer for 10 minutes. Strain the mixture, discarding the spices, return the water to the pot. Add the apple juice to the water, simmer over low heat until thoroughly heated. Serve hot.

Nutritional analysis per 1/2 cup serving: Calories 46, Fat 0, Cholesterol 0, Protein 0, Sodium 4.

JUMP START LATTEÉ

Serving Size: 1

Amount	Measure	Ingredient – Preparation Method
1	cup	decaf coffee or coffee substitute Teccino, Mediterranean Herbal Espresso, Flavor Almond Amaretto
1/2	cup	vanilla flavored soy milk, hot

Place coffee and shake mix in blender, blend until smooth. Pour in your favorite cup and enjoy!

Nutritional analysis: Calories 65, Fat 0, Cholesterol 0, Carbohydrate 16, Protein 5.

PINA COLADA PROTEIN SMOOTHIE

Serving Size: 1

Amount	Measure	Ingredient – Preparation Method
1	cup	Pina Calada bottled mix (non-alcohol)
1	scoop	VEGE FUEL® (TWINLAB® protein powder)
1/2	cup	chopped ice

Place all ingredients in a blender, blend until smooth. Serve immediately.

Nutritional analysis: Calories 93, Fat .5, Cholesterol 0, Carbohydrate 8, Protein 15.

POTASSIUM PACKED PROTEIN SMOOTHIE

Serving Size: 1

Amount	Measure	Ingredient – Preparation Method
1	cup	orange juice
1	medium	banana
1	scoop	VEGE FUEL® (TWINLAB® protein powder)
1/2	cup	chopped ice

Place all ingredients in a blender, blend until smooth. Serve immediatley.

Nutritional analysis: Calories 275, Fat 1.1, Cholesterol 0, Carbohydrate 53, Protein 16.4.

PROTEIN FRUIT SMOOTHIE

Serving Size: 1

Amount	Measure	Ingredient – Preparation Method
1	cup	pineapple juice
1/2	cup	mango, chopped
1/2	cup	papaya, chopped
1	scoop	VEGE FUEL® (TWINLAB® protein powder)
1/2	cup	chopped ice

Place all ingredients in a blender, blend until smooth. Serve immediately. Comment: since fresh mango and papaya are not always in season, we use the Sun Burst Brand. Found in the produce section, refrigerated. Both fruits are in jars and keep well in the refrigerator.

Nutritional analysis: Calories 330, Fat 1, Cholesterol 0, Carbohydrate 67, Protein 16.

SUPER SMOOTHIE

Serving Size: 1

Amount	Measure	Ingredient – Preparation Method
1	6 ounce	container, fat-free lemon yogurt
1	6 ounce	soy milk
1	scoop	VEGE FUEL® (TWINLAB® protein powder)
1	tablespoon	Flax powder
1/2		banana
3		strawberries

Combine all ingredients, in a blender. Blend until smooth.

Nutritional analysis: Calories 230, Fat 1, Cholesterol 0, Carbohydrate 18, Protein 25.

NOTES:

BREAKFAST/BRUNCH

Breakfast Popovers, page 47

BREAKFAST POPOVERS

♥

Serving Size: 9

Amount	Measure	Ingredient – Preparation Method
1	16 ounce	MORNINGSTAR FARMS® Ground Meatless – thawed
1	teaspoon	ground cumin
1/2	teaspoon	ground thyme
1	teaspoon	ground sage
1	teaspoon	salt
1/2	teaspoon	pepper
1/2	teaspoon	cayenne pepper
2	stalks	celery – grated
2	slices	onion – grated
1/2	cup	oatmeal
1 1/2	cups	flour, all-purpose
1	cup	skim milk
1		egg white
1/2	cup	water

Place thawed Ground Meatless in bowl, add the spices and oatmeal. Mix well. Place celery and onion in food processor and process until minced. Add to Ground Meatless mixture. Mix well. Form into 18 small balls. Place balls into sprayed muffin tins.

Place flour in bowl, make a well in the middle, pour in the milk and egg white, blend well. Gradually add water while mixing. Pour mixture evenly over balls. Bake in 425 degree oven for 20-25 minutes. Serve hot.

Nutritional analysis: Calories 120, Fat 0.7, Cholesterol 0, Carbohydrate 22.6, Protein 10.9, Sodium, 462.

BREAKFAST/BRUNCH CASSEROLE ♥

Serving Size: 6

Amount	Measure	Ingredient – Preparation Method
6	slices	bread slices
6		MORNINGSTAR FARMS® Breakfast Patties – thawed
2	cups	nonfat cheddar cheese, shredded
2	cups	MORNINGSTAR FARMS® Scramblers Egg Product – thawed
¾	cup	EDENSOY® Organic Soy Beverage
1	tablespoon	mustard, dry
1	cup	onion – chopped
1	cup	green pepper – chopped
1	can	Campbell's Healthy Request Mushroom Soup
⅓	cup	EDENSOY® Organic Soy Beverage
		salt and pepper to taste

The day before: spray bottom and sides of 9x13 baking dish, line with bread slices. Crumble thawed Morningstar Breakfast Patties over bread evenly. Top with shredded cheese. Microwave onions and green pepper until tender, spread over cheese. Sprinkle with salt and pepper to taste. In small mixing bowl mix together egg product, 3/4 cup EdenSoy milk and dry mustard. Pour evenly over the layers. Cover with plastic and store in refrigerator over night.

Next day: in small mixing bowl, mix together the cream of mushroom soup and 1/3 cup EdenSoy milk. Salt and pepper to taste. Spread evenly over the entire top of casserole. Bake at 350 degrees 60 to 90 minutes. Let set about 10 minutes after removing from oven before serving.

Comment: 2 cans of drained mushrooms can be added to onion and pepper layer for variety.

Nutritional analysis: Calories 258, Fat 4.6, Cholesterol 7, Carbohydrate 34.5, Protein 21, Sodium 1230, Potassium 263, Calcium 94.

BREAKFAST FAJITAS ♥

Serving Size : 4

Amount	Measure	Ingredient – Preparation Method
4	flour	tortillas
½	cup	frozen hash brown potatoes
½	cup	onion – chopped
½	cup	green pepper – chopped
½	cup	red bell pepper – chopped
2		MORNINGSTAR FARMS® Breakfast Patties – thawed
1	cup	Egg Beaters® (egg substitute)
		Salt and pepper to taste
4	slices	American or cheddar – grated, fat-free
		salsa, picante, taco sauce of your choice

Sauté potatoes, onion, and peppers in small amount of water or vegetable broth until tender. Crumble thawed breakfast patties and add to vegetables. Pour 1 cup of Egg Beaters over mixture, stirring until eggs have set. Remove from heat. In a 9-11 sprayed baking dish place tortillas, fill one at a time. Place 1/4 of the egg mixture down the center of each, fold ends and secure with a tooth pick. Place a slice of cheese over each (I cut the slice in half to cover the entire top). Place in microwave just long enough to melt cheese. Serve with your favorite salsa, picante or taco sauce.

Excellent served with fresh fruit.

Nutritional analysis: Calories 240.1, Fat 4.1, Cholesterol 4, Carbohydrate 167.6, Protein 19.3, Sodium 859, Potassium 202, Calcium 95.

BREAKFAST IN A LOAF

Serving Size: 8

Amount	Measure	Ingredient – Preparation Method
1	8-9 inch	round loaf bread
4		MORNINGSTAR FARMS® Breakfast Patties – crumbled
1	cup	red bell pepper – chopped
1	cup	onion – chopped
1	cup	grated fat-free cheese of choice
6		Egg Beaters® (egg substitute)
1	medium	tomato – thinly sliced
1	can 4 ounce	mushroom pieces

Cut 2 inch slice from top of loaf; set aside for lid. Remove soft interior of loaf, leaving a 1-inch thick wall and bottom. Place crumbled sausage patties in bottom of loaf. Top with half of the cheese. Set aside. In small microwave bowl with cover, microwave chopped peppers and onion on high for 3-4 minutes, drain well. In a medium sized, sprayed sauté pan, scramble the Egg Beaters, to which you have added the chopped peppers and onion. When done, layer this mixture over the sausage and cheese. Top with thinly sliced tomato, mushrooms and the remaining cheese. Place lid on loaf. Wrap in foil. Place on baking sheet. Bake in a 350 degree oven for 45 minutes. Cut into wedges or slices and serve.

Nutritional analysis: Calories 177, Fat 2.1, Cholesterol 5, Carbohydrate 157.3, Protein 21.8, Sodium 674.

BROCCOLI-CAULIFLOWER FRITTATA

Serving Size: 6

Amount	Measure	Ingredient – Preparation Method
1	10 ounce	package frozen cauliflower, thawed
1	10 ounce	package frozen broccoli, thawed
1	cup	Egg Beaters® (egg substitute)
½		envelope onion soup mix
½	cup	KRAFT® Miracle Whip Nonfat Dressing
½	cup	fat-free cracker crumbs

Drain thawed cauliflower and broccoli. Mash vegetables and mix with egg substitute, onion soup mix, and Miracle Whip. Lightly spray a 9x13 inch baking dish and sprinkle with cracker crumbs. Pour vegetable mixture in baking dish, top with additional cracker crumbs, and bake in a 350 degree oven for 45 minutes, or until set.

Nutritional analysis: Calories 70, Fat 0, Cholesterol 0, Carbohydrate 13, Protein 5, Sodium 615.

CHILI RELLENO CASSEROLE

Serving Size: 8

Amount	Measure	Ingredient – Preparation Method
2	16 ounce	cans fat-free refried beans
2-4	teaspoons	chili powder
2	4 ounce	cans hot diced green chilies, drained
1	pound	fat-free shredded Monterey Jack cheese
1	cup	Egg Beaters® (egg substitute)
4	tablespoons	flour, all-purpose
1	cup	skim milk

Preheat oven to 350 degrees. Season the refried beans with chili powder and spread over the bottom of a 9x13 inch baking dish that has been sprayed with cooking spray. Layer chilies and cheese on top of beans. In a medium bowl mix the eggs flour and milk blending well. Spread egg mixture on top of cheese. Bake in preheated oven 30 to 45 minutes, or until egg mixture is set and slightly brown.

Nutritional analysis: Calories 259, Fat 0, Cholesterol 0, Carbohydrate 31, Protein 29, Sodium 1168.

CRAB ASPARAGUS PIE

Serving Size: 4

Amount	Measure	Ingredient – Preparation Method
4	ounces	artificial crabmeat – shredded
12	ounces	fresh asparagus – cooked
1	cup	onion,chopped – cooked
1	cup	grated fat-free cheese of choice
3/4	cup	all-purpose flour
3/4	teaspoon	baking powder
1/2	teaspoon	salt
1/2	teaspoon	pepper
1	tablespoon	WONDERSLIM® Fat/Egg Substitute
1 1/2	cups	soy milk lite
4		Egg Beaters® 99% egg substitute

Spray a 10 inch quiche dish or pie plate. Layer crabmeat, cooked asparagus and onion in prepared dish. Top with cheese. Season with salt and pepper. In large bowl combine flour, baking powder and salt. With pastry blender, cut in Wonderslim Fat/Egg Substitute. Add milk and eggs; stir until blended. Pour over crab, vegetables and cheese. Bake in a 350 degree oven 30 minutes or until filling is puffed and a knife inserted near center comes out clean. Serve hot.

Nutritional analysis: Calories 305.2, Fat 2.0, Cholesterol 30, Carbohydrate 32.9, Protein 37, Sodium 628, Potassium 465, Calcium 174.

Comment: crabmeat could be omitted.

CRUSTLESS SPINACH QUICHE

Serving Size: 8

Amount	Measure	Ingredient – Preparation Method
2	cups	Egg Beaters® 99% egg substitute
1/3	cup	flour, all-purpose
1	teaspoon	baking powder
2	cups	nonfat cottage cheese
1	10 ounce	package frozen chopped spinach, thawed and squeezed dry
1/2	cup	thinly sliced green onions
1/4	teaspoon	cayenne pepper
		salt to taste

Preheat oven to 400 degrees. Lightly spray a 10 inch quiche or pie dish with cooking spray. Mix all of the ingredients in a large bowl. Pour into baking dish and bake 15 minutes. Lower heat to 350 degrees and bake 35 to 40 minutes more, or until filling is set and a toothpick inserted in the center comes out clean. Let cool 10 minutes on wire rack before serving.

Nutritional analysis: Calories 92, Fat 0, Cholesterol 1, Carbohydrate 9, Protein 12, Sodium 279.

HAM OR "VEGETARIUN" CANADIAN BACON QUICHE

Serving Size: 2

Amount	Measure	Ingredient – Preparation Method
6		egg whites
1	cup	non-fat milk
2	scoops	VEGE FUEL® (TWINLAB® protein powder)
4	ounces	turkey ham or "Ives Canadian Bacon", cubed
½	teaspoon	salt
½	teaspoon	pepper
2	ounces	Alpine Lace non-fat cheese

Preheat oven to 325 degrees. Combine the egg whites, milk, Vege Fuel, salt and pepper in a blender. Pulse several times, just enough to eliminate any lumps. Pour into an aluminum pie tin and set aside to rest, allowing the bubbles caused by blending to dissipate. Meanwhile, brown the ham pieces in a non-stick pan. Pat dry on a paper towel to remove any fat. (If using the Ives Canadian Bacon, you do not have to brown as this is a vegetable product.) Add this to the egg mixture. Add the cheese and stir the mixture to evenly distribute the ingredients. Cover the tin with aluminum foil and bake for about 1 hour, until a knife inserted into the center of the quiche can hold a small slit open. Allow the quiche to cool slightly and serve.

Nutritional analysis: Calories 318, Fat 3, Carbohydrate 15, Protein 55.

LOW FAT EGG SAUSAGE BREAKFAST SANDWICH

Serving Size: 1

Amount	Measure	Ingredient – Preparation Method
1		English muffin, low fat – toasted
¼	cup	MORNINGSTAR FARMS® Scramblers Egg Product – thawed
1	serving	Gimme Lean Sausage
1	slice	fat-free American cheese

Toast muffin. Layers: slice of cheese. Sauté breakfast pattie according to package directions, place on top of cheese. Pour Scramblers in small sauté pan, prepare over medium high, heat omelet style, fold in half and place over breakfast pattie, top with second half of muffin.

Nutritional analysis: Calories 210, Fat 1, Cholesterol 0, Carbohydrate 32, Protein 26, Sodium 610.

MUSHROOM AND ONION EGG BAKE

Serving Size: 6

Amount	Measure	Ingredient – Preparation Method
2	tablespoons	vegetable broth
1	bunch	green onions – chopped
4	ounces	mushrooms – sliced
1	cup	ricotta cheese fat-free
1	cup	sour cream, fat-free
6		Egg Beaters® (egg substitute)
3	tablespoons	all-purpose flour
½	teaspoon	salt
½	teaspoon	pepper
	dash	hot pepper sauce

Heat broth in medium skillet over medium heat. Add onions and mushrooms; cook until tender. Set aside.

In food processor or blender, process ricotta cheese until almost smooth. Add sour cream, eggs, flour, salt, pepper and hot pepper sauce; process until combined. Stir in onions and mushrooms. Pour into a sprayed 1-quart baking dish. Bake in a 350 degree oven about 40 minutes or until a knife inserted in the center comes out clean.

Nutritional analysis. Calories 133.1, Fat 0.2, Cholesterol 0, Carbohydrate 16.1, Protein 16.1, Sodium 101, Potassium 326, Calcium 101.

QUICK BREAKFAST CASSEROLE

Serving Size: 10

Amount	Measure	Ingredient – Preparation Method
1	24 ounce	frozen hash brown potatoes – thawed
1 ½	cups	onion – chopped
1	14 ounce	Gimme Lean Sausage
		salt and pepper to taste
2	cups	nonfat cheddar cheese, shredded
1	package	Pioneer fat-free gravy mix prepared according to package directions
1	tablespoon	dry mustard
1	cup	MORNINGSTAR FARMS® Scramblers – thawed

In a lightly sprayed 9x13 inch baking dish layer hash browns, chopped onion, crumbled breakfast patties, 1 1/2 cup shredded cheddar cheese. Salt and pepper to taste. In a medium bowl, mix together the prepared gravy, dry mustard and egg substitute. Pour over the potato layer evenly. Garnish with remaining 1/2 cup of cheese. Cover with foil and bake in a 350 degree oven for 1 hour and 15 minutes. Let sit for 5 to 10 minutes before serving.

Nutritional analysis: Calories 120, Fat 0, Cholesterol 0, Carbohydrate 17, Protein 12, Sodium 764.

SAUSAGE BROCCOLI BAKE

Serving Size: 6

Amount	Measure	Ingredient – Preparation Method
1	10 ounce	frozen chopped broccoli
8	ounces	Gimme Lean Sausage flavor thawed and crumbled
3	cups	fat-free croutons, seasoned
2	cups	nonfat cheddar cheese, shredded
1	cup	Pioneer Gravy made according to package directions
1	cup	Egg Beaters® (egg substitute)
10 ¾	ounces	EDENSOY® Organic Soy Beverage

Cook broccoli according to package directions. Drain and place in large bowl. Crumble thawed sausage, add to broccoli. Add croutons and cheese. Combine well, arrange the mixture in a sprayed 8 x 12 inch baking dish. In the same bowl, mix gravy and egg substitute until smooth. Mix well. Pour over the broccoli mixture, covering all ingredients. Bake for 45 minutes in a 375 degree oven. Let stand 10 minutes before serving.

Nutritional analysis: Calories 250, Fat 4.9, Cholesterol 2, Carbohydrate 24.5, Protein 27, Sodium 1138.

SCRAMBLED EGGS WITH TAMALES

Serving Size: 6

Amount	Measure	Ingredient – Preparation Method
1	15 ounce	can tamales, meatless
8		Egg Beaters® (egg substitute)
2	tablespoons	soy milk lite
½	teaspoon	salt
3	tablespoons	vegetable broth
1	large	tomato – chopped
2	tablespoons	onion – minced
2	tablespoons	green chiles – diced
1	cup	grated fat-free cheese of choice

Drain tamales, reserving 1/2 of the sauce from can. Remove wrappings from tamales; place tamales in a single layer in a 10x6 inch sprayed baking dish. Cover with the reserved sauce. Bake 10 minutes in a 350 degree oven or until heated through.

Whisk eggs, milk and salt in medium bowl. Set aside. In a large skillet over medium heat, place broth, tomato, onion and chiles. Cook 2 minutes or until vegetables are heated through. Add egg mixture. Cook, stirring gently, until eggs are set. Remove tamales from oven. Spoon eggs over tamales; sprinkle with cheese. Return to oven for a few minutes, until cheese melts. Serve hot.

Nutritional analysis: Calories 164.5, Fat 1.5, Cholesterol 7, Carbohydrate 13.9, Protein 23.2, Sodium 584, Potassium 309, Calcium 114.

SOY YUMMY BREAKFAST PUDDING

Serving Size: 6

Amount	Measure	Ingredient – Preparation Method
1 $\frac{1}{2}$	cups	oatmeal, (quick or old fashioned)
2 $\frac{1}{2}$	cups	EDENSOY® Organic Soy Beverage – Vanilla
$\frac{1}{2}$	cup	raisins or chopped dried fruit of choice
$\frac{2}{3}$	cup	applesauce
$\frac{3}{4}$	cup	lemon flavored fat-free yogurt
1		banana – sliced
1	small	orange, peeled and chopped

In large saucepan combine oatmeal and soy milk, cook according to package directions. Add raisins, chopped dry fruit, applesauce, yogurt, and chopped oranges. Stir gently to thoroughly heat fruits, add banana. Serve.

Nutritional analysis: Calories 105, Fat .8, Cholesterol .9, Protein 3.9, Sodium 29 3

Comments: Left overs can be chilled and served as a dessert! Wonderful!

SPINACH-CHEESE BAKE

Serving Size: 4

Amount	Measure	Ingredient – Preparation Method
8	ounces.	fat-free shredded cheddar cheese
1	10 ounce	package frozen chopped spinach, thawed and well-drained
2	cups	fat-free cottage cheese
$\frac{3}{4}$	cup	Egg Beaters® (egg substitute)
3	tablespoons	flour, all-purpose
$\frac{3}{4}$	teaspoon	garlic powder
2	ounces	fat-free shredded mozzarella cheese
		salt and pepper to taste

Preheat oven to 375 degrees. Combine all the ingredients except mozzarella cheese in a large bowl, mix well. Pour into a baking dish lightly sprayed with cooking spray. Top with mozzarella cheese and bake in preheated oven for 45 minutes or until set. Allow casserole to cool 10 minutes before serving.

Nutritional analysis: Calories 148, Fat 0, Cholesterol 3, Carbohydrate 11, Protein 23, Sodium 602.

SPINACH CHEESE STRATA

Serving Size: 6

Amount	Measure	Ingredient – Preparation Method
6		whole wheat bread slices, low fat
2	tablespoons	WONDERSLIM® Fat/Egg Substitute
1	cup	nonfat cheddar cheese, shredded
8	ounces	American or cheddar – grated, fat-free
1 ¼	cups	soy milk lite
6		Egg Beaters® (egg substitute)
1	10 ounce	frozen spinach – thawed and drained
		salt and pepper to taste

Spread bread with Wonderslim Fat/Egg Substitute. Arrange bread slices in a single layer in a sprayed 13x9-inch baking dish. Sprinkle with cheeses. In a large bowl combine milk, eggs, well drained spinach salt and pepper; stir well. Pour over bread and cheese. Cover; refrigerate at least 6 hours or overnight. Bake uncovered, in a 350 degree oven about 1 hour or until puffy and lightly golden.

Nutritional analysis: Calories 267.2, Fat 1.8, Cholesterol 11, Carbohydrate 29.3, Protein 35.8, Sodium 1,257, Potassium 453, Calcium 159.

STRAWBERRY & BANANA STUFFED FRENCH TOAST

Serving Size: 4

Amount	Measure	Ingredient – Preparation Method
1	12 " loaf	french bread loaf
2	tablespoons	strawberry jam
4	ounce	cream cheese fat-free – softened
1	pound	strawberries
3		bananas
6		Egg Beaters® (egg substitute)
¾	cup	soy milk lite
½	cup	apple juice, frozen concentrate

Cut French bread into 1 1/2 inch slices. Make pocket in each slice by cutting slit from top of bread almost to bottom. Combine jam, cream cheese, 1/4 cup chopped strawberries and 1/4 cup chopped bananas. (Use remaining strawberries and sliced bananas for garnish.) Place heaping tablespoon of strawberry filling into each pocket. Press back together. Beat eggs and milk in wide shallow bowl. Add bread; let stand to coat, then turn to coat other side. Place half of the frozen apple juice in large skillet ,over medium heat, add four bread slices. Cook until brown, turn and cook other side. Remove and keep warm. Repeat with remaining four bread slices. Garnish each plate with remaining strawberries and sliced bananas. Can be served with warm syrup or a warm strawberry sauce of your choice.

Nutritional analysis: Calories 630, Fat 5.1, Cholesterol 4, Carbohydrate 119.7, Protein 28.1, Sodium 1,180, Potassium 1,172, Calcium 235

STUFFED TOMATOES AND CREAMED SPINACH

Serving Size: 4

Amount	Measure	Ingredient – Preparation Method
4	medium	tomatoes
1/4	cup	grated parmesan cheese fat-free
4		Egg Beaters® (egg substitute)
4	teaspoons	green onions – minced
		salt and pepper to taste

CREAMED SPINACH

1	10 ounce	package spinach, frozen — chopped
1	tablespoon	WONDERSLIM® Fat/Egg Substitute
2	tablespoons	all-purpose flour
1	cup	soy milk lite
		salt and pepper to taste
1	tablespoon	grated parmesan cheese fat-free

Cut thin slice off top of each tomato; remove seeds and pulp, being careful not to pierce side of tomato. Place tomato shells in shallow sprayed baking dish. Sprinkle 1 tablespoon parmesan cheese inside each tomato. Pour 1/4 cup Egg Beater into each tomato. Top with onion, salt and pepper. Bake 15 to 20 minutes in a 375 degree oven until eggs are set.

Creamed Spinach:
Thaw chopped spinach, press to remove all moisture; set aside. In a medium saucepan over medium heat, mix together Wonderslim Fat/Egg Substitute and flour; stir and cook until bubbly. Slowly stir in milk. Stir and cook until thickened. Add spinach; continue cooking over low heat, stirring constantly, about 5 minutes or until spinach is tender. Season with salt, pepper and cheese. Serve with baked tomatoes.

Nutritional analysis: Calories 207.7, Fat 1.5, Cholesterol 0, Carbohydrate 26.6, Protein 19.4, Sodium 494, Potassium 698, Calcium 132.

VEGE FUEL OATMEAL

Serving Size: 1

Amount	Measure	Ingredient – Preparation Method
2/3	cup	oatmeal
1 1/4	cups	cold water
2	scoops	VEGE FUEL® (TWINLAB® PROTEIN POWDER)
1	tablespoon	vanilla
1	teaspoon	cinnamon
4		packets Equal® sweetener
1/4	teaspoon	salt

Pour the water into a saucepan and add the Vege Fuel. Mix well with a wire whisk until all lumps are gone. Add the oatmeal and bring to a boil, stirring constantly. Once the mixture starts to thicken, cover the pot and turn off the heat. Let the oatmeal steep undisturbed for 10 minutes. Add the remaining ingredients and mix well.

Nutritional analysis: Calories 456, Fat 5, Carbohydrate 37, Protein 60.

VEGETABLE QUICHE

Serving Size: 1

Amount	Measure	Ingredient – Preparation Method
6		egg whites
1	cup	non-fat milk
2	scoops	VEGE FUEL® (TWINLAB® PROTEIN POWDER)
1	teaspoon	salt
1/4	teaspoon	black pepper
1	cup	sliced onion
1/2	cup	green pepper, chopped
1/2	cup	sliced mushrooms
		cooking spray

Preheat the oven to 325 degrees. Combine the Vege Fuel, milk and egg white in a blender. Pulse several times, just enough to eliminate any lumps. Pour into an aluminum pie tin and set aside to rest, allowing the bubbles caused by blending to dissipate. Meanwhile, coat a pan with cooking spray and add the onion and salt. Sauté over medium heat until the onions start to brown. Add the green peppers and mushrooms. Sauté until all of the water from the mushrooms has evaporated and the peppers are soft. Add the pepper, remove from the heat, and allow to cool slightly. Add the vegetables to the egg mixture and stir to evenly distribute the ingredients. Cover the tin with aluminum foil and bake until a knife inserted into the center of the quiche can hold a small slit open. Allow the quiche to cool slightly and serve.

Nutritional analysis: Calories 457, Fat 1, Carbohydrate 32, Protein 80.

WHEAT N SOY STRAW CAKES

Serving Size: 4

Amount	Measure	Ingredient – Preparation Method
4		Quaker Oats Shredded Wheat Rounds
1	cup	EDENSOY® Organic Soy Beverage – Vanilla
1	teaspoon	vanilla
1	tablespoon	soy flour
1	teaspoon	cinnamon
4	tablespoons	apple juice, frozen concentrate

In shallow bowl pour milk, add vanilla, flour and cinnamon, mix well.

Dip wheat rounds in the milk mixture, covering both sides. Grill on nonstick griddle that has been sprayed. Use apple juice to keep from sticking, grill until golden brown on both sides. Sprinkle with sugar and cinnamon, top with lite pancake syrup if desired. Another great topping is a small amount of roasted soy nuts and syrup. Place soy nuts and syrup in small sauté pan, heat thoroughly. Pour over straw cakes. Serve with a grilled banana, lightly seasoned with lime juice.

Comment: for an alternative you can dip the wheat rounds in frozen apple juice only, prior to grilling and top with no-fat yogurt ice cream.

Nutritional analysis: Calories 141, Fat 1, Cholesterol 0, Carbohydrate 28, Protein 5, Sodium 31.

SANDWICHES/SOUPS

Corn Potato Chowder, page 59

CORN POTATO CHOWDER

Serving Size: 6

Amount	Measure	Ingredient – Preparation Method
1	bunch	scallions – sliced
2	medium	onions – diced
2	cups	potatoes – peeled and diced
3 ½	cups	EDENSOY® Organic Soy Beverage
½	teaspoon	salt
1	cup	corn kernels
		(optional) liquid smoke to taste

Garnishes:
Green: Chopped chives, parsley or scallion tops. Red: Sweet red pepper or finely chopped cherry tomatoes.

In large microwave bowl, place sliced scallions, diced onions and diced potatoes, microwave on high until tender, 3-5 minutes. Transfer to large soup pot, add milk. Bring to boil, stirring constantly. Reduce heat. Add salt, pepper and liquid smoke if desired. Simmer covered with lid tilted for about 5 minutes. Add corn kernels, cook just until heated through. Ladle into soup bowls and garnish with either a green or red garnish.

Nutritional analysis: Calories 132.9, Fat 2.1, Cholesterol 0, Carbohydrate 20.2, Protein 7.4, Sodium 424, Potassium 511, Calcium 28.

APPLE CHEDDAR CHEESE SPREAD

Amount	Measure	Ingredient – Preparation Method
8	ounce	nonfat cream cheese, softened
1	cup	cottage cheese, fat-free
1 ½	cups	finely chopped tart apples
1	cup	shredded nonfat cheddar cheese

Place the cheeses in a food processor or blender and process until smooth. Place in a bowl with cover. Stir in the apples and cheddar cheese. Cover and chill for several hours. Excellent served with bagels, crackers or celery sticks.

Nutritional analysis per tablespoon: Calories 15, Fat 0, Cholesterol 0, Protein 1, Sodium 29.

BEAN AND CHEESE PITAS

Serving Size: 4

Amount	Measure	Ingredient – Preparation Method
⅔	cup	canned kidney or black beans, drained
½	cup	onions, finely diced
1	cup	tomatoes, chopped, drain juice
4	ounce	fat-free shredded mozzarella cheese
1 ½	tablespoons	fat-free Italian dressing
4	1 ounce	pita breads

Preheat oven to 400 degrees. In a large bowl, combine all ingredients, except pita breads. Mix well. Split open one end of each pita. Divide filling evenly and spoon into open end. Wrap each pita tightly in a piece of aluminum foil. Bake 20 minutes. Serve hot.

Nutritional analysis: Calories 195, Fat 2, Cholesterol 2, Carbohydrate 27, Protein 12, Sodium 445.

BLACK BEAN BURRITOS

Serving Size: 4

Amount	Measure	Ingredient – Preparation Method
4		flour tortillas, fat-free
1	8 ounce	cream cheese fat-free
		garlic powder to taste
1	15 ounce can	EDENSOY® Organic Black Soy Beans – drained
1	bunch	green onions – chopped fine
4	tablespoons	salsa sauce
¾	cup	nonfat cheddar cheese, shredded

Divide cream cheese equally onto the 4 tortillas, spread evenly over the tortillas. Sprinkle with garlic powder. Divide the drained beans equally onto the tortillas, then layer with chopped onion, salsa sauce and shredded cheese. Roll up each tortilla, (I use cocktail picks to hold them in rolls) and wrap each one in plastic wrap to keep them from drying out. Great lunch treat!

Nutritional analysis: Calories 219, Fat 0.5, Cholesterol 6, Carbohydrate 32.4, Protein 20.6, Sodium 453.

BLACK SOY BEAN BURGERS

Serving Size: 4

Amount	Measure	Ingredient – Preparation Method
1	14 ounce can	black soybeans – drained, divided
1	small	onion
2	cloves	garlic – crushed fine
2	teaspoons	cajun seasoning
1/2	cup	seasoned bread crumbs
1/4	cup	Egg Beaters® (egg substitute)

Place onion and garlic in food processor, process until fine, add 1/2 can well drained black soybeans, process until beans are in mashed consistency. Place in medium mixing bowl, add remaining beans, cajun seasoning, bread crumbs and Egg Beaters. Mix thoroughly. Shape into 4 patties. Spray large fry pan, sauté on med-high heat, brown both sides. Lower heat and continue sautéing until heat thoroughly. Serve with your favorite salsa, or on buns as a sandwich.

Nutritional analysis: Calories 97.6, Fat 0.9, Cholesterol 0, Carbohydrate 16.5, Protein 5.9, Sodium 664, Potassium 110.

CARROT DOG

Serving Size: 2

Amount	Measure	Ingredient – Preparation Method
2	medium	carrots – peeled
1/4	cup	balsamic vinegar
1/4	cup	soy sauce, low sodium
2	tablespoons	Pickapeppa Sauce

Place peeled carrots in marinate sauce, of vinegar, soy sauce and Pickapeppa Sauce. Marinate overnight in refrigerator. Place carrots in a microwave dish with small amount of marinate sauce. microwave until tender. Remove from dish, place on grill, grill until browned. Place on hot buns, serve with all of your favorite hot dog garnishes.

Nutritional analysis: Calories 50.5, Fat 0.2, Cholesterol 0, Carbohydrate 11.5, Protein 2, Sodium 992.

CINNAMON RAISIN BAGEL SPREAD

Amount	Measure	Ingredient – Preparation Method
8	ounce	nonfat cream cheese
1	cup	cottage cheese, fat-free
		1-2 teaspoons cinnamon
½	cup	raisins

Place cheeses in a food processor or blender, and process until smooth. Stir in the cinnamon and raisins. Place the spread to a serving dish, cover and chill for several hours. Serve with sliced toasted whole grain bagels. Keeps well in refrigerator, or cut recipe in half for small family.

Nutritional analysis per tablespoon: Calories 15, Fat 0, Cholesterol 0.5, Protein 2, Sodium 40.

EGG SALAD

Serving Size: 6

Amount	Measure	Ingredient – Preparation Method
3	medium	potatoes – boiled
3	ounces	MORI-NU® Lite SILKEN TOFU, EXTRA FIRM – diced fine
¾	cup	KRAFT® Miracle Whip Nonfat Dressing
1	tablespoon	mustard
1	tablespoon	Dijon mustard
2	teaspoons	sweet pickle juice
		salt and pepper to taste
		paprika

Peel and boil potatoes until done. Mash potatoes to a very fine consistency, when cool add finely diced tofu, Miracle Whip, mustards, pickle juice, dry salad mix, salt and pepper to taste. Best if made a day ahead and chilled in refrigerator.

Nutritional analysis: Calories 93.5, Fat 0.5, Cholesterol 0, Carbohydrate 16.2, Protein 2.1, Sodium 298, Potassium 312, Calcium 8.

EGGPLANT SPREAD

Amount	Measure	Ingredient – Preparation Method
2	1 pound	eggplant
2	heads	garlic, separated into cloves and peeled
¼	cup	chopped sun-dried tomatoes
2	tablespoons	lemon juice
1 ½	teaspoons	dried oregano
¼	teaspoon	ground cumin
¼	teaspoon	crushed red pepper
		salt to taste

Cut each eggplant in half lengthwise. Cut 2 deep slits down the length of each half. Insert the garlic cloves and dry tomatoes in the slits. Place the eggplants in a baking pan. Cover and bake in a 425 degree oven for 60 minutes, or until very tender. Cool to room temperature. Scoop out the eggplant flesh along with the garlic and tomatoes, placing in a food processor or blender with remaining ingredients. Process until smooth. Transfer the spread to a serving dish. Serve at room temperature with crusty french bread slices.

Nutritional analysis per tablespoon: Calories 12, Fat 0, Cholesterol 0, Protein 0.5, Sodium 25.

FRUIT AND CHEESE PITAS

Serving Size: 2

Amount	Measure	Ingredient – Preparation Method
½	cup	fat-free cottage cheese
½	cup	shredded fat-free cheddar cheese
½		kiwi fruit, peeled and sliced
½	cup	strawberries, sliced
¼	cup	pineapple tidbits, drained
1	tablespoon	green onions, sliced
2		pita pockets

In a medium bowl stir together all of the ingredients, except the pita pockets. To serve open one end of each pocket. Spoon the fruit and cheese mixture into the pitas.

Nutritional analysis: Calories 160, Fat 2.5, Cholesterol 0, Carbohydrate 23, Protein 6.

GORGEOUS GEORGE BURGER

Serving Size: 1

Amount	Measure	Ingredient – Preparation Method
1		MORNINGSTAR FARMS® Better N Burger
1		burger bun
1	slice	pineapple
1	slice	onion
1	slice	Swiss cheese, no fat
1	tablespoon	no fat Thousand Island salad dressing
1		lettuce leaf
3	tablespoons	vegetable broth

Grill Better N Burger and slice of pineapple slowly in sprayed grill pan until thoroughly heated. Use 2-3 tablespoons of vegetable broth in grill pan to prevent sticking. Place burger, pineapple, Swiss cheese, onion and lettuce leaf on bun, top with or serve on side Thousand Island salad dressing. Wonderful!

Nutritional analysis: Calories 250, Fat 1.5, Cholesterol 6, Carbohydrate 33, Protein 21.

HAWAIIAN CHEESE SANDWICH

Serving Size: 2

Amount	Measure	Ingredient – Preparation Method
4	slices	lite whole wheat bread
2	slices	fat-free cheddar or American cheese
¼	cup	canned pineapple tidbits, unsweetened – drained
2	tablespoons	green pepper, finely chopped
2	tablespoons	tomato, finely chopped, drain juice

Place 2 slices of bread on a broiler pan. Place 1 slice of cheese on each slice of bread. In a small bowl, combine pineapple, green pepper and tomato. Divide evenly and arrange on top of cheese. Place under a preheated broiler and broil until cheese starts to melt. Top with remaining bread slices and return to broiler. Broil just until top slices of bread are toasted.

Nutritional analysis: Calories 180, Fat 2, Cholesterol 2, Carbohydrate 20, Protein 11, Sodium 380.

HEALTHY HOAGIES ♥

Serving Size: 4

Amount	Measure	Ingredient – Preparation Method
4		hoagie buns
1	large	onion – chopped
1		green pepper – chopped
1	clove	garlic – chopped
4	tablespoons	vegetable broth
1	8 ounce	White Wave Filly Slices, chopped
4	slices	mozzarella cheese fat-free – diced

Sauté onion, green pepper and onion in vegetable broth to desired doneness. Add Filly Slices, heat thoroughly, add cheese until melted. Serve on hoagie buns.

Nutritional analysis: Calories 237, Fat 2, Cholesterol 0, Carbohydrate 32, Protein 14, Sodium 724.

HOT BEAN SANDWICH SPREAD

Serving Size: 3

Amount	Measure	Ingredient – Preparation Method
1	cup	canned vegetarian baked beans
1-2	tablespoons	horseradish
2-3	tablespoons	onion, minced

Mash the beans in a bowl. Add the horseradish and onion. Mix well. Spread on two slices of low-fat bread. Excellent served with lettuce leaf and tomato slice.

Nutritional analysis, does not include bread: Calories 100, Fat 1, Carbohydrate 25, Protein 5, Sodium 425.

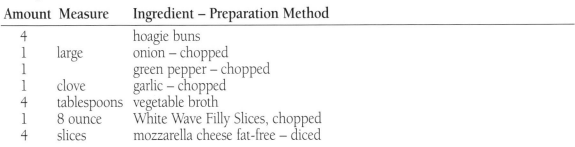

ITALIAN TOFU PITAS

Serving Size: 6

Amount	Measure	Ingredient – Preparation Method
1	12.3 ounce	package firm tofu
1	10 ounce	package frozen chopped spinach, thawed well drained
1	teaspoon	dried oregano
1/2	teaspoon	dried basil
1	teaspoon	garlic powder
6	1 ounce	pita breads
3/4	cup	low fat spaghetti or marinara sauce

Preheat oven to 375 degrees. Drain tofu slightly. Place in a food processor or blender and process until smooth. Spoon into a bowl and add well drained spinach and spices. Mix well. Split open one end of each pita. Divide filling evenly and spoon into open end. Spoon 2 1/2 tablespoons of sauce into each pita. Wrap each pita in a piece of aluminum foil. Bake 20 to 25 minutes. Serve hot.

Nutritional analysis: Calories 160, Fat 3.5, Carbohydrate 26, Cholesterol 0, Sodium 385.

MOCK BARBECUE BEEF

Serving Size: 12

Amount	Measure	Ingredient – Preparation Method
3	cups	textured vegetable protein, chunks
2	large	bottles barbecue sauce, fat-free
1 1/2	cups	water – heated to boiling

In large crockpot put 3 cups textured vegetable protein, rehydrate the textured vegetable protein with 1/2 cup barbecue and 1 1/2 cups hot water. Let sit for 15 minutes. Add the remaining barbecue sauce, cook on low 5-6 hours. Serve on low fat whole grain buns.

Nutritional analysis per serving, includes bun: Calories 135, Fat 0, Cholesterol 0, Protein 14.8, Sodium 806.

MOCK CHICKEN SALAD

Serving Size: 6

Amount	Measure	Ingredient – Preparation Method
1	16 oz. box	Chicken Style Wheat Meat – chopped fine
2	cups	celery – chopped fine
1/3	cup	parsley – dry
1/2	large	red onion – chopped fine
1/4	cup	sweet pickle relish
1	cup	KRAFT® Miracle Whip Nonfat Dressing
2	tablespoons	Grey Poupon Mustard
1/2	teaspoon	celery seed

Cut Chicken Style into small pieces or chop in a food processor for a few seconds. In a large bowl, mix together chicken, celery, parsley, onion and pickle relish. In a separate bowl, combine Miracle Whip, mustard, and celery seeds, mix well and add to chicken mixture.

Comment: flavors blend the best when made the day ahead.

Nutritional analysis: Calories 75.5, Fat 0.4, Cholesterol 0, Carbohydrate 15.7, Protein 2, Sodium 437.

MOCK TUNA SALAD

Serving Size: 4

Amount	Measure	Ingredient – Preparation Method
1	can	garbanzo beans – drained
1/2	cup	celery – chopped fine
2	tablespoons	green onion – chopped fine
1	tablespoon	sweet pickle relish
1/2	cup	KRAFT® Miracle Whip Nonfat Dressing
2	teaspoons	soy sauce, low sodium
		salt and pepper

Mash the drained garbanzo beans with a pastry blender. Leave some chunks. Add celery, onion, relish, soy sauce and Miracle Whip. Mix well.

Spread on your favorite bread (toasted or plain). Garnish with lettuce and tomato, if desired. For a change, use pita bread instead of regular bread.

Nutritional analysis for salad ingredients only: Calories 158, Fat 1.3, Cholesterol 0, Protein 5.8, Sodium 625.

ONION BURGER

Serving Size: 1

Amount	Measure	Ingredient – Preparation Method
2	patties	MORNINGSTAR FARMS® Better N Burgers – thawed
2	slices	onion – chopped
2	tablespoons	vegetable broth
		pepper to taste
		garlic salt to taste

Crumble the Better N Burgers in small mixing bowl, add pepper and garlic salt to taste, set aside. Sauté chopped onion in broth until tender. Add to burger mixture, mix well and shape into pattie. Grill slowly until nicely browned and heated thoroughly. Serve on your favorite hamburger bun.

Nutritional analysis: Calories 140, Fat 0, Cholesterol 0, Carbohydrate 12, Protein 22, Sodium 720, Potassium 780.

Comment: nutritional analysis does not include hamburger bun. If out-door grilling, use low heat. Do not over cook. If burger begins to become dry, spray with vegetable broth seasoned with hickory smoke flavor.

PIMENTO CHEESE SPREAD

Amount	Measure	Ingredient – Preparation Method
1	cup	cottage cheese, fat-free
2	tablespoons	nonfat mayonnaise
2	teaspoons	spicy mustard
½	teaspoon	crushed fresh garlic
		ground white pepper to taste
3	tablespoons	finely chopped onion
1	cup	nonfat shredded cheddar cheese
1	4 ounce jar	chopped pimentos, drained

Place the cottage cheese, mayonnaise, mustard, garlic and pepper in a food processor or blender and process until smooth. Add the onion and cheddar cheese, process to the desired consistency. Transfer to serving bowl, stir in the pimentos. Cover and chill for several hours. Serve with crackers, as a sandwich filler, or as a dip for celery sticks or carrots.

Nutritional analysis per tablespoon: Calories 12, Fat 0, Cholesterol 0, Protein 2, Sodium 45.

SALSA BURGERS

Serving Size: 4

Amount	Measure	Ingredient – Preparation Method
1	pound	MORNINGSTAR FARMS® Ground Meatless – thawed
½	cup	seasoned bread crumbs
¾	cup	finely chopped onions
½	cup	prepared thick salsa
1-2	teaspoons	chili powder
4		burger buns

Combine the ground meatless, bread crumbs, onion, salsa and chili powder in a mixing bowl. Mix the ingredients thoroughly. Shape the mixture into 4 patties. Spray a large grill pan with cooking spray. Over medium heat grill patties on both sides until heated through. Can be basted with small amount of vegetable broth to keep from sticking. Remove from grill pan, serve on buns with your favorite garnishes.

Nutritional analysis, burger with bun: Calories 170, Fat 1.5, Cholesterol 0, Protein 15, Sodium 480.

SEAFOOD SALAD SANDWICH

Amount	Measure	Ingredient – Preparation Method
2	cups	imitation crab, chopped
½	cup	KRAFT® Miracle Whip Nonfat Dressing
2	stalks	celery, diced fine
3	tablespoons	onion, diced fine
		fat-free bread slices, or pita pockets

Chop the crab and combine with the Miracle Whip, celery and onion. Serve as a sandwich or a pita pocket.

Nutritional analysis: Calories 137, Fat 0, Cholesterol 0, Carbohydrate 24, Protein 9, Sodium 950.

SMOKED SALMON BAGEL SPREAD

Amount	Measure	Ingredient – Preparation Method
1	12 ounce	smoked salmon
1	cup	no-fat cream cheese, softened
3	teaspoons	prepared horseradish
2	tablespoons	finely chopped onion
1	tablespoon	lemon juice
1/2	cup	minced fresh parsley

Place the salmon in a medium-sized bowl, separate it into flakes. Add the remaining ingredients except for the parsley. Stir until the mixture is the consistency of a spread. Shape the salmon mixture into a log. Spread the parsley on waxed paper, and roll the log in the parsley to coat evenly. Transfer to a serving plate, cover and refrigerate for several hours.

Nutritional analysis per tablespoon: Calories 16, Fat 0.5, Cholesterol 3, Protein 2.6, Sodium 108.

SOYBUTTER AND JELLY SANDWICH

Serving Size: 1

Amount	Measure	Ingredient – Preparation Method
2	slices	bread
2	tablespoons	Natural Touch soybutter
1	tablespoon	grape jelly

Spread soybutter on one slice of bread and jelly on the other. Fold together and slice in half or quarters.

Nutritional analysis: Calories 340, Fat 13, Cholesterol 0, Carbohydrate 46, Protein 10, Sodium 370.

SWEET BEAN SANDWICH SPREAD

Serving Size: 3

Amount	Measure	Ingredient – Preparation Method
1	cup	canned vegetarian baked beans
2-3	tablespoons	sweet pickle relish

Mash the beans in a bowl. Add the relish and mix well. Spread on low-fat bread.

Nutritional analysis, does not include bread: Calories 100, Fat 1, Carbohydrate 27, Protein 5, Sodium 520.

SUPER SOY SLOPPY JOES

Serving Size: 8

Amount	Measure	Ingredient – Preparation Method
1	pound	MORNINGSTAR FARMS® Ground Meatless – thawed
1	large	onion – chopped
1	large	green pepper – chopped
2	cloves	garlic – coarsely crushed
½	cup	catsup
2	cans	Campbell's Fiesta Tomato Soup
		salt and pepper to taste

In large sauce pan sauté onion, green pepper and garlic in small amount of water or a vegetable broth until tender, add Ground Meatless, catsup, Fiesta Tomato Soup, slowly simmer for 20-30 minutes. Add additional water or broth if it becomes to thick.

Serve on your favorite kaiser or low fat whole grain bun.

Nutritional analysis does not include roll served on: Calories 97.8, Fat 0.1, Cholesterol 0, Carbohydrate 12.9, Protein 11, Sodium 687.

TOFU SALAD SANDWICH

Serving Size: 4

Amount	Measure	Ingredient – Preparation Method
1	10.5 ounce	package extra-firm tofu
1	cup	seedless green grapes, halved
¼	cup	celery, sliced
¼	cup	green onions, sliced
¼	cup	raisins
½	cup	KRAFT® Miracle Whip Nonfat Dressing
½	teaspoon	curry powder
¼	teaspoon	ground ginger
		salt to taste
		lettuce leaves
4	slices	whole grain toast

Drain the tofu between paper towels, 10 to 15 minutes. Finely chop tofu. In a large bowl combine the chopped tofu, grapes, celery, onions and raisins. For dressing, stir together the Miracle Whip, curry powder, ginger and salt. Add dressing to tofu mixture, stirring to combine well. Cover and chill 2 to 24 hours, prior to serving. To serve, spread the tofu mixture on the lettuce-lined whole wheat bread slices. If you desire, the bread can be toasted. Excellent in pita bread.

Nutritional analysis: Calories 165, Fat 4, Cholesterol 0, Carbohydrate 33, Protein 8.

TUNA BURGERS

Serving Size: 4

Amount	Measure	Ingredient – Preparation Method
5	ounces	tuna in water – drained
5	ounces	tofu lite firm – crumbled
1/4	cup	seasoned bread crumbs
2	tablespoons	Egg Beaters® (egg substitute)
3	tablespoons	green onion – diced fine
		vegetable broth

Place tofu in medium bowl, crumble with pastry cutter or fork. Add well drained tuna, bread crumbs, Egg Beaters and onion. Blend well, shape into 4 patties. Spray non-stick skillet. Over medium heat brown patties on both sides. (I use a small amount of broth to keep them from sticking). When browned, remove and serve on your favorite buns.

Nutritional analysis: Calories 109.8, Fat 0.6, Cholesterol 11, Carbohydrate 8.2, Protein 14.3, Sodium 413, Potassium 207, Calcium 55.

VEGGIE-CHEESE SANDWICH

Serving Size: 8

Amount	Measure	Ingredient – Preparation Method
1/3	cup	vegetable broth
3	tablespoons	white wine
2	cups	mushrooms, sliced
1		red bell pepper, seeded and sliced
1	cup	scallions, sliced (whites only)
2	cups	fat-free grated mozzarella cheese
8	slices	fat-free sourdough bread
		spicy mustard

Heat vegetable broth and wine in a nonstick skillet. Add mushrooms, red pepper and scallions. Cook until liquid is evaporated, stirring often. Toast the bread lightly. Place on broiler pan. Spread each bread slice with mustard and top with veggie mixture. Sprinkle grated mozzarella cheese over top of each slice of bread. Place under preheated broiler until cheese is melted. Serve sandwich open-faced.

Nutritional analysis: Calories 150, Fat 0, Cholesterol 1, Carbohydrate 13, Protein 20, Sodium 619.

VEGGIE PITAS

Serving Size: 4

Amount	Measure	Ingredient – Preparation Method
4	6 inch	pita pockets
1	cup	broccoli flowerets, chopped fine
1	cup	carrots, grated
1	cup	mushrooms, sliced
4		green onions, thinly sliced
4	tablespoons	fat-free ranch salad dressing
1	cup	alfalfa sprouts

Combine broccoli, carrots, mushrooms and green onions in a microwave-safe baking dish, cover with vented plastic wrap, and cook 6 to 8 minutes, or until all the vegetables are tender. Cut a slice from the top of each pita pocket and fill with the warm vegetable mixture. Top with alfalfa sprouts and ranch dressing. Serve.

Nutritional analysis: Calories 140, Fat 0, Cholesterol 0, Carbohydrate 28, Protein 6, Sodium 295.

VEGGIE SUBMARINE

Serving Size: 8

Amount	Measure	Ingredient – Preparation Method
2	cups	onions, thinly sliced, separate into rings
3	cups	zucchini, thinly sliced
3	cups	sweet yellow peppers, seeded and thinly sliced
3	cups	mushrooms, sliced
1/4	cup	vegetable broth
1	teaspoon	garlic powder
1	teaspoon	dried oregano
1/2	teaspoon	black pepper
1	1 pound	loaf French or sourdough bread, unsliced
8	ounces	sliced fat-free cheddar cheese

Heat vegetable broth in a large nonstick skillet over medium-high heat. Add vegetables. Sprinkle with spices. Cook, stirring frequently, until vegetables are tender. Cut bread in half lengthwise and open to make a sandwich. (Do not cut all the way through.) Pile the vegetables on the bread and top with cheese slices. Close the sandwich and secure with toothpicks. Slice and serve.

Nutritional analysis: Calories 247, Fat 2.5, Carbohydrate 40, Cholesterol 0, Protein 15, Sodium 536.

WHOLESOME HOAGIES

Serving Size: 6

Amount	Measure	Ingredient – Preparation Method
1/2	cup	green onions, finely diced
1	cup	tomatoes, finely chopped
1/4	cup	carrots, finely shredded
1/2	cup	green pepper, finely chopped
1	tablespoon	dried parsley flakes
1	teaspoon	garlic powder
		black pepper to taste
3	tablespoons	fat-free Italian dressing
4	ounce	fat-free shredded Cheddar cheese
6		hoagie rolls

Cut each roll in half lengthwise. With a sharp knife scoop out the inside of each roll leaving a 1/2 inch shell. Crumble the insides of the rolls into a large bowl. (Place the roll shells into a plastic bag to retain freshness.) Add the remaining ingredients to the bread crumbs. Mix well. Pat mixture down firmly in the bowl, cover, and chill at least 1 to 2 hours. Stir the vegetable mixture, then, using a spoon, stuff the mixture into each roll evenly. Wrap each roll and chill several hours or overnight.

Nutritional analysis: Calories 220, Fat 15, Cholesterol 0, Carbohydrate 35, Protein 10, Sodium 640.

AUTUMN SQUASH SOUP

Serving Size: 8

Amount	Measure	Ingredient – Preparation Method
2	cups	acorn squash, baked and cooled
2	tablespoons	frozen apple juice
1	medium	onion – chopped
2		carrots, diced
1	medium	potato, diced
2		apples, peeled, cored and diced
3 1/2	cups	water
1 1/2	cups	soy milk lite
1/8	teaspoon	cinnamon
		salt and pepper to taste

Sauté onion in apple juice until translucent, add carrots, potato, apples and water. Bring to a boil, reduce heat and simmer for 20 minutes or until vegetables are tender. Place cooled squash, vegetables along with stock from vegetables in a food processor in several batches. Process each batch to a smooth consistency. Place processed vegetables in a saucepan, add soy milk, stir and heat on low until thoroughly heated. Add cinnamon, salt and pepper to taste.

Nutritional analysis: Calories 80, Fat 0, Cholesterol 0, Carbohydrate 16.5, Protein 2.8, Sodium 100.

BARLEY MUSHROOM SOUP

Serving Size: 8

Amount	Measure	Ingredient – Preparation Method
1	cup	onions, chopped
1/2	cup	carrots, diced
1	cup	celery, thinly sliced
3	cups	mushrooms, sliced
5	cups	water
4	teaspoons	instant vegetable broth mix
1/2	cup	barley, uncooked
		salt and pepper to taste

In a large soup pot, combine all the ingredients. Bring to a boil. Cover, reduce heat to low and simmer 1 hour.

Nutritional analysis: Calories 80, Fat 0, Cholesterol 0, Carbohydrate 14, Protein 3, Sodium 335.

BEET BORSCHT

Serving Size: 6

Amount	Measure	Ingredient – Preparation Method
3	cups	beets, peeled and shredded
1	cup	carrots, shredded
1	cup	onion, shredded
2	cups	cabbage, finely shredded
4	cups	water
1/2	teaspoon	salt
1/2	teaspoon	pepper
1/2	teaspoon	paprika
1	tablespoon	lemon juice
6	tablespoons	fat-free sour cream (optional)

Combine all ingredients, except lemon juice and sour cream, in a large saucepan. Bring to a boil over medium heat. Reduce heat to low, cover, and simmer 30 to 40 minutes. Stir in lemon juice and serve. Garnish with sour cream if desired.

Nutritional analysis: Calories 60, Fat 0, Cholesterol 0, Carbohydrate 12, Protein 2, Sodium 165.

BLACK BEAN SOUP

Serving Size: 4

Amount	Measure	Ingredient – Preparation Method
1 2/3	cups	vegetable broth, divided
1	large	onion, chopped
3	cloves	garlic, minced
1	15 ounce	can tomato sauce
1/4	teaspoon	ground thyme
1/4	teaspoon	ground cumin
2	teaspoons	Cajun seasoning
2	15 ounce	cans, black beans, drained

In a large saucepan over moderate heat, heat 1/4 cup of the vegetable broth, add the onion and garlic and cook, uncovered, until the onion is soft. Stir in the spices and cook for 1 to 2 minutes, stirring continuously. Place 1 can of black beans in a blender or food processor and puree for 30 seconds. Add the bean puree, the remaining beans, and the remaining vegetable broth to the saucepan, bring to a boil, reduce the heat to low and cook, uncovered, about 30 minutes. Add tomato sauce, continue to simmer the soup 10 to 15 minutes.

Nutritional analysis: Calories 100, Fat 0, Cholesterol 0, Carbohydrate 20, Protein 7, Sodium 380.

CABBAGE AND BEAN SOUP

Serving Size: 6

Amount	Measure	Ingredient – Preparation Method
4	cups	vegetable broth
1	cup	water
1	tablespoon	dry minced onion
1	medium	head of cabbage – chopped coarse
1 1/2	cups	carrots – sliced thin
1	large	onion – sliced and chopped
1	teaspoon	allspice
2	15.8 ounce	cans great northern beans
2	tablespoons	dried dill weed
		fat-free sour cream

Bring broth, water, cabbage, carrots, dry minced onion, onions, and allspice to a boil in a large soup pot. Reduce heat, cover and simmer until vegetables are tender. Add beans and dill and simmer uncovered for 15 minutes. Garnish with sour cream, if desired. Store left-over soup in the refrigerator, even better the second day!

Nutritional analysis: Calories 220, Fat 0.5, Cholesterol 3, Carbohydrate 45, Protein 12, Sodium 1392.

CABBAGE AND POTATO SOUP

Serving Size: 8

Amount	Measure	Ingredient – Preparation Method
4	cups	cabbage, coarsely shredded
4	medium	potatoes, peeled and cubed
1 ½	cups	onion, chopped
3	cups	water
2	16 ounce	cans tomatoes, undrained, chopped
3	tablespoons	lemon juice
2	tablespoons	sugar
¼	teaspoon	thyme
		salt and pepper to taste

In a large soup pot, combine cabbage, potatoes and onions. Add 2 cups of the water, cover and cook on medium heat 15 minutes. Add remaining ingredients. Bring to a boil, reduce heat, cover and simmer about 1 hour, or until potatoes and cabbage are tender. Serve with crusty rye bread. Refrigerate any left over soup, as this soup is even better the next day.

Nutritional analysis: Calories 95, Fat 0, Cholesterol 0, Carbohydrate 20, Protein 3, Sodium 195.

COLD CUCUMBER SOUP

Serving Size: 4

Amount	Measure	Ingredient – Preparation Method
2	medium	cucumbers, peeled, seeded and chopped
1	medium	red onion, sliced thin
1 ½	teaspoons	dill weed
2	teaspoons	mint flakes
2	cups	buttermilk, low fat
½	cup	fat-free plain yogurt
½	cup	vegetable broth
3	tablespoons	red wine vinegar
½	teaspoon	salt
½	teaspoon	pepper
⅛	teaspoon	cayenne pepper

Place the cucumbers, onion, dill and mint in a food processor, whirl for 30 seconds. Add the buttermilk, yogurt and vegetable broth, whirl 20 seconds longer or until blended. Transfer to a medium size bowl, stir in the vinegar, salt, black pepper and cayenne pepper. Cover and chill in the refrigerator at least 5 hours before serving.

Nutritional analysis: Calories 114, Fat 0.5, Cholesterol 0, Carbohydrates 14, Protein 7, Sodium 300.

CONSOMME'

Serving Size: 12

Amount	Measure	Ingredient – Preparation Method
2	quarts	tomato juice
2	quarts	V-8® vegetable juice
3	cups	egg whites,approximately 2 dozen eggs
2	cups	onion, diced
2	cloves	garlic, minced

VEGETABLE GARNISH, if desired:

1	cup	carrots, diced
1	cup	frozen green peas
1	cup	leeks, diced, white part only
2	tablespoons	minced parsley or chives

Put tomato juice and V-8 juice in a large pot. In a bowl, whisk together egg whites, onion, and garlic to break up the whites. Add them to the pot, whisking. Bring mixture to a boil over moderate heat, stirring occasionally. Adjust heat to maintain a simmer and cook, uncovered, for 20 minutes. Strain mixture through a sieve lined with a double thickness of cheesecloth, or with paper towels or a coffee filter. The consomme' should be crystal-clear.

If you wish the vegetable garnish: return consomme' to a clean saucepan. Taste and adjust seasoning. Bring to a boil over moderately high heat. Add carrots, peas, and leeks. Simmer 2 minutes. Serve in bowls or cups, garnished with a little minced parsley or chives.

Nutritional analysis for serving size one cup: Calories 30, Fat 0, Cholesterol 0, Carbohydrate 1.3, Protein 0.1, Sodium 300.

This recipe was developed by Jean-Marc Fulsack and appears in Dr. Dean Ornish's book, "Everyday Cooking With Dean Ornish".

CREAM OF BROCCOLI SOUP

Serving Size: 4

Amount	Measure	Ingredient – Preparation Method
1	pound	bag frozen chopped broccoli
3	cups	vegetable broth
2	tablespoons	dry minced onions
2	cups	EDENSOY® Organic Soy Beverage
1/4	cup	cornstarch
1/2	teaspoon	ground thyme

In a large saucepan, combine the broccoli, 1 cup vegetable broth and dry minced onion. Bring to a boil. Reduce the heat. Cover and simmer for 8 to 10 minutes or until broccoli is tender. Transfer the broccoli mixture to a blender or food processor. Process until nearly smooth. Return the mixture to the saucepan and set aside. In a small bowl, stir together 1/4 cup of the soy milk and the cornstarch until smooth. Then stir the cornstarch mixture into the broccoli mixture. Add the remaining 2 cups of broth and 1 3/4 cups soy milk. Cook and stir until thickened. Do not boil. Add the thyme, continue cooking and stirring 2 to 3 minutes more.

Nutritional analysis: Calories 220, Fat 1, Cholesterol 0, Carbohydrate 35, Protein 9, Sodium 1,295.

CREAM OF MUSHROOM SOUP

Serving Size: 4

Amount	Measure	Ingredient – Preparation Method
1	pound	mushrooms – sliced
1	cup	onions – chopped
2	tablespoons	dry white wine
1 1/2	cups	vegetable broth
1	teaspoon	garlic powder
		pepper to taste
1	cup	EDENSOY® Organic Soy Beverage
2	tablespoons	cornstarch

Lightly spray an unheated medium saucepan with cooking spray. Add the mushrooms, onion and wine. Cook and stir over medium heat until tender. Stir in the broth, garlic powder and pepper. Transfer the mixture to a blender or food processor. Blend until smooth. Return the mixture to the saucepan and set aside. In small bowl, stir together 1/4 cup of the milk and the cornstarch until smooth. Stir the cornstarch mixture into the mushroom mixture, then stir in the remaining soy milk. Cook and stir over medium, heat until thickened. Do not boil. Simmer for 3-4 minutes more.

Nutritional analysis: Calories 126, Fat 1, Carbohydrate 25, Protein 8, Sodium 800.

CREAM OF POTATO SOY SOUP

Serving Size: 4

Amount	Measure	Ingredient – Preparation Method
2 ½	cups	potatoes – peeled and diced
2	cups	onions – chopped
3	cloves	garlic – minced
2	cups	vegetable broth
5	ounces	tofu lite firm
¼	cup	fresh parsley – chopped
1	cup	soy milk
		salt to taste
		cracked red pepper or black pepper to taste
		fresh parsley, chopped

Place potatoes, onions and garlic in large soup pot, add vegetable broth. Cover and bring to a boil. Lower heat and simmer until potatoes are soft. While this is cooking, place tofu in small food processor and process to a creamy consistency. Set aside.

When potatoes are soft, remove from heat. With a hand mixer, blend until creamy. Stir in the processed tofu, mix well. Add 1/4 cup fresh parsley, soy milk, salt and pepper. Return to stove, heat until almost boiling, but do not boil. Serve garnished with fresh parsley.

Nutritional analysis: Calories 118, Fat 1, Cholesterol 0, Carbohydrate 15.2, Protein 5.3, Sodium 622, Potassium 458, Calcium 51.

CREAM OF VEGETABLE SOUP

Serving Size: 6

Amount	Measure	Ingredient – Preparation Method
2	cups	vegetable broth
1	tablespoon	dry minced onion
1	teaspoon	onion powder
1	teaspoon	garlic powder
½	teaspoon	ground thyme
2	10 ounce	packages frozen vegetables (spinach, broccoli, carrot, zucchini, etc. or combination)
1	cup	cooked rice
2	cups	EDENSOY® Organic Soy Beverage
		salt and pepper to taste

Place vegetable broth, frozen vegetables and spices in a large saucepan over high heat and bring to boil. Reduce heat to low, cover and simmer until vegetables are tender. Stir vegetables several times during cooking. Pour half of the broth, half of the vegetables and cooked rice into a food processor or blender and process on low until smooth. Pour soup mixture into a large bowl and repeat blending with the remaining broth, vegetables and rice. Stir soy milk into soup and refrigerate until chilled. The soup can be served hot or cold.

Nutritional analysis: Calories 115, Fat 1.5, Cholesterol 1, Carbohydrate 18, Protein 7, Sodium 387.

CREAMY ASPARAGUS SOUP

Serving Size: 4

Amount	Measure	Ingredient – Preparation Method
1	pound	asparagus
1 ½	teaspoons	Chicken Not®*
1	cup	boiling water
1	medium	leek, white and some green stem, chopped
1	medium	onion, chopped
1	medium	potato, peeled and chopped
1	large	stalk celery, chopped
2	cups	fat-free buttermilk
2	tablespoons	flour, all purpose
		salt and pepper to taste
2	teaspoons	fat-free parmesan cheese

Remove the tough ends from the asparagus. Chop the tips finely and set aside. Place the stalks in a medium size stock pot. Add the boiling water mixed with the Chicken Not, leeks, onions, potatoes and celery. Cover and simmer over medium-low heat until the asparagus is very tender. Season to taste with salt and pepper. Whisk in the flour. Pour the soup into a food processor. Process until very smooth. Return the soup to the stock pot. Whisk in the buttermilk and reserved asparagus tips. Cover and simmer, stirring occasionally for 3 to 4 minutes. Do not boil. Garnish with fat-free parmesan topping before serving.

Nutritional analysis: Calories 108, Fat 0.4, Cholesterol 0, Carbohydrate 14, Protein 3, Sodium 315.

Reference to Chicken Not® is located on page 216.

CREAMY CAULIFLOWER SOUP

Serving Size: 6

Amount	Measure	Ingredient – Preparation Method
2 ½	cups	vegetable broth
1	pound	package frozen cauliflower
1 ½	cups	onions, chopped
1	cup	celery, chopped
1		bay leaf
½	teaspoon	garlic powder
¼	teaspoon	marjoram
¼	teaspoon	thyme
¼	teaspoon	turmeric
¼	teaspoon	ground sage
⅛	teaspoon	dried basil
⅛	teaspoon	dried tarragon
		pepper to taste
1 ½	cups	EDENSOY® Organic Soy Beverage

In a large saucepan place frozen cauliflower, onions, celery and 1 cup of broth. Bring to a boil, reduce heat, cover, simmer for 10 minutes. Add the remaining broth and all the seasonings. Mix well. Bring mixture back to a boil, reduce heat, cover and simmer until vegetables are tender. Transfer the vegetables to a food processor or blender. Process until smooth, add a little of the soup liquid if necessary. Return vegetable mixture to liquid in saucepan. Add Soy milk and heat through. (Do not boil.)

Nutritional analysis: Calories 110, Fat 2.5, Cholesterol 0, Carbohydrate 14, Protein 8, Sodium 400.

CREAMY DILL SOUP

Serving Size: 4

Amount	Measure	Ingredient – Preparation Method
2	cups	V-8® vegetable juice
1	cup	EDENSOY® Organic Soy Beverage
1	14 oz. can	stewed tomatoes – pureed
4	tablespoons	dry cultured buttermilk
		salt and pepper to taste
2	teaspoons	dry dill weed

Place stewed tomatoes in food processor, puree until smooth. Pour vegetable juice in a medium size sauce pan, add tomatoes. In a small bowl place dry buttermilk mix, pour EdenSoy over mix, whisk thoroughly to a very fine consistency. Add to vegetable juice. Heat thoroughly over medium to low heat, stirring often. (Do not boil.) Season with dill weed, salt and pepper to taste. Pour into 4 serving cups, 3/4 cup each.

This would serve 2 as a main dish, of 1 1/2 cup per serving.

Nutritional analysis based on 4 servings: Calories 61.4, Fat 1.2, Cholesterol 0, Carbohydrate 9.8, Protein 3.6, Sodium 480, Potassium 348, Calcium 14.

CROCKPOT CHILI

Serving Size: 8

Amount	Measure	Ingredient – Preparation Method
2	15 ounce	chili beans in chili sauce – canned
1	medium	green pepper – chopped
1	medium	onion – chopped
1	tablespoon	garlic powder
1/2	teaspoon	crushed oregano
2	tablespoons	chili powder
1	16 ounce	tomatoes, canned – drained
1	23-24 ounce	tomato sauce
1	pound	MORNINGSTAR FARMS® Ground Meatless – thawed
		salt and pepper to taste

Put all ingredients in a large crock pot. Mix well. Cook on low for 6 to 8 hours. Additional chili powder my be added if you prefer very spicy chili.

Nutritional analysis: Calories 215, Fat 0.5, Cholesterol 0, Carbohydrate 25.3, Protein 15.2, Sodium 939.

DILLY POTATO BEAN SOUP

Serving Size: 12

Amount	Measure	Ingredient – Preparation Method
2	cups	celery – sliced 1/4" thick
1	pound	carrots, baby – shredded
1	large	onion – shredded
2	cups	Chicken Not®*
6	medium	potatoes – diced
2	cloves	garlic – shredded
1	can	soybeans
2	cans	great northern beans
4	teaspoons	dill weed – dried
1	cup	vegetable broth
		salt and pepper to taste

Process celery, carrots, onion and garlic in food processor. Place vegetables in large stock pot, add 1 cup oriental broth, bring to a boil, lower heat and simmer slowly about 20 minutes or until tender. Stir in chicken broth, potatoes and dillweed. Bring back to boil, reduce heat, simmer covered 20-30 minutes or until potatoes are tender. With a potato masher lightly mash the potatoes in the broth. Add the soybeans and 1 can of great northern beans, (in small bowl mash the other can of great northern beans before adding). Simmer 30 minutes more.

Nutritional analysis: Calories 239, Fat 4, Cholesterol 0, Carbohydrate 39, Protein 41, Sodium 271, Potassium 1.196, Calcium 130.

Comment: this soup is best when made the day before and chilled in the refrigerator. Heat well before serving.

Reference to Chicken Not® is located on page 194.

FRENCH ONION SOUP

Serving Size: 4

Amount	Measure	Ingredient – Preparation Method
1/4	cup	vegetable broth
4	medium	yellow onions, sliced
1/8	teaspoon	sugar
2	tablespoons	flour
5	cups	vegetable broth
1/2	cup	dry white wine
1/2	teaspoon	ground thyme
1		bay leaf
1/2	teaspoon	black pepper
1	tablespoon	brandy
4	slices	toasted French bread, about 1/4 inch thick-sliced
1	clove	garlic, split lengthwise
2	tablespoons	grated parmesan cheese, fat-free

In a large heavy saucepan, heat the 1/4 cup vegetable broth, add the onion slices and cook, uncovered, until golden, about 10 minutes. Blend in the sugar and flour and cook, stirring 3 minutes longer. Add the 5 cups of vegetable broth, wine, thyme, bay leaf and pepper. Raise the heat to high and bring to a boil, stirring constantly, about 6 minutes. Adjust the heat so the mixture simmers, partly covered, for 30 minutes. Remove and discard the bay leaf, then stir in the brandy. Preheat the broiler. Rub each piece of toast with garlic clove and sprinkle with the cheese. Ladle the soup into 4 flameproof bowls and float a piece of toast, cheese side up, in each one. Place the bowls in the broiler, 4 to 6 inches from the heat, and broil until the cheese is golden brown. About 2 minutes.

Nutritional analysis: Calories 120, Fat 0.5, Cholesterol 0, Carbohydrate 28, Protein 4, Sodium 128.

GAZPACHO SOUP

Serving Size: 8

Amount	Measure	Ingredient – Preparation Method
3	large	cans Mexican-style stewed tomatoes
3	stalks	celery, diced
1	medium	green pepper, seeded and diced
1	medium	red pepper, seeded and diced
1	bunch	green onions, diced
1	4 ounce	can chopped hot green chilies
2	medium	cucumbers, diced
3	tablespoons	Worcestershire sauce
1 1/2	teaspoons	garlic powder
1 1/2	teaspoons	onion powder
		pepper to taste

Pour the stewed tomatoes, with juice, into a large bowl with cover. Add all the diced vegetables, Worcestershire sauce and seasonings. Mix well. Cover bowl. Refrigerate for 4 to 6 hours prior to serving.

Nutritional analysis: Calories 94, Fat 0, Cholesterol 0, Carbohydrate 24, Protein 3, Sodium 890.

GO BIG RED TAIL GATE SOUP

Serving Size: 12

Amount	Measure	Ingredient – Preparation Method
1 1/2	cups	TVP Granules
3	cans	vegetable broth plus 2 teaspoons soy sauce
1	large	onion – chopped
2	cloves	garlic – crushed
2	cans	tomatoes, stewed – 14 ounce size
		salt and pepper – to taste
16	ounces	mixed vegetables, frozen

Stir together and set aside: 1 1/2 cup TVP granules with 1 cup hot oriental broth.

Into a large soup pot sauté onion in 1/4 cup oriental broth for 5 to 10 minutes.

Add the TVP, 2 – 14 ounce cans stewed tomatoes, crushed garlic, 4 cups hot oriental broth.

When soup begins to boil, drop in: 1 16 ounce package mixed frozen vegetables. Simmer soup until vegetables are tender, about 20 minutes.

Comments: any type of frozen vegetables may be used, I use carrots, broccoli, and cauliflower. (This soup is best if made 24 hours in advance and stored in refrigerator, flavors blend!) Wonderful!

Serve with crusty sourdough bread.

Nutritional analysis: Calories 125, Fat 0.6, Cholesterol 0, Carbohydrate 19, Protein 17.5, Sodium 439, Potassium 197, Calcium 30.

HEARTY BEAN SOUP

Serving Size: 10

Amount	Measure	Ingredient – Preparation Method
1	cup	textured vegetable protein, granules
1	large	onion – chopped
3	cloves	garlic – minced
4		carrots – sliced
3	stalks	celery – chopped
3	medium	potatoes – diced
1	16 oz can	stewed tomatoes
4	cups	cabbage – shredded
1	tablespoon	parsley
1	can	soybeans
1	can	great northern beans, canned
4	cans	vegetable broth – divided
1 ½	teaspoon	lite soy sauce
4	tablespoons	tomato paste
		salt and pepper to taste

Rehydrate textured vegetable protein with 3/4 cup oriental broth, set aside. In stock pot place onion, garlic, carrots, celery and potatoes, add 1 can broth, bring to boil, turn down heat and simmer 15 minutes. Add TVP, tomatoes, cabbage, parsley, beans, tomato paste and 2 additional cans broth, and 1 1/2 teaspoon lite soy sauce. Bring to boil, lower heat and simmer slowly, stirring occasionally for 45 minutes.

Comment: this soup is best if made the day before and chilled overnight in the refrigerator. Heat well before serving. Serve with toasted sourdough bread slices. (Analysis does not include bread.)

Nutritional analysis: Calories 266.7, Fat 4.3, Cholesterol 0, Carbohydrate 35, Protein 24, Sodium 583, Potassium 961, Calcium 118.

MINESTRONE SOUP

Serving Size: 6

Amount	Measure	Ingredient – Preparation Method
2	15 ounce	cans kidney beans
2	cloves	garlic, minced
1/2	teaspoon	pepper
1/4	cup	chopped fresh parsley
1		unpeeled zucchini, diced
3	stalks	celery, chopped
2		carrots, diced
1	bunch	green onions, including greens, diced
1	10 ounce	package frozen spinach, thawed and drained well
1	8 ounce	can tomato sauce
2 1/2	cups	water
1/2	cup	dry sherry
1/2	cup	rotini, or other small pasta shells

Place kidney beans in a large soup pot and mash until 2/3 of the beans are broken. Add garlic, pepper and parsley, mix well. Add the remaining vegetables, tomato sauce and water. Bring to a boil, lower heat and simmer 1 hour. Stir occasionally. Add sherry, simmer 10 minutes. Add pasta and cook over high heat, until pasta is tender. Garnish with grated low-fat parmesan cheese.

Nutritional analysis: Calories 225, Fat 0.5, Cholesterol 0, Carbohydrate 40, Protein 12, Sodium 860.

MISO SOUP

Serving Size: 6

Amount	Measure	Ingredient – Preparation Method
1	small	onion, sliced thin and chopped
2	cloves	garlic, minced
1	cup	carrots, grated
1	cup	mushrooms, sliced
1/4	cup	vegetable broth
1/4	cup	miso
4	cups	water

Miso is a thick paste, that is made from soybeans. It has been used in Japan for years to promote good health and aid digestion. Miso is found in Health Food stores. Choose a medium to dark miso for a rich, full bodied flavor.

In a large saucepan combine the onion, garlic, carrots, mushrooms and 1/4 cup broth. Over medium heat, cook, stirring frequently 10 minutes, or until vegetables are tender. In a small bowl gradually stir 1/4 cup of the water into the miso, mixing until smooth. Add to the saucepan, along with the remaining water. Cook until hot.

Comment: for a thicker soup, add cooked noodles or brown rice.

Nutritional analysis: Calories 50, Fat 0, Cholesterol 0, Carbohydrate 6, Protein 2, Sodium 425.

MOCK CHICKEN-CHEESE SOUP

Serving Size: 2

Amount	Measure	Ingredient – Preparation Method
½	cup	TVP Granules
¼	cup	vegetable broth plus 2 teaspoons soy sauce
1	medium	onion – chopped fine
2	stalks	celery – chopped fine
2	medium	potatoes – chopped fine
2	cups	Chicken Not®*
1	teaspoon	garlic powder
		salt and pepper to taste
4	ounces	American or cheddar – grated, fat-free
		fresh parsley, garnish

Rehydrate TVP granules with 1/4 cup broth, set aside for 10 minutes. In large sauce pan put onion, celery, potatoes, garlic powder, salt, pepper and 2 cups of broth. Bring to boil, lower heat, add TVP and simmer until vegetables are tender. Add cheese, stir constantly until cheese is melted. Serve garnished with fresh parsley.

This serves 2-3 if used as a main dish, 4-6 if used as a starter. Great served with green salad and hot crusty bread as main dish.

Comment: if you make this soup a day ahead of time, you may want to add a small amount of milk while slowly heating.

Analysis based on two servings.

Nutritional analysis: Calories 355, Fat 0, Cholesterol 0, Carbohydrate 55.3, Protein 51.8, Sodium 2532, Potassium 821, Calcium 58.

Reference to Chicken Not® is located on page 194.

PUMPKIN-BARLEY SOUP

Serving Size: 6

Amount	Measure	Ingredient – Preparation Method
4	cups	water
1	15 ounce	can pumpkin
1	medium	onion, chopped
1/2	cup	quick-cooking barley
4	teaspoons	instant vegetable bouillon granules
1		clove garlic, minced
1	teaspoon	curry powder
1/2	teaspoon	ground thyme
1 1/4	cups	soy milk

In a medium size stock pot combine all ingredients, except the milk. Bring to a boil, reduce heat. Cover and simmer for 45 minutes or until barley and onions are tender. Cool slightly. Place half of the pumpkin mixture in a food processor and process until smooth. Pour into a bowl. Repeat with remaining mixture. Return all to saucepan. Stir in the milk. Cook and stir over low heat until thoroughly heated. Do not boil.

Nutritional analysis: Calories 194, Fat 2, Protein 6, Carbohydrate 28, Cholesterol 0, Sodium 950.

QUICK N SLAW SOUP

Serving Size: 6

Amount	Measure	Ingredient – Preparation Method
2	cups	TVP flakes/chunks
2	cups	water – heated to boiling
1	tablespoon	kitchen bouquet
2	large	potatoes – peeled and cubed
2	cups	celery – sliced
2	large	onions – chopped
2	cups	cabbage – shredded
		salt to taste
1	46 ounce	V-8® vegetable juice

Place TVP in large crockpot, mix kitchen bouquet with hot water. Pour over TVP, let set for 10 minutes to rehydrate. Add remaining ingredients to crockpot and cook on low for 8 hours or until vegetables are tender.

Nutritional analysis: Calories 111, Fat 0.4, Cholesterol 0, Protein 11.7, Sodium 337, Potassium 488.

RATATOUILLE SOUP

Serving Size: 8

Amount	Measure	Ingredient – Preparation Method
1 ¼	cups	onions, chopped
1	cup	green pepper, chopped
2	cloves	garlic, chopped
3	cups	eggplant, peeled and cubed
2	16 ounce	cans tomatoes, undrained, chopped
3	cups	zucchini, unpeeled and chopped
4	cups	vegetable broth
1		bay leaf
1 ¼	teaspoons	dried basil
1 ¼		dried oregano
⅔	cup	orzo, or any type of very small pasta
		salt and pepper to taste

In a large soup pot place onions, green pepper, garlic and 1 cup of the vegetable broth, cook 6 to 8 minutes. Add eggplant, cook another 5 minutes, stirring frequently. Add remaining ingredients (except orzo). Bring mixture to a boil, reduce heat to low, cover and cook 45 minutes. Add orzo and cook, covered 10 minutes. Remove and discard bay leaf before serving.

Nutritional analysis: Calories 110, Fat 0, Cholesterol 0, Carbohydrate 20, Protein 4, Sodium 190.

SPLIT PEA SOUP, WITH SPICY GARNISH

Serving Size: 4

Amount	Measure	Ingredient – Preparation Method
1	cup	dry split peas
4	cups	vegetable broth
1/4	teaspoon	dried rosemary, crushed
1		bay leaf
1	medium	onion, chopped
2	stalks	celery, sliced
2	medium	carrots, sliced
2	medium	potatoes, peeled and cubed
2	cloves	garlic, minced
2	tablespoons	dry sherry
1/2	cup	fat-free yogurt
1/4	teaspoon	ground turmeric
1/4	teaspoon	paprika
1/4	teaspoon	ground cumin
1/8	teaspoon	cayenne pepper

Rinse peas. In a large saucepan combine the split peas, vegetable broth, rosemary and bay leaf. Bring to a boil, reduce heat. Cover and simmer 1 hour, stirring occasionally. Stir in the onion, celery, carrots, potatoes and garlic. Return to boiling, reduce heat. Cover and simmer until vegetables are tender. Discard bay leaf. Remove soup from heat and allow to cool 10 minutes. In a food processor or blender puree the vegetables and small amount of liquid in several batches. Return puréed vegetables and liquid to saucepan, bring back to serving temperature.

While vegetables are simmering. In a small bowl stir together the yogurt, turmeric, paprika, cumin and pepper.

To serve, ladle soup into individual bowls, garnish each serving with the spiced yogurt mixture.

Nutritional analysis: Calories 260, Fat 2, Cholesterol 2, Carbohydrate 40, Protein 20, Sodium 850.

SUNDAY NIGHT CHILI

Serving Size: 8

Amount	Measure	Ingredient – Preparation Method
2	cups	TVP Granules
1 ½	cups	vegetable broth – hot
2	15 ounce	chili beans in chili sauce – canned
1	medium	onion – chopped
1	medium	green pepper – chopped
1	tablespoon	garlic powder
½	teaspoon	crushed oregano
2	tablespoons	chili powder
1	16 ounce	tomatoes – canned
1	24 ounce	tomato sauce – canned

Rehydrate TVP with hot broth for 10-15 minutes. Place all ingredients in a large crockpot. Mix well. Cook on low for 6-8 hours. Additional chili powder may be added if you prefer very spicy chili.

Nutritional analysis: Calories 244, Fat 1.0, Cholesterol 0, Carbohydrate 26.4, Protein 32.4, Sodium 1024.

QUICK MOCK HAMBURGER, VEGETABLE SOUP

Serving Size: 8

Amount	Measure	Ingredient – Preparation Method
1	cup	tvp granules
2	cups	water
1	package	Lipton onion soup mix
1	15 ounce	tomato sauce – canned
2	cups	V-8® vegetable juice
1	pound	mixed vegetables, frozen
1	cup	hashed brown potatoes – frozen
1	cup	frozen corn
¼	teaspoon	oregano
1	teaspoon	Cajun seasoning
		salt and pepper to taste

Place TVP, onion soup mix and 2 cups water in large sauce pan. Bring to a boil, lower heat and simmer for 10 minutes, stirring frequently. Turn heat off, cover and let sit for 10 minutes. Add tomato sauce, V-8 Juice, 1 cup water and frozen vegetables. Bring slowly back to a boil, lower heat cover and simmer for 40-50 minutes. Stir occasionally. Wonderful served with hot crusty bread on a cold winter night!

Nutritional analysis: Calories 138, Fat0.5, Cholesterol 0, Carbohydrates 24.6, Protein 9.5.

VEGETABLE BROTH

Serving Size: 4

Amount	Measure	Ingredient – Preparation Method
4	large	carrots, minced
4	medium	onion, minced
2		leeks, white part only, minced
1	cup	tomatoes, peeled and seeded
2	stalks	celery, minced
2	medium	parsnips, peeled and minced
4		sprigs parsley
2	cloves	garlic
10		whole black peppercorns
1		bay leaf
1		celery knob
½	teaspoon	sugar
2	teaspoons	lemon juice
2	tablespoons	fresh chives, minced
		salt and pepper to taste

Bring 8 cups of cold water to a boil. Add all the vegetables (except for the celery knob), 1 1/2 teaspoons salt, the peppercorns, and the bay leaf. Peel and chop the celery knob and immediately add it to the rest of the vegetables, as it darkens quickly when left exposed to air. Reduce the heat and simmer the broth gently, partially covered, for 2 hours. As the water level lowers, you must replace the evaporated liquid with fresh cold water, keeping the level constant throughout the 2 hours. Skim the top occasionally. After 2 hours, strain the soup and discard the solids. Return the strained liquid to the saucepan, and over medium heat, reduce the broth until only 4 cups remain. Add the sugar and lemon juice. Taste for seasoning and adjust, if necessary. Ladle into soup bowls and sprinkle with chives before serving.

Nutritional analysis: Calories 18, Fat 0, Cholesterol 0, Carbohydrate 3, Protein 0, Sodium 100.

VEGETABLE CHEESE SOUP

Serving Size: 6

Amount	Measure	Ingredient – Preparation Method
4	cups	Chicken Not®* or Consomme, see recipe on page 52
1	medium	onion – diced
1 ½	cups	carrots – diced
1 ½	cups	potatoes – diced
1	cup	zucchini – diced
1	cup	broccoli – diced
1	cup	cauliflower flowerets – diced
1	cup	celery – diced
2	cans	Campbell's Healthy Request Mushroom Soup
16	ounces	American or cheddar – grated, fat-free

In large soup pot cook vegetables with chicken broth until desired doneness. Add mushroom soup and cheese. Heat until cheese is melted, stirring often. If soup becomes to thick, small amount of chicken broth may be added.

Nutritional analysis: Calories 155, Fat 0.6, Cholesterol 0, Carbohydrate 22, Protein 14.

Reference to Chicken Not® is located on page 194.

VICHYSSOISE

Serving Size: 4

Amount	Measure	Ingredient – Preparation Method
2	cups	vegetable broth – divided
1	medium	yellow onion, chopped
1	medium	leek, chopped
2	medium	stalks, celery, chopped
2	medium	potatoes, peeled and diced
1	cup	fat-free buttermilk
1	tablespoon	fresh chives, minced
2	tablespoons	lemon juice
		hot red pepper sauce to taste

In a large saucepan, heat 1/4 cup broth. Add the onion, leek and celery. Cook uncovered until vegetables are tender, 6-8 minutes. Add more broth if necessary. Add the potatoes and cook, stirring occasionally, until potato are tender, 3-4 minutes more. Stir in the remaining broth and bring to a boil. Adjust the heat, cover and simmer until potatoes are tender 15-20 minutes. Remove from heat. In a food processor or blender, puree the soup in 2 or 3 batches, whirling each batch about 30 seconds. Pour into large serving bowl. Stir in the buttermilk, chives, lemon juice and red pepper sauce. Cover the soup and refrigerate at least 3-4 hours before serving.

Nutritional analysis: Calories 120, Fat 0, Cholesterol 1, Carbohydrate 17, Protein 5, Sodium 78.

WHITE CHILI

Serving Size: 4

Amount	Measure	Ingredient – Preparation Method
1	cup	tvp granules
1 ½	cups	boiling water, mixed with 2 tsps. Chicken Not®*
1	large	onion, chopped
2	cloves	garlic, minced
2 ½	cups	water
1	15 oz can	cannellini beans, drained
1	cup	tomatoes, diced
1	cup	white whole-kernel corn
¼	cup	canned green chili peppers, diced
1	teaspoon	cajun seasoning
½	teaspoon	ground cumin
1	teaspoon	chili powder
1	teaspoon	vinegar
		salt and pepper to taste
½	cup	fat-free Swiss cheese, shredded

In a medium bowl combine the TVP with Chicken Not dissolved in the boiling water. Set aside. In a medium stock pot, combine the onions, garlic and 1/2 cup of the water. Stir over medium-high heat for 5 to 6 minutes, or until onions are soften. Add the TVP, beans, tomatoes, corn, chili peppers, cajun seasoning, cumin, chili powder, vinegar, salt and pepper to taste and the remaining 2 cups of water. Cover and simmer over low heat for 45 to 60 minutes. Add small amount of additional water if necessary. Sprinkle with grated Swiss cheese before serving.

Nutritional analysis: Calories 340, Fat 1, Cholesterol 0, Carbohydrate 70, Protein 19, Sodium 265.

Reference to Chicken Not® is located on page 216.

YUMMY YUMMY SOUP

Serving Size: 8

Amount	Measure	Ingredient – Preparation Method
3 1/4	cups	vegetable broth
2		yams, peeled and cubed
4		carrots, peeled and sliced
1	large	onion, diced
8	ounces	mushrooms, sliced
3	cloves	garlic, chopped
2	teaspoons	Italian seasoning
		salt and pepper to taste
5	cups	water
1	small	can tomato paste
3/4	cup	small pasta
1	10 ounce	package frozen peas
1	10 ounce	package frozen chopped spinach

Pour vegetable broth into a large soup pot, add yams, carrots, onion, mushrooms, garlic, i\Italian seasoning, salt and pepper. Bring to a boil, reduce the heat to low, cover and simmer until vegetables are tender. Add water and tomato paste, mixing well. Bring the soup back to a boil, over medium-high heat, stir in the pasta. Cook uncovered 5 minutes. Stir in the peas and spinach and return soup to a boil, lower heat and continue cooking until pasta is tender.

Nutritional analysis: Calories 250, Fat 0.5, Cholesterol 0, Carbohydrate 56, Protein 7, Sodium 445.

NOTES:

MAIN DISHES

Eggplant Rollups, page 97

EGGPLANT ROLLUPS

Serving Size: 6

Amount	Measure	Ingredient – Preparation Method
1	medium	eggplant
1	cup	fat-free ricotta cheese
1/4	cup	MORI-NU® Lite SILKEN TOFU, FIRM
1	package	spinach, frozen – chopped fine
4	tablespoons	onion – chopped fine
1	26 ounce jar	Healthy Choice Extra Chunky Mushroom Pasta Sauce
		salt and pepper

Slice eggplant lengthwise 1/4 inch thick. Discard the first slice as you do not want the whole skin. Spray a large cookie sheet, lay eggplant slices on sheet, place under oven broiler, broil both sides very carefully, 1-2 minutes each side. Set aside.

In a large mixing bowl, mix together ricotta cheese, tofu, spinach (thawed and very well drained) onion, salt and pepper to taste. Spread this mixture evenly over each eggplant slice. Roll up each slice and place in a sprayed 3 quart casserole dish. Pour the pasta sauce over the rollups. Cover and bake in 350 degree oven for one hour.

Nutritional analysis: Calories 118, Fat .9, Cholesterol 2, Protein 10.9, Sodium 950.

BAKED MACARONI AND EGGPLANT

Serving Size: 2

Amount	Measure	Ingredient – Preparation Method
4	ounces	fusilli (twist) pasta
1/2	cup	whole peeled tomatoes
1	cup	eggplant, peeled and cut in small cubes
1/2		medium onion, chopped
1	cup	non-fat milk
2	tablespoons	flour
2	scoops	VEGE FUEL® (TWINLAB® protein powder)
2	teaspoons	salt
3	cloves	garlic, minced
1/4	cup	fresh basil, chopped
1/2	teaspoon	black pepper
2	tablespoons	grated fat-free parmesan cheese
		olive-oil-flavored cooking spray

Preheat oven to 350 degrees. Coat a sauté pan with olive-oil-flavored cooking spray and sauté the garlic and onion with the salt. Once the liquid has evaporated and the onions begin to brown, add the eggplant and continue to cook for about 10 minutes, until the eggplant is tender but not mushy. Add the tomatoes, basil, and pepper. Continue to cook for another 10 minutes.

Meanwhile, cook the pasta according to package directions. While the pasta cooks, mix the Vege Fuel and the milk in a blender. Pour the mixture into small saucepan and whisk in the flour. Bring the mixture to a boil over medium heat, whisking constantly, until the mixture is smooth.

Remove from the heat and whisk in the grated cheese. Add the eggplant mixture to the Vege Fuel mixture and blend well. Add the pasta and toss to coat. Coat a 9 by 9 inch baking dish with olive-oil-flavored spray and fill with the mixture. Bake for about 30 minutes, until golden brown.

Nutritional analysis: Calories 475, Fat 0, Carbohydrates 64, Protein 43.

Optional: You could substitute soy beverage for the skim milk for added protein, but would add 2 grams of fat.

BAKED STEW

Serving Size: 6

Amount	Measure	Ingredient – Preparation Method
1 ½	cups	TVP Flakes/Chunks
1	cup	tomato juice – hot
1	envelope	dry onion soup mix
1	package	fat-free brown gravy mix – vegetarian
1	tablespoon	horseradish
5	medium	potatoes – peeled and quartered
5	medium	carrots – peeled and sliced
6	small	onions – peeled and halved
1	can	mushrooms
		salt and pepper to taste

Place TVP and dry soup mix in sprayed 3 qt. casserole, pour hot tomato juice to rehydrate. Mix well and let set for 1 hour. Add gravy horseradish and mushrooms, mix well. Add potatoes, carrots, and onions, mix well. Cover and bake in a 350 degree oven until vegetables are tender, about 1 1/2 hours. Stir occasionally while baking, if the stew becomes dry add a small amount of water or tomato juice.

Nutritional analysis: Calories 182, Fat 0, Cholesterol 0, Carbohydrates 38, Protein 12.5, Sodium 1119, Potassium 974, Calcium 95.

BAKED STUFFED PORTABELLO CAPS

Serving Size: 6

Amount	Measure	Ingredient – Preparation Method
6		portabello mushrooms
1/4	cup	MORI-NU® Lite SILKEN TOFU, FIRM
2	tablespoons	Pickapeppa sauce
1	tablespoon	soy sauce, low sodium
1	tablespoon	Grey Poupon Mustard
1	teaspoon	honey
2	tablespoons	apple juice, frozen concentrate
1/2	teaspoon	garlic – minced
1/4	teaspoon	red pepper flakes
1	teaspoon	salt, coarse
1	cup	red pepper – diced
1	tablespoon	parsley sprigs – chopped fine
1	teaspoon	thyme leaves – chopped
1/4	teaspoon	black pepper
		parsley sprigs for garnish

Slice tofu in one inch slices, then cube. In a shallow dish whisk together Pickapeppa sauce, soy sauce, mustard and honey. Place cubed tofu in marinating sauce for one hour. Meanwhile mix together your topping of apple juice, minced garlic, pepper flakes, salt, red bell pepper, parsley, thyme and black pepper.

After marinating cubes for 1 hour, remove from sauce (reserve sauce) gently sauté them in a sprayed sauté pan. Place portabello caps, bottom side up on a large baking sheet, put equal amounts of cubes onto each cap. Top these with the red bell pepper topping. Pour equal amounts of reserved marinating sauce over each. Bake at 350 degrees for 30 minutes.

Nutritional analysis: Calories 55, Fat 0.1, Cholesterol 0, Carbohydrate 5, Protein 0.6, Sodium 86.

CABBAGE CASSEROLE

Serving Size: 4

Amount	Measure	Ingredient – Preparation Method
1 ½	cups	TVP Granules
1	cup	water – hot
1	envelope	Butter Buds®
2	cups	onion – chopped
1	medium	cabbage head – shredded
8	ounces	American or cheddar – grated, fat-free
1	can	Campbell's Healthy Request Tomato Soup
		salt and pepper to taste

Rehydrate TVP with 1 cup hot water, to which you have added dry Butter Buds. Set aside. In a small microwave dish, microwave chopped onion on high for 4 minutes. Add to TVP mixture. In a 2 quart sprayed casserole put half of the shredded cabbage, half of the TVP mixture and half of the cheese. Make another layer ending with the cheese on top. Salt and pepper each layer to your liking. Pour the tomato soup over the top. Cover and bake at 350 degrees for 1 hour.

Nutritional analysis: Calories 338, Fat 0, Cholesterol 0, Carbohydrate 48, Protein 25.9, Sodium 772, Potassium 648, Calcium 144.

CABBAGE PATCH STEW

Serving Size: 6

Amount	Measure	Ingredient – Preparation Method
1	package	Green Giant Harvest Burgers for Recipes Prebrowed Vegetable Crumbles
16	ounces	can stewed tomatoes
1	cup	V-8® Vegetable Juice
1	medium	onion, sliced
1	cup	celery, diced
2	cups	cabbage, chopped
1	10 ounce	package frozen peas

Combine all ingredients except for the peas in a large crockpot, cook on low for 7 to 8 hours. Add thawed peas the last hour.

Nutritional analysis: Calories 167, Fat 0.4, Cholesterol 0, Carbohydrate 23, Protein 19, Sodium 876.

CABBAGE ROLLS

Serving Size: 6

Amount	Measure	Ingredient – Preparation Method
6	large	cabbage leaves – washed
1	cup	Minute Rice
1	cup	water
1	cup	onion – diced fine
1	package	gimme lean beef – thawed
1	clove	garlic
½	cup	Egg Beaters® (egg substitute)
		salt and pepper to taste
1	14 ounce	can, tomato sauce

In large sauce pan steam cabbage leaves in small amount of water, 3 minutes. Remove from heat, drain and place on paper towels.

Place 1 cup Minute Rice and 1 cup of water in small microwave dish with cover. Microwave on high 6 minutes.

Dice onion very fine or process in food processor. Place in another small microwave bowl with cover and microwave on high for 3 minutes.

In large mixing bowl place Gimme Lean, rice, onion, garlic, Egg Beaters, salt and pepper to taste. Mix well. (I use my hands, as if preparing a meat loaf.)

Spray a 9x13 inch baking dish. Place small amount of tomato sauce on bottom. Divide stuffing mixture equally by placing down the center of leaf. Roll one side and then the other, place seam side down in the baking dish. Pour remaining tomato sauce over rolls.

Cover and bake in a 350 degree oven for 50 minutes.

Nutritional analysis: Calories 165, Fat 0.1, Cholesterol 9, Carbohydrate 18, Protein 13.7, Sodium 658, Potassium 213, Calcium 33.

CARIBBEAN MOCK CHICKEN AND RICE STEW

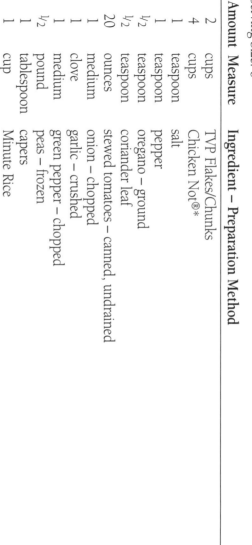

Serving Size: 6

Amount	Measure	Ingredient – Preparation Method
2	cups	TVP Flakes/Chunks
4	cups	Chicken Not®*
1	teaspoon	salt
1	teaspoon	pepper
½	teaspoon	oregano – ground
½	teaspoon	coriander leaf
20	ounces	stewed tomatoes – canned, undrained
1	medium	onion – chopped
1	clove	garlic – crushed
1	medium	green pepper – chopped
½	pound	peas – frozen
1	tablespoon	capers
1	cup	Minute Rice

Reference to Chicken Not® is located on page 216

Place TVP in dutch oven, add spices and Chicken Not. Bring to boil, lower heat to simmer for 10 minutes, stirring occasionally. Add tomatoes, onion, garlic and green pepper, cover and simmer for 45 minutes. Add peas and capers, simmer for 10 minutes. Add Minute Rice, stirring well. Let set, covered with no heat for 10 minutes. Garnish with grated parmesan cheese.

Nutritional analysis: Calories 168, Fat 0, Cholesterol 0, Carbohydrate 20, Protein 11, Sodium 1,170, Potassium 379.

CHEESE ENCHILADAS

Serving Size: 4

Amount	Measure	Ingredient – Preparation Method
8		fat-free corn tortillas
1	cup	fat-free ricotta cheese
1	bunch	green onions, chopped fine
½	teaspoon	ground coriander
¾	teaspoon	ground cumin
1	teaspoon	chili powder
¼	teaspoon	cayenne pepper
2	teaspoons	lemon juice
1	cup	fat-free shredded mozzarella cheese

Preheat the oven to 350 degrees. Wrap the tortillas in aluminum foil and warm in the oven for 10 minutes, or until warm and soft. Remove the tortillas, set aside, increase the oven temperature to 375 degrees. Combine the ricotta cheese, green onions, spices and lemon juice in a small bowl, mixing well. Spread 2 tablespoons of cheese mixture in the center of each tortilla and fold one side over the filling.

Place the tortillas in a lightly sprayed baking dish. Cover the dish and bake for 20 minutes. Uncover, sprinkle the enchiladas with mozzarella cheese, bake 5 minutes more, or until cheese is melted. Serve immediately.

Nutritional analysis: Calories 274, Fat 0.5, Cholesterol 5, Carbohydrate 32, Protein 32, Sodium 630.

CHEESE/SPINACH STUFFED MANICOTTI

Serving Size: 6

Amount	Measure	Ingredient – Preparation Method
12	shells	manicotti,
1	cup	ricotta cheese fat-free
¼	cup	MORI-NU® Lite SILKEN TOFU, EXTRA FIRM
1	package	spinach, frozen – chopped fine
4	tablespoons	onion – chopped fine
1	26 ounce jar	pasta sauce
		(or delicious served with beer/cheese sauce) recipe found in comments

Cook manicotti shells according to package directions. Place the tofu in food processor and process well to creamy consistency, pour into large mixing bowl, add ricotta cheese, spinach, thawed and very well drained and onion. Mix well. Place in pasty tube to fill manicotti shells, fill shells. Put small amount of sauce of your choice on bottom of baking dish, place manicotti shells on top. Pour small amount of sauce of your choice over the top of shells. Set sauces aside to be heated and serve over finished dish. Cover baking dish and bake in 350 degree oven for 30-40 minutes. Serve with additional sauce of choice. Garnish with fresh parsley or basil.

Serve with leafy salad or vegetable of choice and hot crusty bread. Delicious.

Comment: beer/cheese sauce: slowly melt one half carton fat-free cheese loaf with 1/4 to 1/2 cup of dark ale beer.

(Nutritional analysis contains break down for pasta sauce and does not contain break down for cheese sauce): Calories 262, Fat 1.3, Cholesterol 0, Carbohydrate 46.5, Fiber 3.3, Protein 16, Sodium 285, Potassium 137, Calcium 48.

CORN AND TOMATO CASSEROLE

Serving Size: 2

Amount	Measure	Ingredient – Preparation Method
1	can	peeled whole tomatoes, chopped and drained
2	cups	canned corn, drained
½	cup	red bell pepper, chopped
½	cup	onion, chopped
3	cloves	garlic, minced
2	tablespoons	cilantro, finely chopped
2	teaspoons	salt
½	teaspoon	pepper
1	cup	non-fat milk
2	scoops	VEGE FUEL® (TWINLAB® protein powder)
2	tablespoons	flour
		cooking spray

Preheat oven to 350 degrees. Coat a saucepan with cooking spray. Sauté the bell pepper, onion, garlic and salt until the liquid has evaporated and the onion begins to brown. Add the corn and continue to sauté until the corn starts to brown. Add the tomatoes, cilantro, and pepper. Mix well and remove from the heat. Using a blender, dissolve the Vege Fuel in the milk and pour the mixture into a small saucepan. Bring to a boil while whisking in the flour. As the mixture comes to a boil, reduce the heat and continue whisking until it thickens. Continue to cook, whisking constantly, until it is smooth.

Cook a baking dish with cooking spray. Mix the Vege Fuel mixture with the corn mixture in the dish until well blended. Bake for about 30 minutes, until golden brown.

Nutritional analysis: Calories 470, Fat 2, Carbohydrate 78, Protein 37.

CRUSTLESS VEGGIE PIE

Serving Size: 4

Amount	Measure	Ingredient – Preparation Method
1		eggplant, peeled and cubed
1	large	green pepper, chopped
1	large	onion, diced
3	stalks	celery, diced
8	ounces	mushrooms, sliced
4		tomatoes, seeded and chopped
1	cup	Egg Beaters® (egg substitute)
1	teaspoon	garlic powder
¼	teaspoon	oregano
		salt and pepper to taste
8	ounces	fat-free shredded mozzarella cheese
4	ounces	fat-free parmesan cheese

Preheat oven to 350 degrees. In a nonstick skillet, sprayed with cooking spray, over medium-high heat, cook eggplant cubes, bell pepper, onion and celery for 10 minutes. If to dry, add small amounts of water or vegetable broth. Add mushrooms and chopped tomatoes and simmer on low for 20 minutes. Remove vegetables from heat and allow to cool. Add garlic powder, oregano, salt and pepper into egg substitute, blending well. Add cooled sautéed vegetables to the egg mixture and mix well. Pour mixture into a 9 inch pie pan, lightly sprayed. Top with the two cheeses. Bake for 35 minutes or until a crust forms.

Nutritional analysis: Calories 184, Fat 0, Cholesterol 0, Carbohydrate 24, Protein 21, Sodium 423.

FAUX CHICKEN, BROCCOLI AND RICE

Serving Size: 8

Amount	Measure	Ingredient – Preparation Method
2	cups	textured vegetable protein, flakes/chunks
1 ½	cups	Chicken Not®*
1	envelope	Butter Buds®
2	cups	quick cook rice
1	16 ounce	broccoli, frozen
1	cup	onion – chopped
2	cans	Campbell's Healthy Request Mushroom Soup
6	slices	fat-free American cheese
1	teaspoon	dry mustard
		salt and pepper to taste

Place textured vegetable protein in large bowl. Place Chicken Not in small bowl; heat in microwave. Add 1 envelope Butter Buds. Pour this over the dry textured vegetable protein. Set aside.

Take frozen broccoli and add chopped onions. Cook according to package directions. Add drained broccoli and onion to textured vegetable protein.

In sauce pan or microwave prepare quick cook rice according to package directions. Add this to textured vegetable protein and broccoli mixture.

In small bowl, place soup, dry mustard, salt and pepper to taste. Pour over the textured vegetable protein and broccoli mixture, stir well to get all evenly mixed. Pour into a sprayed 9x13 inch baking dish. Cover lightly with foil. Bake in 350 degree oven for 40 minutes. Remove from oven and top with cheese slices. Place back in oven until cheese melts.

Nutritional analysis: Calories 235, Fat 0.9, Cholesterol 7, Carbohydrate 25, Protein 24.5, Sodium 737.

Reference to Chicken Not® is located on page 216.

GIMME LEAN POTATO BOATS

Serving Size: 4

Amount	Measure	Ingredient – Preparation Method
4	large	potatoes – baked
1/2	cup	soy milk lite
1	14 oz	gimme lean sausage
1	small	onion – chopped fine
1/2	cup	sour cream, fat-free
3	teaspoons	horseradish sauce
1/4	cup	grated parmesan cheese fat-free
2	teaspoons	liquid smoke flavoring
		salt and pepper
		paprika

Wash potato skins and prick with a fork. Bake at 400 degrees for 60-70 minutes or until tender. Allow potatoes to cool to the touch. Slice a small portion off the top of each potato, carefully scoop out the pulp, leaving a 1/4 inch shell. In a bowl mash the pulp with milk, sour cream, horseradish, salt and pepper to taste. Set aside.

In a saucepan sauté onion in small amount of water until tender, season with salt and pepper. Add the gimme lean and liquid smoke, mix well. Spoon into the potato shells, top each with 1/4 of the mashed potato mixture; sprinkle with parmesan cheese and paprika. Bake in shallow baking dish for 20-25 minutes or until thoroughly heated. Set oven at 400 degrees.

Comment: serve with fresh steamed asparagus, cranberry relish and low fat bread sticks.

Nutritional analysis: Calories 322, Fat 1.6, Cholesterol 2, Carbohydrate 46, Protein 27, Sodium 965.

GREAT BALLS OF FIRE

Serving Size: 12

Amount	Measure	Ingredient – Preparation Method
14	oz	Gimme Lean Beef
14	oz	Gimme Lean Sausage
4		Egg Beaters® (egg substitute)
1	cup	seasoned bread crumbs
1 1/2	cups	vegetable broth
1	tablespoon	salt
1 1/2	cups	onion – finely chopped
		pepper, cajun seasoning and tabasco sauce to taste

In large bowl combine Gimme Lean Products, Egg Beaters, bread crumbs, 1 1/2 cup broth, salt, and onion. Form into small meat balls, sauté in a sprayed large sauté pan over medium heat, turning as necessary, when evenly browned.

Nutritional analysis: Calories 148, Fat 0.3, Cholesterol 5, Carbohydrate 16, Protein 15, Sodium 1,397, Potassium 111, Calcium 46.

Comment: analysis does not include rice or pasta. Meatballs can be served with pasta or used as appetizer with fat-free sauces. Just use your imagination.

GREAT PLAINS MEATY BALLS

Serving Size: 12

Amount	Measure	Ingredient – Preparation Method
14	oz	Gimme Lean Beef
14	oz	Gimme Lean Sausage
4		Egg Beaters® (egg substitute)
1	cup	seasoned bread crumbs
1 ½	cups	vegetable broth
1	tablespoon	salt
1 ½	cups	onion – finely chopped

In large bowl combine Gimme Lean Products, Egg Beaters, bread crumbs, 1 1/2 cup broth, salt, and onion. Form into small meat balls, sauté in a sprayed large sauté pan over medium heat, turning as necessary, when evenly browned.

Nutritional analysis: Calories 148, Fat 0.3, Cholesterol 5, Carbohydrate 16, Protein 15, Sodium 1,397, Potassium 111, Calcium 46.

Comment: analysis does not include rice or pasta. Meatballs can be served with pasta or used as appetizer with fat-free sauces. Just use your imagination.

GREEN BEAN – MUSHROOM MEDLEY

Serving Size: 6

Amount	Measure	Ingredient – Preparation Method
4		MORNINGSTAR FARMS® Better N Burgers – thawed
1	medium	onion – chopped
1	cup	green pepper – chopped
1	cup	onion – chopped
1	can	green beans – with liquid
1	can	Campbell's Healthy Request Mushroom Soup
1	can	mushroom stems and pieces – drained
1	cup	soy milk lite
1	tablespoon	worcestershire sauce
1	teaspoon	salt
2	cups	noodles – uncooked

Break up Better N Burgers and place in food processor, process until hamburger like consistency. Place onions, green pepper and celery in medium microwave bowl, cover and microwave on high 4-5 minutes. In large bowl combine Better N Burger mixture with all remaining ingredients, add vegetables; mix well. Pour into a 2 quart casserole dish that has been sprayed. Cover and bake in a 350 degree oven for 45 minutes.

Nutritional analysis: Calories 152.7, Fat 1.5, Cholesterol 14, Carbohydrate 22.3, Protein 12, Sodium 915, Potassium 293, Calcium 39.

HOT TAMALE CASSEROLE

Serving Size: 6

Amount	Measure	Ingredient – Preparation Method
1	1 pound	tube fat-free polenta, Sun Dried Tomato
1	cup	TVP granules
1	cup	hot water
1	tablespoon	WONDERSLIM® Fat/Egg Substitute
1/4	cup	water
1	large	onion, chopped
1	large	green pepper, chopped
1		jalapeno pepper, chopped
1	tablespoon	chili powder
2	teaspoons	cumin
1	teaspoon	garlic powder
1	teaspoon	salt
1	16 ounce	can tomatoes, chopped
1	16 ounce	package frozen corn
		hot sauce to taste

In a small bowl, pour hot water over TVP granules, mix well and set aside. In a large saucepan pour 1/4 cup of water and Wonderslim fat/egg substitute. Add onion, green and jalapeno peppers. Sauté over medium heat until soften. Add TVP and spices. Stir well, simmer for 10 to 15 minutes. Add frozen corn and hot sauce. Simmer for 3 to 5 minutes. Spray a 8 x 8 x 3 inch baking dish with no-stick cooking spray. Slice tube of polenta in half. Slice first half into 11 thin slices and place on the bottom of the baking dish. Spread TVP corn filling on top. Slice second half of polenta into 11 thin slices and place evenly on top of filling. Bake in a 350 degree oven for 30 to 45 minutes.

Nutritional analysis: Calories 220, Fat 0, Carbohydrate 34, Protein 11.

LASAGNA ♥

Serving Size: 6

Amount	Measure	Ingredient – Preparation Method
1 ½	cups	TVP granules
1 ½	cups	water – heated to boiling
1	tablespoon	kitchen bouquet
1	envelope	Butter Buds®
1	large	onion – chopped
3	cloves	garlic – minced
1	teaspoon	garlic powder
2	teaspoons	Italian seasoning
1	28 ounce can	stewed tomatoes
1	6 ounce can	tomato paste
1	24 ounce	cottage cheese
1	15 ounce	ricotta cheese fat-free
8	ounces	nonfat mozzarella cheese, shredded
6		oven ready lasagna pasta

In a small mixing bowl combine TVP granules with hot water, kitchen bouquet and Butter Buds, set aside. In a large saucepan sauté onion and garlic in small amount of water or vegetable broth until tender. Season to taste with salt and pepper. Add garlic powder, Italian seasoning, stewed tomatoes and tomato paste. Mix well. Simmer mixture for 10 minutes. Add TVP mixture to tomato sauce and simmer an additional 10 minutes. Remove from heat. In a medium size mixing bowl combine cottage cheese with ricotta cheese, mixing well. In a lightly sprayed 9x13 inch baking dish, place a small amount of tomato mixture in bottom of dish to keep pasta from sticking. Place a layer of 3 lasagna noodles on top of this, then a layer of tomato mixture, two cheese mixture and a layer of grated mozzarella cheese. Repeat layers. Bake covered in a 350 degree oven for 45 to 60 minutes. After removing from oven, let set for 10 minutes to set.

Traditional lasagna pasta may be used, but would have to be cooked according to package direction, prior to using in this recipe.

Nutritional analysis: Calories 205, Fat 1.7, Cholesterol 7, Carbohydrate 20, Protein 18.4, Sodium 608.

LITE, HIGH PROTEIN ALFREDO SAUCE

Serving Size: 8

Amount	Measure	Ingredient – Preparation Method
1	15.8 ounce	can great northern beans, drained
1	clove	garlic, minced
4	tablespoons	dry cultured buttermilk
2	cups	EDENSOY® Organic Soy Beverage
½	teaspoon	dry basil leaves
		pepper to taste
½	cup	Romano cheese, grated
1-2	tablespoons	cornstarch
		water

Place drained beans and minced garlic in the food processor, process until smooth. Place in a medium size saucepan. In a medium size bowl, blend together the dry buttermilk mix with the soy beverage until smooth. Add this to the bean mixture, blend well. Add the basil, pepper and Romano cheese. Heat over low heat until the cheese has melted, stirring constantly. In a small bowl blend together the cornstarch and water. Add to the milk mixture. Continue stirring until thicken. Serve over your favorite prepared according to package directions linguine.

Nutritional analysis (does not include linguine): Calories 117, Fat 3, Cholesterol 6.2, Carbohydrate 12.6, Protein 9.

LOW-FAT QUICHE CRUST

Serving Size: 6

Amount	Measure	Ingredient – Preparation Method
2	cups	brown rice – cooked
1		egg white
1	teaspoon	dry parsley flakes
1	teaspoon	garlic powder
1	teaspoon	seasoned salt

In a medium mixing bowl, combine all the ingredients. Mix well. Press the mixture over the bottom and up the sides of a 9 inch pie plate. Microwave on high power, 1 to 2 minutes until the crust is set. Fill with your favorite quiche mixture and bake according to recipe instructions.

Nutritional analysis: Calories 130, Fat 1, Carbohydrate 22.6, Protein 3.2, Sodium 240.

MACARONI AND CHEESE WITH VEGE FUEL

Serving Size: 2

Amount	Measure	Ingredient – Preparation Method
4	ounces	elbow macaroni, uncooked
1	cup	non-fat milk
2	slices	KRAFT® fat free cheddar cheese singles
2	scoops	VEGE FUEL® (TWINLAB® protein powder)
1	teaspoon	salt
1/2	teaspoon	pepper
2	tablespoons	flour

Preheat oven to 350 degrees. Boil the macaroni in 1 quart of lightly salted water until tender. Meanwhile, mix the Vege Fuel with the milk until blended. Pulse several times, until all of the lumps have dissipated. Pour the mixture into a small saucepan and whisk in the flour. Bring the mixture to a boil over medium heat, whisking constantly, until the mixture begins to thicken. Once the mixture starts to boil, reduce the heat to just barely boiling and continue to stir as the mixture begins to thicken. Continue to cook for 2 or 3 minutes, stirring constantly, until the mixture is smooth and free of lumps. Break the cheese into small pieces and whisk them into the Vege Fuel mixture. Once the cheese is melted and blended, add the drained macaroni, remove from the heat and stir to evenly coat the pasta. Pour the macaroni and cheese into a lightly sprayed baking dish and bake for 20 to 30 minutes, until golden brown on top.

Nutritional analysis: Calories 403, Fat 0, Carbohydrate 55, Protein 39.

Optional: For a quick high protein dish, add 1-1/2 to 2 scoops of Vege Fuel® to the dry cheese mix of Kraft® Macaroni and Cheese Dinner.

MEAT BALLS

Serving Size: 6

Amount	Measure	Ingredient – Preparation Method
1	pound	MORNINGSTAR FARMS® Ground Meatless – thawed
1 1/4	cups	seasoned bread crumbs
3/4	cup	MORNINGSTAR FARMS® Scramblers Egg Product – thawed
1 1/2	cups	onion – diced fine
1	teaspoon	garlic powder
		salt and pepper to taste

In large bowl combine all ingredients. Mix well. Form into small meat balls. Place on sprayed baking sheet. Bake in a 350 degree oven 35-45 minutes, or until browned. Serve with your favorite pasta sauce over pasta of your choice.

Nutritional analysis does not include sauce or pasta: Calories 198.5, Fat 0.7, Cholesterol 1, Carbohydrate 25.9, Protein 20.3, Potassium 280, Sodium 1,205.

MEXICAN MOCK MEATLOAF

Serving Size: 6

Amount	Measure	Ingredient – Preparation Method
12	ounces	package MORNINGSTAR FARMS® Sausage Style Recipe Crumbles – thawed
1 ½	cups	picante sauce
1	can	Campbells Healthy Request Cream of Chicken soup
1	6 ounce	can tomato paste
1	small can	green chiles, diced
1	small	onion, diced
1-2	large	flour tortillas'
1	cup	fat-free cheddar cheese, grated

In a large saucepan, mix together crumbles and all ingredients except tortillas and cheese. Bring to a boil, stirring. Heat 1-2 minutes. Remove from heat and pour one half of the mixture into a sprayed 9 x 13 inch baking dish. Top with a layer of flour tortillas'. Pour remaining crumbles mixture over the tortillas'. Top with grated cheese. Cover with foil, (very important). Bake in a 350 degree oven for 30 to 40 minutes.

Nutritional analysis: Calories 413, Fat 3, Cholesterol 7, Protein 23, Sodium 1460.

MOCK CHICKEN ENCHILADAS

Serving Size: 6

Amount	Measure	Ingredient – Preparation Method
6		low fat flour tortillas
2	cups	fat-free sour cream
2	packages	Hidden Valley Ranch dressing/dip mix
2	cups	fat-free cheddar cheese, shredded
4 ½	ounces	can chopped black olives
2	cups	White Wave Chicken Slices, cubed

Mix together sour cream, 1 package dry dressing, 1 cup of the cheese, olives and cubed chicken. (Trim tortillas on two sides so that they roll and fit in the pan better.) Use a 9 x 13 inch baking dish that you have sprayed with cooking spray. Place filling on tortillas and roll up. Place seam side down in baking dish. Sprinkle with remaining cup of cheese and 1 package of dressing. Bake in a 350 degree oven or 20 minutes. Serve with extra salsa or taco sauce.

Nutritional analysis: Calories 360, Fat 3, Cholesterol 5, Carbohydrate 50, Protein 29, Sodium 2120.

MOCK STROGANOFF

♥

Serving Size: 6

Amount	Measure	Ingredient – Preparation Method
2	cups	TVP flakes/chunks
1	can	ARROWHEAD MILLS, Mushroom Broth
1	tablespoon	Kitchen Bouquet
1	large	onion – chopped
1	clove	garlic – crushed
1	can	Campbell's Healthy Request Mushroom Soup
1	cup	sour cream, fat-free
1/2	cup	EDENSOY® Organic Soy Beverage
1	3 ounce can	mushroom pieces – drained
2	tablespoons	worcestershire sauce
2	tablespoons	catsup
		salt and pepper to taste
		Minute Rice or fat-free noodles

Pour mushroom broth in large sauté pan, heat to boiling. Turn off heat, stir in the TVP, cover and let soak for 10 minutes. Add onion, garlic and salt and pepper to taste, to the TVP. Turn heat back up and simmer for 15 - 20 minutes until TVP and onion are fork tender but not mushy. Add soup, soy milk, mushroom pieces, sour cream, worcestershire sauce and catsup. Simmer for an additional 15-20 minutes, stirring often. Serve over rice or noodles.

Comment: Nutrition analysis does not include rice or noodles.

Nutritional analysis: Calories 121.5, Fat 0.7, Cholesterol 2, Carbohydrate 16.5, Protein 14, Sodium 745

NANCY'S NEW NINE LAYER CASSEROLE ❤

Serving Size: 10

Amount	Measure	Ingredient – Preparation Method
6	slices	white bread
2	cups	TVP flakes/chunks
1 ½	cups	Chicken Not®*
8	ounces	mushrooms – sliced
3	tablespoons	vegetable broth
1	8 ounce	water chestnuts, canned – drained/chopped
1	cup	KRAFT® Miracle Whip Nonfat Dressing
6	ounces	mozzarella cheese fat-free slices
6	ounces	nonfat cheddar cheese, shredded
3		Egg Beaters® 99% egg substitute
1 ½	cups	EDENSOY® Organic Soy Beverage
2	jars	Heinz White Gravy Low Fat
¼	cup	Butter Buds®
¾	cup	seasoned bread crumbs

Rehydrate TVP flakes with 1 1/2 cups hot Chicken Not, set aside for 10-15 minutes. Spray a 13x9x2 inch baking dish or pan. Line with bread slices. Sprinkle mock chicken over bread. In saucepan, cook mushrooms slices in 3 tablespoons vegetable broth. Using a slotted spoon, spoon over the mock chicken. Combine water chestnuts and Miracle Whip, spoon over mushrooms. Top with cheeses. Combine egg beaters and soy milk, pour over entire dish evenly. Spread soup over cheese. Cover, chill 3 to 24 hours. Bake, uncovered in a 350 degree oven 1 1/4 hours. Combine Butter Buds mixed to package directions with bread crumbs. Sprinkle over casserole. Bake 10 minutes longer. Remove from oven and let sit for 10 minutes before serving.

Nutritional analysis: Calories 211, Fat 1.8, Cholesterol 4, Carbohydrate 26, Protein 17.4.

Reference to Chicken Not® is located on page 216.

NO LOAF-N-MEAT LOAF

Serving Size: 6

Amount	Measure	Ingredient – Preparation Method
2	cups	TVP Granules
1 1/2	cups	vegetable broth – heated
2	small	potatoes – grated
1/2	medium	onion – grated
1	cup	bread crumbs, seasoned
1/2	cup	Egg Beaters® (egg substitute)
1/4	cup	WONDERSLIM® Fat/Egg Substitute
2	teaspoons	garlic powder
2	teaspoons	seasoned salt
1	teaspoon	pepper, coarse ground
1	teaspoon	Italian seasoning
1	envelope	Lipton Onion Soup Mix

In large bowl place TVP and 1 envelope of Lipton Onion Soup Mix, rehydrate with 1 1/2 cups hot oriental broth. Set aside for 10-15 minutes. Peel and grate the potatoes and onion, add to TVP mixture. Add all the remaining ingredients, mix very well. Form into a loaf, place in sprayed loaf pan. Bake in a 350 degree oven for 45 minutes.

Nutritional analysis: Calories 330, Fat 0, Cholesterol 0, Carbohydrate 51.7, Protein 46.9, Sodium 1,283, Potassium 311, Calcium 42.

OH SOY GOOD MEATLESS LOAF

Serving Size: 6

Amount	Measure	Ingredient – Preparation Method
1	pound	MORNINGSTAR FARMS® Ground Meatless – thawed
1/2	medium	onion – chopped fine
1 1/2	cups	bread crumbs, seasoned
3/4	cup	MORNINGSTAR FARMS® Scramblers Egg Product – thawed
1/4	cup	WONDERSLIM Fat/Egg Substitute
2	teaspoons	garlic powder
2	teaspoons	seasoned salt
1	teaspoon	pepper
1	teaspoon	Italian seasoning
1	envelope	Lipton Onion Soup Mix

In large mixing bowl combine grated onion, bread crumbs, Scramblers, fat/egg substitute, seasonings and soup mix. Blend well. Add Ground meatless and blend well. Form into a loaf, place in a sprayed loaf pan. Bake in a 350 degree oven for 45 minutes.

Nutritional Analysis: Calories 222, Fat 0.9, Cholesterol 1, Carbohydrate 30.6, Protein 21.3, Sodium 1,695, Potassium 274, Calcium 38

Comment: serve with mashed potatoes and a fat-free gravy. This "meatless" loaf is great served as a cold loaf sandwich the next day.

POLENTA WITH SOUTHWEST SAUCE

Serving Size: 4

Amount	Measure	Ingredient – Preparation Method
1	16 ounce	tube prepared fat-free polenta
1/2	teaspoon	ground cumin
1/2	teaspoon	ground oregano
1	cup	chunky fat-free salsa
1	cup	canned black beans, drained
6		green onions, finely chopped
1/4	cup	fat-free sour cream
1	tablespoon	chopped fresh cilantro

Cut the polenta into 8 slices. Sprinkle evenly with the cumin and oregano. Spray a large no-stick skillet. Warm over medium heat. Place the polenta in the skillet in a single layer. Reduce the heat to low and cook for 4 to 5 minutes on each side, or until heated through. Remove the polenta to a platter, cover loosely to keep warm. Add the salsa, beans and onions to the skillet. Simmer 3 to 5 minutes or until hot. Spoon the salsa over the polenta. Top with sour cream and sprinkle with cilantro.

Nutritional analysis: Calories 190, Fat 0.5, Cholesterol 0, Carbohydrate 38, Protein 8, Sodium 690.

POTATO LASAGNA ♥

Serving Size: 8

Amount	Measure	Ingredient – Preparation Method
1	package	Gimme Lean Beef – thawed
1	package	Lipton Onion Soup Mix
1	clove	garlic – minced
1	15 oz can	tomato sauce
		salt and pepper to taste
1	cup	fat-free ranch dressing
1	jar	Heinz White Gravy
1	tablespoon	parsley, freeze-dried
5	cups	frozen hash brown potatoes – thawed
8	ounces	American or cheddar – grated, fat-free

Place Gimme Lean Beef Flavor in mixing bowl, add soup mix, garlic, tomato sauce and salt and pepper to taste. Mix well, set aside. In another mixing bowl combine potatoes, salad dressing, soup and parsley, mix well. Spray 9x13 inch baking dish. Layer one: spread one half of the potato mixture over bottom. Layer two: spread entire Gimme Lean mixture over the potatoes evenly. Layer three: spread remaining potato mixture over Gimme Lean. Bake in 350 degree oven for one hour, or until potatoes are done. Remove from oven, top with cheese, return to oven and bake 5 to 10 minutes longer.

Nutritional analysis: Calories 266, Fat 0, Cholesterol 12, Carbohydrate 42, Protein 19, Sodium 1,214.

POTATO SANTE FE

Serving Size: 6

Amount	Measure	Ingredient – Preparation Method
4	medium	potato – cubed
1	medium	onion – sliced
1	cup	TVP Flakes/Chunks
¾	cup	Chicken Not®*
1	teaspoon	Butter Buds® – dry
1	26 oz jar	Healthy Choice pasta sauce
1	14 oz can	canned whole kernel corn
1	teaspoon	chili powder
½	teaspoon	cilantro
		salt and pepper

Place TVP in small bowl. In glass measuring cup heat chicken broth in microwave oven, 1-2 minutes, remove and add dry Butter Buds. Pour this over TVP to rehydrate, set aside.

In large covered casserole micro wave potatoes and onions until tender, 10-15 minutes, drain if water forms. In sauce pan pour pasta sauce, corn, chili powder, cilantro, salt and pepper to taste. Add TVP mixture, simmer for 10-15 minutes. Pour over the potato mixture. Bake in a 325 degree oven for 40-45 minutes.

Comment: I have found that any dish using TVP has better flavor if made the day before. In this dish you would pour pasta mixture over potato mixture, cover and refrigerate 12-24 hours. You may have to increase the baking time 15 to 20 minutes.

Nutritional analysis: Calories 197, Fat 0.7, Cholesterol 0, Carbohydrate 30, Protein 43, Sodium 284.

Reference to Chicken Not® is located on page 216.

RED PEPPER, EGGPLANT, AND TOMATO PASTA

Serving Size: 6

Amount	Measure	Ingredient – Preparation Method
1	1 pound	eggplant
1	teaspoon	salt
1	cup	vegetable broth
1	cup	onion, chopped
3	large	cloves garlic, minced
6		Roma tomatoes, chopped
1		red bell pepper, seeded and chopped
1	teaspoon	crushed red pepper flakes
4	tablespoons	tomato paste
1	teaspoon	honey
		6 servings of dry pasta of your choice

Peel and dice eggplant, place in a medium bowl and sprinkle with salt. Toss well and let stand at room temperature 15 minutes to soften. Bring vegetable broth to a boil in a large saucepan over medium-high heat. Reduce heat and stir in onion and garlic. Simmer 3 to 4 minutes. Add tomatoes, bell pepper and red pepper flakes. Simmer 10 more minutes. Drain the eggplant and rinse well. Add eggplant, tomato paste and honey to sauce. Simmer 15 minutes until thickened, stirring occasionally. Keep sauce warm while the pasta cooks according to package directions. Serve the sauce over hot drained pasta.

Nutritional analysis: Calories 262, Fat 0, Cholesterol 0, Carbohydrate 54, Protein 9, Sodium 398.

RICE-SEAFOOD CASSEROLE

Serving Size: 6

Amount	Measure	Ingredient – Preparation Method
3	cups	cooked rice
1	cup	green pepper, chopped
1	cup	celery, chopped
1	cup	onion, finely chopped
1	can	water chestnuts, drained and sliced
8	ounces	imitation lobster flakes
12	ounces	imitation crab flakes
1	cup	KRAFT® Miracle Whip Nonfat Dressing
1	cup	tomato juice
		salt and pepper to taste
1	cup	fat-free shredded cheddar cheese

Preheat oven to 350 degrees. Combine all ingredients, except shredded cheese. Mix well. Pour into a sprayed 2-quart casserole. Top with cheese. Bake 25 to 30 minutes.

Nutritional analysis: Calories 230, Fat 0.5, Cholesterol 8, Carbohydrate 35, Protein 16, Sodium 1153.

SALMON PATTIES

Serving Size: 2

Amount	Measure	Ingredient – Preparation Method
7	ounces	canned salmon – drained
5	ounces	MORI-NU® Lite SILKEN TOFU, FIRM – creamed
1/4	cup	MORNINGSTAR FARMS® Scramblers Egg Product – thawed
1/2	cup	seasoned bread crumbs
		SWANSON Vegetable Broth

Place tofu in food processor, process until creamy. Place in medium bowl. Drain, debone and remove skin of salmon before adding to tofu mixture. Add bread crumbs and egg product. Blend well, shape into 4 patties. Spray non-stick skillet. Over medium heat brown patties on both sides. (I use a small amount of broth to keep them from sticking.) When browned on both sides, lower heat to simmer and remain sautéing for 15 – 20 minutes for a firm pattie. Remove from pan and serve.

Nutritional analysis: Calories 247.3, Fat 6.6, Cholesterol 55, Carbohydrate 13.3, Protein 26.5, Sodium 1,049, Potassium 454, Calcium 266

Comment: 1/2 pound of fresh poached salmon may be used in place of the canned salmon. To poach salmon, place salmon fillet in hot but not boiling water, simmer 6 to 10 minutes depending on thickness of fillet. Remove and drain on paper towel. Remove skin and flake before adding to tofu mixture.

SANTE FE STEW

Serving Size: 8

Amount	Measure	Ingredient – Preparation Method
1	package	Vigo Sante Fe Beans & Rice with Corn
1	cup	TVP Flakes/Chunks
3/4	cup	V-8® Vegetable Juice
1	medium	onion – chopped
1	can	Chicken Not®*
1	can	kidney beans
1	can	canned whole kernel corn – drained
3	teaspoons	chili powder
1	cup	V-8® Vegetable Juice

Prepare 1 package of Vigo Sante Fe Beans & Rice with Corn according to package directions. (DO NOT USE THE BUTTER) Set aside.

Rehydrate 1 cup of TVP with 3/4 cup heated V-8 juice. Let set for 10 to 15 minutes.

In large sauce pan sauté chopped onion in 1/4 cup Chicken Not until tender, add more broth if necessary. Add the kidney beans, whole kernel corn, 3 teaspoons chili powder, 1 cup Chicken Not, 1 cup V-8 juice and the TVP mixture, simmer for 15 minutes. Add Vigo Bean & Rice mixture, simmer an additional 15 minutes until well heated.

Serve with fresh fruit salad and crusty sour dough bread.

Comment: for the best flavor, make the day before, cover and refrigerate. Heat thoroughly before serving.

Nutritional analysis: Calories 197, Fat 0.8, Cholesterol 0, Carbohydrate 30, Protein 41.5, Sodium 415.

Reference to Chicken Not® is located on page 216.

SIMPLE MEXICAN RICE

Serving Size: 6

Amount	Measure	Ingredient – Preparation Method
1	medium	onion, chopped
1	medium	green pepper, seeded and chopped
1	10 ounce	package frozen corn, thawed
1 1/4	cups	vegetable broth
1	cup	medium or hot salsa
1 1/2	cups	fat-free Minute Instant Rice
1/2	cup	fat-free shredded cheddar cheese

In a large nonstick skillet over medium heat, heat 1/4 cup vegetable broth. Add onion and green pepper to hot broth and cook until tender. Add corn, remaining 1 cup of vegetable broth and salsa. Bring ingredients to a boil. Stir in rice, cover and remove from heat. Let stand 5 minutes and fluff with a fork. Pour into serving dish, sprinkle with cheese, cover, and let stand until cheese melts.

Nutritional analysis: Calories 151, Fat 0, Cholesterol 0, Carbohydrate 31, Protein 6, Sodium 397.

SLAM BALLS

Serving Size: 4

Amount	Measure	Ingredient – Preparation Method
1	6 ounce	package Yves Canadian Veggie Bacon, cubed
1	6 ounce	package Lightlife Smart Deli Country Ham Style Meatless Fat-Free Slices, cubed
2/3	cup	Egg Beaters® (99% egg substitute)
1/2	cup	seasoned bread crumbs

Place cubed Veggie Bacon and Ham in food processor, process until finely ground. Place in mixing bowl, add Egg Beaters and bread crumbs. Mix well. Lightly spray a baking sheet. Form ham mixture into 12 to 14 balls. Bake in a 350 degree oven for 30 minutes.

Nutritional analysis based on 3 meatballs: Calories 215, Fat 0, Cholesterol 0, Carbohydrate 5, Protein 38.

Serve with Cranberry-Dijon Sauce.

1 can Whole Berry Cranberry Sauce, 2-3 tablespoons Dijon mustard, start with 1 tablespoon and go from there, it is up to you! Based on your taste!

Nutritional analysis: this would depend on the canned cranberry sauce used.

SOUTH OF THE BORDER LASAGNA

Serving Size: 4

Amount	Measure	Ingredient – Preparation Method
4		MORNINGSTAR FARMS® Better N Burgers – thawed
1	cup	onion – chopped
2	tablespoons	jalapeno peppers – chopped fine
2	tablespoons	chili powder
1	14.5 ounce	can, tomatoes, stewed
1	15 ounce	can, Fat-Free Hormel Vegetarian Chili
		salt and pepper to taste
2	cups	baked tortilla chips low-fat – crushed
1 1/4	cup	tofu lite firm
1	envelope	fat-free ranch salad dressing mix

Place chopped onion in a small microwave dish with cover, microwave on high 3 minutes. In large bowl combine crumbled Better N Burgers, onion, jalapeno peppers, chili powder, stewed tomatoes, chili, salt and pepper. Mix well. Place crushed chips on the bottom of a sprayed 9x9 inch baking dish. Spread Better N Burger mixture over chips. Place tofu in a food processor and process until creamy, add dry salad dressing mix, if mixture seems a little thick add very small amount of water. Spread this over the top of casserole. Cover with foil and bake in a 350 degree oven for 35 - 45 minutes.

Nutrition analysis: Calories 146, Fat 2.0, Cholesterol 0, Carbohydrates 25, Protein 11, Sodium 1,546, Potassium 285, Calcium 50.

SPAGHETTI WITH HIGH PROTEIN TOMATO SAUCE

Serving Size: 6

Amount	Measure	Ingredient – Preparation Method
12	ounces	spaghetti

TOMATO SAUCE

Amount	Measure	Ingredient – Preparation Method
2	32 ounce	cans chopped tomatoes with puree added
3	cloves	garlic, finely minced
1/2	cup	fresh basil, chopped
2	teaspoons	salt
1	teaspoon	pepper
6	scoops	VEGE FUEL® (TWINLAB® protein powder) (to be added right before serving) olive-oil-flavored cooking spray

Tomato sauce can be made in advance and stored in refrigerator.

Coat a 2-quart saucepan with olive-oil-flavored cooking spray and sauté the garlic until it just starts to brown. Add the tomatoes, basil, salt and pepper. Bring the sauce to a boil. Reduce the heat and simmer the sauce for about 10 minutes. Transfer the sauce to a large plastic container. Let cool, then refrigerate.

Cook spaghetti according to package directions. While pasta is cooking, combine the Vege Fuel with the unheated sauce in a serving bowl. Add the drained pasta to the sauce. Toss with 2 forks to coat the pasta. The hot pasta will heat the sauce. Serve immediately.

Nutritional analysis: Calories 327, Fat 1, Carbohydrate 47, Protein 32.

SPICY HOT CHILI RICE

Serving Size: 4

Amount	Measure	Ingredient – Preparation Method
2	cups	cooked rice
1	15 ounce	can fat-free vegetarian chili
¾	cup	V-8® vegetable juice
1	teaspoon	chili powder, more if you like
3	cups	frozen mixed vegetables, thawed
1	cup	frozen corn, thawed
1	bunch	green onions, sliced
4	tablespoons	fat-free sour cream
1	cup	fat-free shredded cheddar cheese

In a large saucepan, combine chili, V-8 juice, mixed vegetables and corn. Bring to a boil, cover and simmer over low heat until vegetables are tender. Serve over prepared rice, top with sliced green onions, sour cream and cheese.

Nutritional analysis: Calories 329, Fat 0, Cholesterol 0, Carbohydrate 57, Protein 21, Sodium 870.

SPINACH AND ARTICHOKE PILAF

Serving Size: 2

Amount	Measure	Ingredient – Preparation Method
3	cups	fresh spinach leaves, washed and chopped
1	cup	artichoke hearts, drained and quartered
½	cup	peeled whole tomatoes, chopped and drained
1	medium	onion, chopped
3	cups	white rice
1	cup	vegetable broth
2	scoops	VEGE FUEL® (TWINLAB® protein powder)
2	teaspoons	salt
1	teaspoon	black pepper
½	teaspoon	dried oregano
		olive-oil-flavored cooking spray

Preheat oven to 350 degrees. Coat a large oven-safe pan with olive-oil-flavored cooking spray. Add the onion and salt, sauté until the onion starts to brown. Add the rice and continue to cook, stirring constantly, for about 3 minutes, until the rice starts to become more opaque.

Using a blender, dissolve the Vege Fuel in the vegetable stock. Add to the rice and onion mixture. Bring the mixture to a boil and add the spinach. Stir until the spinach wilts. Add the tomatoes, oregano, artichoke hearts and pepper. Bring the mixture to a boil. Remove from heat. Cover, place in oven for 30 minutes, or until all of the liquid has been absorbed and the rice is tender.

Nutritional analysis: Calories 225, Fat 1, Carbohydrate 28, Protein 30.

SPINACH AND NOODLE KUGAL

Amount	Measure	Ingredient – Preparation Method
8	ounces	wide no-yolk egg noodles
2	cups	nonfat cottage cheese
1 ½	cups	nonfat grated mozzarella cheese
2	10 ounce	packages frozen chopped spinach, thawed and squeezed dry
½	cup	EDENSOY® Organic Soy Beverage
1	cup	fat-free egg substitute
		salt and pepper to taste
¼	cup	grated parmesan cheese fat-free

Cook the noodles al dente according to package directions. Drain and return to the pan. Add the remaining ingredients, except for the parmesan cheese, to the noodles, toss gently to mix. Spray an 8x12 inch baking dish with cooking spray. Transfer the noodle mixture to the dish, top with the parmesan cheese. Bake in a 350 degree oven for 45 to 50 minutes, or until the filling is set and the top brown. Insert a knife into the center of the kugel, it should come out clean. Let set for 5 minutes before serving.

Nutritional analysis per 3/4 cup: Calories 148, Fat 0.5, Cholesterol 5, Protein 14, Sodium 210.

SPINACH LASAGNA

Serving Size: 8

Amount	Measure	Ingredient – Preparation Method
6		1 step lasagna noodles (precooked, dry)
1	medium	onion, chopped
8	ounces	package sliced mushrooms
2	cloves	garlic, minced
		vegetable broth
2	10 ounce	packages frozen chopped spinach, thawed and squeezed dry
2	teaspoons	Italian seasoning
		salt and pepper to taste
1	16 ounce	container fat-free cottage cheese
2		egg whites
½	cup	flour
2	cups	fat-free shredded mozzarella cheese
3	8 ounce	cans tomato sauce
½	cup	fat-free parmesan cheese, grated

In nonstick skillet over medium heat, cook onion, mushrooms and garlic 7 to 8 minutes with small amount of vegetable broth. Remove from heat, stir in squeeze dried spinach, and seasonings. Set aside. Combine cottage cheese, egg whites, flour and 1 cup of the mozzarella cheese in food processor or blender, blend until smooth. Spray a 9x13 inch baking dish. Pour very small amount of tomato sauce in bottom to keep first layer of noodles from sticking. Arrange 3 noodles. top with 12 spinach mixture, half of the cheese mixture and 1/2 of the tomato sauce. Repeat these layers. Top with remaining cup of mozzarella cheese, sprinkle top with parmesan cheese. Bake 50 to 60 minutes in a 350 degree oven. Let stand for 10 minutes before serving.

Nutritional analysis: Calories 253, Fat 0, Cholesterol 1, Carbohydrate 40, Protein 21, Sodium 897.

STUFFED GREEN PEPPERS ♥

Serving Size: 2

Amount	Measure	Ingredient – Preparation Method
2	large	green peppers
1	cup	cooked rice
1/2	cup	onion – chopped
1/4	cup	vegetable broth
1	cup	Green Giant, Harvest Burger, crumbles – thawed
3/4	can	Campbell's Fiesta Tomato Soup

Cut opening in the top of each green pepper. Remove seeds and spines. Rinse out. Place in microwave dish, cover and cook on high for 2-3 minutes. In a medium saucepan, sauté onions in vegetable broth until tender. Add additional broth if necessary to keep from sticking. Add Green Giant Crumbles and Fiesta Tomato Soup. Mixing well, simmer for about 3-4 minutes. Add rice to mixture, mix well. Remove from heat. Spoon mixture into each pepper, if you have additional mixture left over, it can be placed around the peppers, that you have placed in a sprayed baking dish. Bake, covered, in a 350 degree oven for 45 minutes.

Nutritional analysis: Calories 195, Fat 1.0, Cholesterol 0, Carbohydrate 35, Protein 10.5, Sodium 1078.

STUFFED MANICOTTI WITH 4 CHEESES AND MOCK SAUSAGE SAUCE ♥

Serving Size: 7

Amount	Measure	Ingredient – Preparation Method
1	8 ounce	package manicotti
1	small	onion, diced
2	cloves	garlic, minced
1	12 ounce	package Yves Just Like Ground Italian flavor
1	28 ounce	can diced tomatoes
1	6 ounce	can tomato paste
1	teaspoon	dried basil leaves
1	teaspoon	sugar
		salt and pepper to taste
1	15 ounce	container fat-free Ricotta cheese
2	cups	fat-free mozzarella cheese, grated
4	ounces	Sharons Finest Hickory Smoked Tofu Rella, cheese alternative, grated
1/3	cup	fat-free parmesan cheese
1/4	cup	Egg Beaters® (99% egg substitute)

Cook manicotti according to package directions. Drain and set aside. In a large saucepan over medium heat, place onions and garlic, with a small amount of water or vegetable broth. Sauté until tender. Add

Yves Just like Ground, tomatoes, tomato paste, basil, sugar, salt and pepper. Mix well. Bring to a boil, reduce heat and simmer for 15 to 20 minutes. In a medium size bowl, combine Ricotta, 1 cup mozzarella, Tofu Rella, parmesan cheese, and Egg Beaters. Mix well. Place cheese mixture in a large pastry bag. Set aside. Spray a 9 x 13 inch baking dish with cooking spray. Place half of the tomato sauce on the bottom of the dish. Fill each manicotti shell with the cheese mixture, place each one on top of the sauce. Spoon remaining sauce over the manicotti. Cover. Bake in a 350 degree oven until hot and bubbly. Uncover, top with remaining 1 cup of mozzarella cheese, bake for 5 minutes longer or until cheese melts. Remove from oven and let rest for 5 minutes before serving. Refrigerate leftover.

Nutritional analysis: Calories 380, Fat 3.6, Cholesterol 14, Carbohydrate 42, Protein 33.

VEGETABLE BAKE

Serving Size: 4

Amount	Measure	Ingredient – Preparation Method
1		eggplant
3		zucchini
2		onions
4		tomatoes
	slice	fat-free cheddar cheese
1	16 ounce	can crushed tomatoes

Preheat oven to 350 degrees. Cut all vegetables in round thin slices. Spray a 9x12x2 inch baking dish with cooking spray. Layer vegetables, then cheese slices. Continue layering, ending with cheese. Pour crushed tomatoes over the entire casserole. Cover with foil and bake 1 hour.

Nutritional analysis: Calories 178, Fat 0, Cholesterol 0, Carbohydrate 29, Protein 15, Sodium 759.

VEGETABLE QUICHE

Serving Size: 6

Amount	Measure	Ingredient – Preparation Method
1	cup	red Bermuda onion – sliced 1/8" thick
10	ounces	asparagus tips – thawed
1	15 ounce can	carrots – julienne
10	ounces	Egg Beaters® (egg substitute)
1/3	cup	soy milk lite
2	tablespoons	all-purpose flour
1/4	cup	parmesan cheese, shredded, fat-free
1	teaspoon	Italian seasoning

In a 2 quart casserole dish, combine onions and asparagus. Cover. Microwave on high 4-5 minutes. Add drained carrots. In a small mixing bowl combine the remaining ingredients. Mix together the egg mixture with the vegetables. Pour into a Low Fat Quiche Crust. (See recipe in this book.) Bake in a 350 degree oven 45-60 minutes until set.

Optional: For a different flavor 1 add 1/4 cup imitation bacon bits to egg mixture.

VEGETARIAN CHILI CON QUESO CASSEROLE

Serving Size: 8

Amount	Measure	Ingredient – Preparation Method
1 ½	cups	TVP Granules
1	cup	tomato juice
1	teaspoon	chili powder
3 ½	ounces	baked tortilla chips low-fat – crushed
2	4 ounce cans green chili peppers	
16	ounces	American or cheddar – grated, fat-free
2	15 ounce cans Hormel vegetarian chili	
1 ¼	cups	onion – chopped
1	4 ounce jar pimiento – chopped	
		salt and pepper

Add 1 teaspoon chili powder to 1 cup tomato juice, heat 2 minutes in microwave oven. Pour over TVP to rehydrate, let set 10-15 minutes. Sauté onion in small amount of water 6-10 minutes until tender, season with salt and pepper to taste, remove from heat add green chilies and pimentos. Add TVP mixture to onions, peppers and pimentos.

Spray a 9x13 inch baking dish, spread about 1/4 can chili on the bottom of baking dish to prevent crushed chips from burning. Top this with 2 cups of crushed chips, carefully spread half of the chili with beans over the chips, layer half the TVP mixture over this, top with half the cheese. Repeat chili and TVP mixture layers. Top with remaining cheese. Cover lightly with foil and bake in a 350 degree oven for 45 to 50 minutes.

Nutritional analysis: Calories 310, Fat 0.9, Cholesterol 8, Carbohydrate 44, Protein 44, Sodium 1254.

VEGGIE LASAGNA

Serving Size: 12

Amount	Measure	Ingredient – Preparation Method
6	cups	carrots, sliced
3	cups	mushrooms, sliced
2	medium	zucchini, sliced
1 ½	cups	onion, chopped
4	cloves	garlic, minced
2	15.5 ounce	great northern beans or kidney beans, canned
1 ½	teaspoons	Italian seasoning
		salt and pepper to taste
15	ounces	ricotta cheese fat-free
4	cups	nonfat mozzarella cheese, shredded, divided
¼	cup	fat-free parmesan cheese
48	ounces	hearty tomato pasta sauce
12		no-cook lasagna noodles
		vegetable cooking spray

Preheat oven to 350 degrees. Spray large skillet with cooking spray; heat over medium heat until hot. Add carrots, mushrooms, zucchini, onions and garlic. Cook covered, over medium heat until carrots are just tender, about 10 minutes, stirring occasionally. Stir in beans and Italian seasoning; season with salt and pepper. Mix ricotta cheese, 2 cups of mozzarella cheese and parmesan cheese in medium bowl. spread 3/4 cup pasta sauce in bottom of sprayed 14 x 10 x 2 inch baking pan. Top with 4 lasagna noodles, overlapping slightly; cover noodles with 1 cup ricotta mixture, 1/3 of the vegetables and about 1 1/2 cups more sauce. Repeat layers two more times; sprinkle with remaining 2 cups of mozzarella cheese. Bake uncovered, 45 minutes. Cover lightly with foil if cheese browns too much. Let stand 10 to 15 minutes before cutting and serving.

Nutritional analysis: Calories 363, Fat 4, Cholesterol 8, Carbohydrate 56, Protein 30, Sodium 750.

VEGGIE PIZZA

Serving Size: 4

Amount	Measure	Ingredient – Preparation Method
1	12 inch	BOBOLI Thin Crust
1	cup	tomato sauce – canned
1	cup	fat-free pizza cheese – shredded
1/2	cup	parmesan cheese, low fat – grated
1	large	red onion – sliced 1/8" thick
1	small	zucchini – sliced 1/8" thick
2		Roma tomatoes – sliced 1/8" thick
8	ounces	mushrooms – sliced
5	ounces	MORI-NU® Lite SILKEN TOFU, FIRM – drained, crumbled
1	teaspoon	garlic powder
		salt and pepper to taste
		red pepper flakes to taste after baking
		sprinkle with paprika before baking

Place BOBOLI PIZZA CRUST on pizza pan. Place first 7 ingredients in layers on pizza crust. In small bowl, chopped tofu with spoon into about 1/4 inch cubes, season with garlic powder, mixing well. Spread evenly over top of vegetables. Sprinkle with paprika. Bake in 400 degree oven for 30 minutes.

Nutritional analysis: Calories 387, Fat 1.7, Cholesterol 6, Carbohydrate 55.4, Protein 24.6, Sodium 1,162, Potassium 725, Calcium 41.

VEGGIE STEW

Serving Size: 4

Amount	Measure	Ingredient – Preparation Method
1	large	onion, chopped
1		leek, split and finely sliced
3		carrots, sliced
3	medium	potatoes, peeled and diced
1	can	peeled whole tomatoes, drained and chopped
8	ounces	fresh green beans, stemmed and cut in 1" pieces
2	small	zucchini, split and sliced
¼	cup	fresh basil, chopped
3	cloves	garlic, finely minced
3	cups	vegetable broth
1	cup	dry white wine
1	can	corn, or kernels from 2 ears
4	scoops	VEGE FUEL® (TWINLAB® protein powder)
3	teaspoons	salt
2	teaspoons	pepper
		cooking spray

Coat a large saucepan with cooking spray. Sauté the garlic, onion and leek with salt until they are soft and just starting to turn brown. Add the vegetable broth, bring to a boil. Add the potatoes and carrots. Reduce the heat to a slow boil cooking the potatoes and carrots for about 10 minutes, until tender but still firm. Add the remaining vegetables, pepper and basil. Continue cooking for 5 to 7 minutes, until all of the vegetables are tender. Ladle out 1 cup of liquid and combine it with the white wine in the blender. Add the Vege Fuel, pulsing until any lumps have disappeared. Slowly add to the stew, stirring constantly. Once it comes to a boil, it is ready to serve.

Nutritional analysis: Calories 302, Fat 1, Carbohydrate 46, Protein 31.

ZUCCHINI CASSEROLE

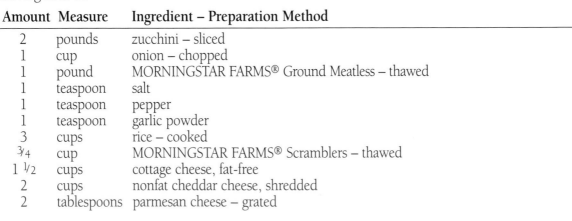

Serving Size: 10

Amount	Measure	Ingredient – Preparation Method
2	pounds	zucchini – sliced
1	cup	onion – chopped
1	pound	MORNINGSTAR FARMS® Ground Meatless – thawed
1	teaspoon	salt
1	teaspoon	pepper
1	teaspoon	garlic powder
3	cups	rice – cooked
¾	cup	MORNINGSTAR FARMS® Scramblers – thawed
1 ½	cups	cottage cheese, fat-free
2	cups	nonfat cheddar cheese, shredded
2	tablespoons	parmesan cheese – grated

Cook zucchini and onion in salted water for 5 minutes. Drain and set aside. Combine Ground Meatless, pepper, garlic powder, rice, Scramblers and cottage cheese. Fold in the zucchini and onion. Turn this into a sprayed 9 x 13 inch baking dish. Top with parmesan cheese. Bake for 30 minutes in a 350 degree oven, remove and top with shredded cheddar cheese, return to oven for 3 to 5 minutes until cheese has melted.

Nutritional analysis: Calories 203.2, Fat 1.2, Cholesterol 3, Carbohydrate 25.7, Protein 22.4, Sodium 1305, Potassium 361, Calcium 80.

ZUCCHINI PASTA CASSEROLE

Serving Size: 6

Amount	Measure	Ingredient – Preparation Method
1	pound	zucchini – sliced
¼	cup	vegetable broth
½	teaspoon	oregano
1	teaspoon	parsley
1	cup	nonfat cheddar cheese, shredded
4	ounces	noodles
1	10.5 ounce	vegetable soup – canned
1	can	water
1	teaspoon	tabasco sauce
		salt and pepper to taste
¼	cup	parmesan cheese – grated, fat-free

Sauté zucchini, oregano and parsley with vegetable broth, until tender. Pour this into a 1 1/2 qt. casserole with cover. Sprinkle with cheddar cheese. Layer uncooked noodles over the cheese. Combine soup, water, tabasco and salt and pepper, pour evenly over the entire casserole. Cover and bake in a 350 degree oven for approximately 30 minutes or until noodles are done. Sprinkle with parmesan cheese. Bake 5 minutes uncovered.

Nutritional analysis: Calories 137, Fat 1, Cholesterol 6, Carbohydrate 21, Protein 7, Sodium 629.

NOTES:

Mock Chicken Pasta Salad, page 147

ANTIPASTO SALAD

Serving Size: 4

Amount	Measure	Ingredient – Preparation Method
1		sweet red peppers
1		yellow pepper
1	teaspoon	dried parsley
¾	cup	celery, diced
½	cup	canned chick-peas, drained
1	medium	onion, chopped
8		cherry tomatoes, halved
3	tablespoons	water
2-3	tablespoons	balsamic vinegar
1	teaspoon	dried oregano
1	large	clove garlic, minced
		pepper to taste

Cut the peppers in half lengthwise. Discard the stems, membranes and seeds. Line a baking sheet with foil and place the peppers, cut side down on the sheet. Broil 4" from the heat for 10 minutes, or until the skins have blackened. Remove from oven and wrap the foil around the peppers, sealing the edges securely. Set aside for 10 to 15 minutes, or until cool enough to handle. In a medium bowl, combine the parsley, celery, chick-peas, onion, tomatoes, water, vinegar basil, oregano and garlic. Mix well. Remove the peppers from the foil. With a paring knife, remove and discard the black skin. Cut the peppers into thin strips. Add to the bowl of vegetables. Season with pepper. Toss before serving.

Nutritional analysis: Calories 75, Fat 0.5, Cholesterol 0, Carbohydrate 14, Protein 2, Sodium 58.

ASPARAGUS VINAIGRETTE

Serving Size: 8

Amount	Measure	Ingredient – Preparation Method
2	packages	frozen cut asparagus, thawed and steamed, al dente, according to package directions
1/2	cup	finely chopped onion
1/2	cup	diced red bell pepper

DRESSING

Amount	Measure	Ingredient
1/4	cup	white wine vinegar
1/4	cup	lemon juice
2	tablespoons	Dijon mustard
1 1/2	teaspoons	dried oregano
2	tablespoons	sugar
1/2	teaspoon	salt

Prepare the asparagus according to package directions. Cool to room temperature. Place in a shallow serving dish, add onion and red pepper. Combine the dressing ingredients in a small bowl, stirring until the sugar and salt dissolves. Pour over the vegetables. Toss to mix well. Cover the salad and chill for several hours or overnight before serving.

Nutritional analysis per 1/2 cup: Calories 30, Fat 0.4, Cholesterol 0, Protein 2, Sodium 90.

ARTICHOKE LUNCHEON SALAD

Serving Size: 4

Amount	Measure	Ingredient – Preparation Method
2	9 ounce	packages frozen artichoke hearts, thawed
1	cup	carrots, shredded
1		sweet red pepper, sliced into matchsticks
1	small	yellow onion, sliced thin
4	ounces	fat-free mozzarella cheese, diced
1	teaspoon	dried thyme
1/4	cup	balsamic vinegar
2	tablespoons	lemon juice
2	tablespoons	water
		coarse ground pepper to taste
1	head	iceberg lettuce
2	tablespoons	fresh parsley, chopped

Place the artichokes on layers of paper towels. Let drain for 10 minutes, then pat dry. Cut the artichokes in half. Place in a large bowl. Add the carrots, red peppers, onions, mozzarella, thyme, vinegar, lemon juice and water. Mix well. Season with black pepper. Remove the outer leaves of the lettuce and arrange on four individual salad plates. Coarsely chop the remaining lettuce. Add to the bowl of vegetables. Toss to combine. Spoon the salad over the lettuce leaves. Sprinkle with the parsley. Excellent served with crusty dinner roll.

Nutritional analysis: Calories 140, Fat 0, Cholesterol 0, Carbohydrate 22, Protein 6, Sodium 230.

BASIC VEGE FUEL PASTA

Serving Size: 2

Amount	Measure	Ingredient – Preparation Method
6		egg whites
4	scoops	VEGE FUEL® (TWINLAB® protein powder)
¾	cup	flour
1	teaspoon	salt

Mix the flour and Vege Fuel in a bowl. Make a well in the center of the mixture and add the egg whites. Gradually mix the ingredients until stiff dough is formed. Don't worry if the dough is too sticky; the texture will change as you work with it. Mix 2 parts Vege Fuel to 1 part flour in a small bow and use the mixture to dust your work surface and your hands as you handle the dough.

Turn the dough onto a dusted work surface and mold it into a ball. Knead the dough between the work surface and the heel of your hand several times, dusting the work surface with the Vege Fuel flour mixture as necessary. Once the dough is firm and elastic, cover it and let rest for 30 minutes.

Divide the dough into fourths and roll it out in your pasta machine. When the dough is rolled out to the thinness you desire, hang the strips on a portable clothes-drying rack. Allow the dough to air for about 30 minutes, until it is no longer damp. Cut the pasta into whatever shapes your machine will do and return the cut pasta to the drying rack to dry out completely. After the pasta dries, it can be cooked or frozen for future use. This recipe makes two 4 ounce portions, and can be doubled as many times as you wish. I would, however, caution you against committing several dozen egg whites to the cause without first perfecting your technique on a smaller batch. After your first success you will find the process easy. It's time-consuming, but it's worth it!

Nutritional analysis: Calories 398, Fat 0, Carbohydrate 36, Protein 62.

BEAN SPROUT SALAD

Serving Size: 4

Amount	Measure	Ingredient – Preparation Method
2	cups	bean sprouts
1	teaspoon	roasted sesame oil plus 1 teaspoon roasted sesame seeds
2		green onions, chopped include greens
1	teaspoon	ketchup
1	teaspoon	imitation bacon soy bits
1	clove	garlic, minced
		pinch of ground ginger
¼	teaspoon	salt
¼	cup	drained, chopped canned pimientos
2	teaspoons	lemon juice
2	tablespoons	rice vinegar

Place the bean sprouts in a colander and rinse under hot tap water just until slightly limp, about 1 minute. Drain well and dry thoroughly between paper towels. Set aside. In a small saucepan over low heat, combine the sesame oil, seeds, green onion, ketchup, bacon bits, garlic, ginger and salt, cook, stirring, about 1 minute or until mixture starts to bubble. Remove from heat. In a medium size bowl, combine the bean sprouts and pimiento. Add the contents of the saucepan and toss well. Cover and chill in the refrigerator for 2 to 3 hours, tossing occasionally. Just before serving, stir in the lemon juice and vinegar that has been combined, toss again.

Nutritional analysis: Calories 53, Fat 1, Cholesterol 0, Carbohydrate 4, Protein 2.

BOWTIE SALAD

Serving Size: 6

Amount	Measure	Ingredient – Preparation Method
9	oz. package	bowtie pasta
1 ½	cups	broccoli flowerets
1 ½	cups	cauliflower flowerets
8	ounce can	pineapple chunks in light syrup
4	tablespoons	balsamic vinegar
1	tablespoon	WONDERSLIM® Fat/Egg Substitute
1	cup	chicken style wheat meat – diced
½	medium	red bell pepper – chopped
½	medium	green bell pepper – chopped
		salt and pepper to taste

Prepare pasta according to package directions, add broccoli and cauliflower last 5-6 minutes of cooking time. Drain pineapple, reserve 1/2 cup juice. in large bowl, combine juice, vinegar and fat substitute. Drain pasta and vegetables. Add pasta, vegetables, chicken style wheat meat, bell peppers and pineapple chucks to dressing, toss well to coat evenly. Can be served at room temperature or chilled. Toss before serving.

Nutritional analysis: Calories 305, Fat 0, Cholesterol 0, Carbohydrate 70, Protein 10.4, Sodium 183, Potassium 557, Calcium 70.

BLACK BEAN SALAD

Serving Size: 8

Amount	Measure	Ingredient – Preparation Method
1	16 ounce	can, black beans, drained
2 ½	cups	cooked brown rice, chilled
1	large	tomato, seeded and chopped
¾	cup	thinly sliced celery
¾	cup	chopped green bell pepper
¾	cup	chopped sweet onion
2	tablespoons	minced fresh cilantro (optional)

DRESSING

½	cup	white wine vinegar
1	tablespoon	olive oil (optional)
2	teaspoons	dried oregano
2	teaspoons	crushed fresh garlic
2	teaspoons	sugar
		salt to taste

Combine the beans, rice, tomato, celery ,green pepper, onion and cilantro in a large bowl, toss to mix well. Combine the dressing ingredients in a small bowl, stir to mix well. Pour the dressing over the bean mixture, toss to mix. Cover the salad and chill 2 to 3 hours before serving.

Nutritional analysis: Calories 115, Fat 0.8, Cholesterol 0, Protein 4.6, Sodium 155.

BLACK EYE PEA SALAD

Serving Size: 4

Amount	Measure	Ingredient – Preparation Method
1	14 ounce	can, black-eyed peas – drained/rinsed
1	large	tomato – chopped
2	stalks	celery – diced fine
½	cup	KRAFT® Miracle Whip Nonfat Dressing
2	tablespoons	fat-free ranch salad dressing mix
3	tablespoons	red wine, garlic vinegar

Mix Black-eyed peas, celery and tomato together. In small bowl mix Miracle Whip, dry ranch dressing and vinegar, blending well. Pour over vegetables. Cover and store in refrigerator until ready to serve.

Nutritional analysis: Calories 130, Fat 0.8, Cholesterol 0, Carbohydrate 25.5, Protein 3.3, Sodium 860.

BROCCOLI-CARROT SALAD

Serving Size: 6

Amount	Measure	Ingredient – Preparation Method
1	pound	broccoli flowerets
2	medium	carrots, grated
1	bunch	green onions – diced fine
¾	cup	fat-free yogurt
1	tablespoon	Dijon mustard
1	tablespoon	lemon juice
2	teaspoons	Worcestershire sauce (vegan)
		pepper to taste

In a large pot of boiling water, cook broccoli until they are bright green and tender-crisp, 5 to 6 minutes. Drain, rinse under cold water and drain again. In a large bowl, combine broccoli, carrots and onions. In small bowl combine yogurt, mustard, lemon juice, Worcestershire sauce and pepper. Mix well and pour over vegetables. Toss until well coated. Serve salad at room temperature.

Nutritional analysis: Calories 55, Fat 0, Cholesterol 0, Carbohydrate 9, Protein 4, Sodium 80.

BROWN RICE SALAD

Serving Size: 4

Amount	Measure	Ingredient – Preparation Method
1 ½	cups	cooked brown rice
1	cup	tomatoes, chopped
½	cup	frozen peas, thawed
½	cup	frozen corn kernels, thawed
½	cup	green onions, chopped fine
1	tablespoon	lemon juice
2	tablespoons	rice vinegar
1	teaspoon	honey
1	clove	garlic, minced
½	teaspoon	crushed dry oregano
½	teaspoon	crushed dried basil
		salt and pepper to taste

Combine rice, tomato, peas, corn and green onions in serving bowl. In a small mixing bowl combine remaining ingredients for dressing, Pour over rice. Mix well. Cover and chill 1-2 hours before serving. Toss again before serving.

Nutritional analysis: Calories 140, Fat 0.8, Cholesterol 0, Protein 1.4.

CAESAR SALAD DRESSING LOW-FAT

Serving Size: 10

Amount	Measure	Ingredient – Preparation Method
1	package	MORI-NU® Lite SILKEN TOFU, FIRM
1/4	cup	lemon juice
1/4	cup	soy sauce, low sodium
2	tablespoons	red wine vinegar
3	tablespoons	grated parmesan cheese fat-free
2	cloves	garlic
1	tablespoon	Dijon mustard
		fresh ground pepper to taste
1	tablespoon	capers – drained

Place all of the ingredients, except the capers and parmesan cheese, in a blender or food processor and process until smooth. Add the capers. Refrigerate until ready to use. Serve over torn romaine lettuce, sprinkle with parmesan cheese.

Nutritional analysis: Calories 28, Fat 0.1, Cholesterol 0, Carbohydrate 3.3, Protein 2.3, Sodium 284.

CARROT RAISIN SALAD

Serving Size: 8

Amount	Measure	Ingredient – Preparation Method
4	cups	grated carrots
3/4	cup	thinly slice celery
2/3	cup	raisins

DRESSING

1/2	cup	nonfat mayonnaise
1/4	cup	frozen apple juice concentrate, thawed

Combine the carrots, celery and raisins in a large bowl. Combine the dressing in a small bowl, pour over the vegetable mixture. Toss to mix well. Cover the salad and chill for several hours or overnight before serving.

Nutritional analysis: Calories 92, Fat 0, Cholesterol 0, Protein 1.5, Sodium 135.

CHERRY TOMATO AND CORN SALAD

Serving Size: 4

Amount	Measure	Ingredient – Preparation Method
6	ounces	nonfat, plain yogurt
2 ½	tablespoons	ketchup
1 ½	teaspoons	prepared mustard
3		green onions, including greens, chopped
1	teaspoon	dill weed
2	cups	frozen whole-kernel corn
12		cherry tomatoes, halved
1	small	green pepper, cored, seeded and chopped
4	large	lettuce leaves

Combine the yogurt, ketchup and mustard in a large bowl, stir in the green onions and dill, set aside. Bring 2 cups unsalted water to a boil in a saucepan, add the corn and cook for 1 minute or until tender. Drain in a colander, rinse under cold running water to stop the cooking, and drain again. Add to the dressing mix, along with the cherry tomatoes and green pepper, toss well to mix. Place the lettuce on individual plates and spoon the corn mixture on top.

Nutritional analysis: Calories 95, Fat 1, Cholesterol 1, Carbohydrate 20, Protein 4, Sodium 50.

CRAB AND VEGETABLE SALAD

Serving Size: 4

Amount	Measure	Ingredient – Preparation Method
8	ounces	sliced mushrooms
1	medium	red onion – sliced thin
2	small	red bell peppers – cut into strips
4	tablespoons	vegetable broth
1	pound	imitation crabmeat flakes
¼	cup	rice vinegar
½	teaspoon	dried oregano leaves
1	tablespoon	Dijon mustard
½	teaspoon	sugar
¼	teaspoon	pepper
		lettuce of your choice for four servings

In a nonstick skillet over medium heat, cook onion and pepper strips in vegetable broth until tender. Add mushrooms toward the end, so as not to over-cook. Remove from skillet and place in bowl. Gently stir in crabmeat. Mix vinegar, oregano, mustard, sugar and pepper in small bowl. Mix well. Pour over crab and vegetable mixture, toss to coat. Arrange lettuce leaves on individual salad plates, spoon crab mixture on top of each.

Nutritional analysis: Calories 168, Fat 0, Cholesterol 20, Carbohydrate 30, Protein 11, Sodium 958.

CRISP APPLE AND CHICKEN SALAD

Serving Size: 6

Amount	Measure	Ingredient – Preparation Method
8	ounces	pasta shells – cooked and drained
2	cups	chicken style wheat meat – cubed
2	cups	celery – diced
2	cups	apples – cored and diced
1/4	cup	raisins
1/4	cup	KRAFT® Miracle Whip Nonfat Dressing
1/4	cup	yogurt, nonfat
1/4	teaspoon	nutmeg
1/4	teaspoon	cinnamon
		salt and pepper to taste

Prepare pasta according to package directions, drain. In large bowl, combine wheat style chicken, celery, apples, raisins and pasta. In small bowl, combine Miracle Whip, yogurt, nutmeg and cinnamon, mix into pasta mixture, combine well. Season to taste with salt and pepper.

Nutritional analysis: Calories 228, Fat 1, Cholesterol 0, Carbohydrate 45.6, Protein 9.5, Sodium 166, Potassium 283, Calcium 44.

CURRIED PASTA SALAD

Serving Size: 4

Amount	Measure	Ingredient – Preparation Method
8	ounces	bow tie pasta
8	ounces	pineapple chunks in light syrup
1/2	cup	KRAFT® Miracle Whip Nonfat Dressing
2	teaspoons	brown sugar, packed
1	teaspoon	curry powder
11	ounces	mandarin oranges in light syrup – drained
1 1/2	cups	chicken style wheat meat – cubed
3/4	cup	celery – sliced
1/4	cup	green onions – chopped
4	large	lettuce leaves

Prepare pasta according to package directions, drain. Drain pineapple, reserve 3 tablespoons of juice. In large serving bowl, stir together reserved juice, Miracle Whip, sugar and curry powder. Add pasta, pineapple, mandarin oranges, wheat style chicken, celery and green onions, toss to coat evenly. Serve on lettuce lined plates.

Nutritional analysis: Calories 357, Fat 1.3, Cholesterol 0, Carbohydrate 74, Protein 12.4, Sodium 308, Potassium 329.

EGGPLANT PASTA SALAD

Serving Size: 6

Amount	Measure	Ingredient – Preparation Method
2	cups	shell pasta
2	cups	eggplant – peeled and cubed
2	small	zucchini – cubed
2	cloves	garlic – minced
1/4	cup	vegetable broth
14 1/2	ounce	tomatoes, canned
1/2	teaspoon	basil
1	teaspoon	garlic powder
1/2	teaspoon	oregano
1/3	cup	feta cheese – crumbled

Prepare pasta according to package directions, drain. In skillet, over medium-high heat cook eggplant, zucchini and garlic in vegetable broth, stirring frequently, 3-5 minutes. Add tomatoes. Cover, cook over medium to low heat 5 – 7 minutes. Cook uncovered about 3 minutes, until thickened. Cool, stir in pasta and cheese. Serve at room temperature or chilled.

Nutritional analysis: Calories 184, Fat 2.4, Cholesterol 6, Carbohydrate 34, Protein 7.2, Sodium 256, Potassium 411, Calcium 72.

FROZEN FRUIT YOGURT SALAD

Serving Size: 1

Amount	Measure	Ingredient – Preparation Method
1	cup	sugar
1	cup	fat-free sour cream
2	8 ounce	cartons fat-free flavored or vanilla yogurt
1	16 ounce	can chunky mixed fruit – drained

Combine the sugar, sour cream and yogurt in a large bowl and mix well. Add the drained mix fruit. Pour mixture into a 9 inch square pan, cover and freeze until firm (about 5 to 6 hours or overnight.). Allow frozen salad to stand at room temperature for 10 to 15 minutes before serving.

Nutritional analysis: Calories 154, Fat 0, Cholesterol 0, Carbohydrate 34, Protein 4, Sodium 43.

FRUIT AND CABBAGE SLAW

Serving Size: 10

Amount	Measure	Ingredient – Preparation Method
4	cups	purchased coleslaw mix
1	cup	unpeeled apple, chopped
1	cup	KRAFT® Miracle Whip Nonfat Dressing
½	teaspoon	celery seed
1	11 ounce	can mandarin orange segments, drained reserving 4 tablespoons liquid

Combine the coleslaw mix and apple in a large bowl. In another bowl, combine the Miracle Whip, celery seed and reserved mandarin orange juice liquid, mix well. Pour over the slaw, toss to coat well. Gently fold in the orange segments. Cover salad and refrigerate until ready to serve.

Nutritional analysis: Calories 56, Fat 0, Cholesterol 0, Carbohydrate 10, Protein 0, Sodium 91.

FRUIT AND CHICKEN PASTA SALAD

Serving Size: 4

Amount	Measure	Ingredient – Preparation Method
2	large	bananas – sliced
8	ounces	macaroni – cooked and cooled
1	cup	celery – sliced
1	cup	seedless red grapes – halved
¼	cup	green onions – sliced
1	cup	chicken style wheat meat – cubed
2	tablespoons	chili sauce
2	tablespoons	lemon juice
½	cup	KRAFT® Miracle Whip Nonfat Dressing

In large bowl, combine bananas, wheat style chicken, macaroni, celery, grapes and green onions. In small bowl stir together miracle whip chili sauce and lemon juice. Pour dressing over salad. Mix well to coat evenly.

Nutritional analysis: Calories 316, Fat 1.3, Cholesterol 0, Carbohydrate 70, Protein 11, Sodium 291, Potassium 445, Calcium 31.

GINGER CHICKEN SALAD

Serving Size: 4

Amount	Measure	Ingredient – Preparation Method
3	tablespoons	red wine vinegar
1 1/2	tablespoons	chili sauce
1	tablespoon	soy sauce, low sodium
1	teaspoon	sesame oil
1	teaspoon	ground ginger
3	teaspoons	teriyaki sauce
8	ounces	bow tie pasta – cooked and drained
2	cups	chicken style wheat meat – cubed
4	ounces	spinach – cut into strips
1/2	cup	bean sprouts
1/2	cup	red bell pepper – cut into strips
4		green onions – sliced

In a small bowl, whisk together vinegar, chili sauce, soy sauce, sesame oil, ginger and teriyaki sauce. In another bowl, combine pasta, chicken, spinach, bean sprouts, bell pepper and green onions, mix well. Add vinegar mixture, tossing to coat. Chill, covered for 2-3 hours before serving.

Comment: 1 tablespoon of fresh grated ginger root can be used in place of the ground ginger.

Nutritional analysis: Calories 308, Fat 0.8, Cholesterol 0, Carbohydrate 60.5, Protein 17.2, Sodium 361, Potassium 750.

HIGH PROTEIN, NO FAT, TOMATO SALAD

Serving Size: 4

Amount	Measure	Ingredient – Preparation Method
4	large	tomatoes
2	cups	fat-free cottage cheese
4	tablespoons	fat-free salad dressing of your choice
		lettuce leaves
		paprika

Place lettuce leaves on 4 individual salad plates. Cut out tomato core (leaving tomato intact), cut into wedges. Place tomato on lettuce leaf and fill each with cottage cheese. Pour a small amount of salad dressing over each and sprinkle with paprika.

Nutritional analysis: Calories 114, Fat 0, Cholesterol 10, Carbohydrate 11, Protein 16, Sodium 414.

HONEY-MUSTARD POTATO SALAD

Serving Size: 12

Amount	Measure	Ingredient – Preparation Method
2	pounds	small red potatoes, washed and sliced
		water
1	cup	KRAFT® Miracle Whip Nonfat Dressing
1	teaspoon	honey
2	tablespoons	Dijon mustard
1	teaspoon	celery seed
1	clove	garlic, minced
1	cup	red bell pepper, diced
½	cup	carrots, grated
1	cup	celery, diced
1	cup	green onions, diced

Place potato slices in a 4 quart Dutch oven and add enough water to cover. Bring to a boil for 10-12 minutes or until cooked through. Drain and rinse the potatoes in cold water. Combine the Miracle Whip, honey, mustard, celery seed and garlic in a large bowl mixing well. Add the cooked potatoes, bell pepper, carrots, celery and onions, mix lightly until evenly coated. Refrigerate until ready to serve.

Nutritional analysis: Calories 60, Fat 0, Cholesterol 0, Carbohydrate 11, Protein 0, Sodium 104.

HOT SPINACH SALAD

Serving Size: 8

Amount	Measure	Ingredient – Preparation Method
8	cups	fresh spinach, cut up
1	medium	red onion, sliced thin, separated in rings
1	8 ounce	can sliced water chestnuts, drained
1	8 ounce	can mandarin oranges, drained
¾	cup	fat-free croutons
4		hard-cooked egg whites, chopped
		fat-free Italian dressing
		(optional) artificial bacon flavored chips for garnish

Wash and drain spinach, then cut up. Add onions, water chestnuts and oranges, toss lightly. Add croutons and cooked egg whites. Heat dressing and pour over salad just before serving. If desired garnish with bacon chips.

Nutritional analysis: Calories 91, Fat 0, Cholesterol 0, Carbohydrate 17, Protein 6, Sodium 124.

ITALIAN VEGETABLE SALAD

Serving Size: 6

Amount	Measure	Ingredient – Preparation Method
1 1/4	cups	water
3	tablespoons	balsamic vinegar
1/3	cup	apple cider vinegar
2	tablespoons	lemon juice
2	teaspoons	Italian seasoning
2	cloves	garlic – minced
1/4	cup	parsley – chopped fine
		pepper to taste
3	cups	mixed cut vegetables, (carrots and celery cut in 1/4 inch slices, red onion rings, red and green peppers cut in 1 inch pieces, small flowerets of broccoli or cauliflower.)

Combine water, vinegars, lemon juice, seasonings, garlic and parsley in large saucepan. Add vegetables. Bring to boil, cover and simmer 10-15 minutes until desired tenderness. Remove from heat. Cool to room temperature, cover and chill for at least 3 hours before serving. Will keep for several weeks if refrigerated.

Nutritional analysis: Calories 34, Fat 2, Cholesterol 0, Carbohydrate 10.

LETTUCE LAYER SALAD

Serving Size: 12

Amount	Measure	Ingredient – Preparation Method
1	large	head of lettuce
4	ribs	celery, thinly sliced
3	bunches	green onions, sliced thin
1	large	red bell pepper, chopped fine
1	10 ounce	package frozen peas, thawed
1	cup	KRAFT® Miracle Whip Nonfat Dressing
2	cups	fat-free sour cream
1	envelope	fat-free dry ranch style dressing mix
3	tablespoons	sugar
8	ounces	fat-free shredded cheddar cheese
		artificial flavored soy bacon chips (optional)

In a glass 9x13 baking dish, layer the torn lettuce. Top with a layer of celery, followed by a layer of green pepper, onions and peas. In medium bowl combine Miracle Whip, sour cream, ranch style dressing mix., mixing well. Spread this mixture over the entire top of the salad so that it will stay crisp. Sprinkle 3 large tablespoons of sugar over dressing mixture. Sprinkle with bacon bits if desired. Top with grated cheese before serving. This can be made 3 days ahead and kept refrigerated.

Nutritional analysis: Calories 96, Fat 0, Cholesterol 0, Carbohydrate 14, Protein 8, Sodium 370.

MOCK CHICKEN PASTA SALAD

Serving Size: 6

Amount	Measure	Ingredient – Preparation Method
4	ounces	pasta
1	cup	TVP Flakes/Chunks
1 1/4	cups	Chicken Not®*
1	teaspoon	Butter Buds® – dry
1	bunch	green onion – chopped fine
2	stalks	celery – chopped fine
3/4	cup	fat-free salad dressing of choice

Cook pasta of choice according to package directions, drain and cool.

In medium saucepan rehydrate 1 cup of TVP with 1 1/4 cup Chicken Not, when broth has come to a boil, add 1 teaspoon Butter Buds. Simmer TVP and Chicken Not for about 20 minutes. Sit aside until cool. When pasta and TVP mixtures have cooled, combine and add chopped onion and celery, mix well. Top this with your favorite fat-free salad dressing. Cover and chill for 2-3 hours before serving.

Nutritional analysis does NOT include fat-free salad dressing, since amounts may vary.

Nutritional analysis: Calories 183, Fat 0, Cholesterol 0, Carbohydrate 28, Protein 43, Sodium 136.

Reference to Chicken Not® is located on page 216.

MOLDED CABBAGE SALAD

Serving Size: 4

Amount	Measure	Ingredient – Preparation Method
2	cups	grapefruit juice
1	envelope	unflavored gelatin
2	tablespoons	sugar
1 1/2	cups	shredded cabbage
1/4	cup	shredded carrots
1/4	cup	sweet red pepper, chopped
2	teaspoons	yellow onion, grated
		lettuce leaves

In a large heat proof bowl, pour 1 cup of the grapefruit juice. Sprinkle the gelatin over it, let soften for 2 to 3 minutes. In a small saucepan pour the remaining cup of grapefruit juice and sugar, bring to a boil over moderate heat, stirring occasionally to dissolve the sugar. Add to the gelatin mixture and stir until gelatin dissolves completely. Chill in the refrigerator for 1 to 1 1/4 hours. Fold in the cabbage, carrot, red pepper and onion. Turn the mixture into a 4 cup mold. Cover and chill overnight for best results. Unmold onto a chilled platter, garnished with lettuce leaves.

Nutritional analysis: Calories 90, Fat 0, Cholesterol 0, Carbohydrate 20, Protein 3, Sodium 10.

MOLDED GAZPACHO SALAD

Serving Size: 4

Amount	Measure	Ingredient – Preparation Method
2	cups	tomato juice
1	envelope	unflavored gelatin
2	cloves	garlic, minced
1	tablespoon	red wine vinegar
1/4	teaspoon	hot red pepper sauce
1/2	medium	green pepper, cored, seeded and chopped
1/2	small	cucumber, peeled, halved, seeded and chopped
1	small	stalk celery, diced
3	tablespoons	green onions, diced
		lettuce leaves

In a large heat proof bowl, pour 1 cup tomato juice. Sprinkle the gelatin over it. Let soften for 2 to 3 minutes. In a small saucepan pour the remaining cup of tomato juice and garlic. Bring to a boil over moderate heat. Add to the gelatin mixture and stir until the gelatin dissolves completely. Stir in the vinegar and pepper sauce. Chill in the refrigerator about 1 to 1 1/4 hours. Fold in the green pepper, cucumber, celery and green onion. Turn this mixture into a small loaf pan or 4 cup mold. Cover and chill overnight for best results. Unmold onto a chilled platter, garnished with lettuce leaves.

Nutritional analysis: Calories 40, Fat 0, Cholesterol 0, Carbohydrate 8, Protein 3, Sodium 35.

ORIENTAL MUSHROOM-BEANSPROUT SALAD

Serving Size: 4

Amount	Measure	Ingredient – Preparation Method
3	teaspoons	honey
3	teaspoons	soy sauce, low sodium
1/4	teaspoon	ground ginger
3	teaspoons	rice vinegar
1	teaspoon	roasted sesame oil
1/2	pound	mushrooms, sliced
3		green onions, sliced, including greens
3/4	cup	bean sprouts, drained
2	teaspoons	fresh coriander, minced
1	teaspoon	toasted sesame seeds (optional)

In a large bowl, whisk together the honey, soy sauce, ginger, vinegar and sesame oil. Add the mushrooms, onions and bean sprouts. Toss well. Cover and refrigerate for 2 to 3 hours. Transfer the salad to a serving platter and sprinkle with the coriander and sesame seeds.

Nutritional analysis: Calories 37, Fat 1, Cholesterol 0, Carbohydrate 7, Protein 2, Sodium 110.

PAPAYA-KIWI FRUIT SALAD WITH ORANGE DRESSING

Serving Size: 4

Amount	Measure	Ingredient – Preparation Method
1		papaya
4		kiwi fruit
6	tablespoons	frozen orange juice concentrate – thawed
3	tablespoons	honey
1	cup	sour cream, fat-free
1	tablespoon	orange peel – grated
1	tablespoon	lemon peel – grated

Peel and remove seeds from papaya. Slice lengthwise into thin slices. Peel kiwi fruit and cut crosswise into thin slices. Arrange papaya and kiwi fruit on 4 salad plates. Combine orange juice and honey in small bowl. Stir in sour cream. Spoon over salads, sprinkle with grated peels.

Nutritional analysis: Calories 166.4, Fat 0.5, Cholesterol 0, Carbohydrate 42.6, Protein 1.9, Sodium 8, Potassium 640, Calcium 52

PICKLED BEET SALAD

Serving Size: 4

Amount	Measure	Ingredient – Preparation Method
1	16 ounce	can sliced beets, reserve 1/2 cup liquid
1/2	cup	cider vinegar
2	teaspoons	sugar
2	teaspoons	horseradish
1	teaspoon	Dijon mustard
6		black peppercorns
4		whole cloves
1		bay leaf
3		green onions, including greens, chopped
1	tablespoon	snipped fresh dill or minced parsley

Drain beets, reserving 1/2 cup liquid. Place beets in a medium size heat proof bowl and set aside. In a small saucepan over moderate heat, bring the 1/2 cup beet liquid, vinegar, sugar, horseradish, mustard, peppercorns, cloves and bay leaf to a boil. Pour the mixture over the beets and cool to room temperature. Cover and chill in the refrigerator for 3 to 4 hours. Just before serving, remove the bay leaf, sprinkle the beets with the green onions and dill, toss well to mix.

Nutritional analysis: Calories 68, Fat 0, Cholesterol 0, Carbohydrate 5, Protein 2, Sodium 123.

PRETTY PASTA SALAD

Serving Size: 6

Amount	Measure	Ingredient – Preparation Method
1 1/4	cups	pasta shells
1 1/4	cups	cottage cheese, fat-free
1/2	cup	green pepper – chopped
1/4	cup	chives – chopped fine
1/4	cup	onions – chopped fine
4		radishes – sliced
1/4	cup	French salad dressing, fat-free
3/4	cup	sour cream, fat-free
1 1/4	tablespoons	lemon juice
1/2	teaspoon	dry mustard
1/2	cup	green picked soy beans cooked

Prepare pasta according to package directions; drain and chill. Combine cottage cheese, shopped green pepper, chives, onions and radish slices; add chilled pasta. In small bowl, combine French dressing, sour cream, lemon juice, mustard, salt and pepper to taste. Add to pasta mixture along with soy beans, gently mix together to blend.

Optional: salad can be garnished with red or green bell peppers.

Nutritional analysis: Calories 205, Fat 5, Cholesterol 3, Carbohydrate 26.7, Protein 11.5, Sodium 380, Potassium 325.

PRIMAVERA PASTA SALAD

Serving Size: 4

Amount	Measure	Ingredient – Preparation Method
1/2	cup	yogurt, nonfat
2	tablespoons	red wine vinegar
2	teaspoons	WONDERSLIM® Fat/Egg Substitute
		salt and pepper to taste
2	cups	penne pasta shells – cooked and drained
2 1/2	cups	mixed vegetables, broccoli, red pepper, carrot, tomatoes – cooked and drained
1/4	cup	red onion – sliced 1/8" thick

In large bowl, combine yogurt, vinegar and fat substitute. Add salt and pepper to taste. Mix well. Add pasta, vegetables and onion. Toss. Refrigerate at least 1 hour.

Nutritional analysis: Calories 228, Fat 0.9, Cholesterol 1, Carbohydrate 46, Protein 8, Sodium 21, Potassium 163, Calcium 55.

QUICK PASTA SALAD

Serving Size: 6

Amount	Measure	Ingredient – Preparation Method
1	pound	fat-free pasta, cooked, drained and cooled
2	cups	assorted fresh vegetables, chopped
1	medium	green pepper, chopped
2	tablespoons	fresh parsley, chopped
1	8 ounce	bottle fat-free Italian dressing
2	tablespoons	Dijon mustard
		pepper to taste

Cook the pasta according to package directions, drain and cool. Combine the Italian dressing, mustard and pepper, mixing well. Combine the cooled pasta with the fresh vegetables in large bowl. Pour the dressing over the pasta and vegetables, mixing well. Cover and chill thoroughly before serving.

Nutritional analysis: Calories 153, Fat 0, Cholesterol 25, Carbohydrate 28, Protein 5, Sodium 360.

SESAME BROCCOLI SALAD

Serving Size: 4

Amount	Measure	Ingredient – Preparation Method
2	teaspoons	sesame seeds
1	pound	package frozen chopped broccoli
2	tablespoons	soy sauce, low sodium
4	tablespoons	rice vinegar
1	teaspoon	sesame oil
2	teaspoons	honey

To toast the sesame seed, place in a small sauté pan over medium to high heat, toast for 2-3 minutes stirring frequently. Remove from heat and set aside. Cook broccoli according to package directions. Drain in a colander, rinse under cold running water to stop the cooking and to cool. Transfer to a serving dish. Combine the soy sauce, vinegar, sesame oil and honey. Pour over the broccoli and toss well. Sprinkle with the sesame seeds and serve.

Nutritional analysis: Calories 60, Fat 2, Cholesterol 0, Carbohydrate 10, Protein 5, Sodium 190.

SILLY-DILLY POTATO SALAD

Serving Size: 6

Amount	Measure	Ingredient – Preparation Method
1	cup	nonfat sour cream
4	teaspoons	dried dill weed
2	tablespoons	lemon juice
		coarse ground pepper to taste
12	small	new red potatoes, washed and quartered
1	medium	red bell pepper, seeded and chopped
2	cups	slice fresh mushrooms
1	9 ounce	package frozen sugar snap peas, thawed

Combine sour cream, dill, lemon juice and pepper in a large bowl, mixing well. Place potatoes in a medium sauce pan, cover with water and bring to a boil. Reduce heat cover and simmer 10 to 15 minutes or until tender. Drain and rinse potatoes with cold water to cool. Add cooked potatoes and remaining salad ingredients to dressing and mix well.

Nutritional analysis: Calories 85, Fat 0, Cholesterol 0, Carbohydrate 14, Protein 4, Sodium 18.

SLAM SALAD

Serving Size: 6

Amount	Measure	Ingredient – Preparation Method
1	6 ounce	package Yves Canadian Bacon
1	6 ounce	package Yves Veggie Deli Slices
3	tablespoons	KRAFT® Miracle Whip Nonfat Dressing
1	tablespoon	sweet pickle relish

Place slices of both Yves products in food processor and process until consistency of ham salad. Place in bowl, add Miracle Whip and pickle relish. Mix well. Serve on bread of your choice.

Nutritional analysis: Calories 136, Fat 0, Cholesterol 0, Carbohydrate 6, Protein 16, Sodium 850.

SOYS ME SALAD

Serving Size: 4

Amount	Measure	Ingredient – Preparation Method
2	bunches	romaine lettuce – washed /drained
¼	cup	soy sauce, low sodium
1	tablespoon	Dijon mustard
1	teaspoon	honey
2	tablespoons	rice vinegar
2	tablespoons	sesame seeds
1	teaspoon	sesame oil

In small non-stick fry pan, roast sesame seeds until golden brown. Set aside. In small bowl combine all the other ingredients, whisk until well blended. Set aside. Tear romaine lettuce into bite size pieces and place in 4 individual salad bowls. Pour salad dressing over each and sprinkle with roasted sesame seeds. Wonderful!

Garnish salad with Easy Oven Tofu Sticks. (see recipe)

Nutritional analysis: Calories 94.8, Fat 4.3, Cholesterol 0, Protein 6.4, Sodium 507, Potassium 835, Calcium 106.

SWEET AND SOUR SALAD

Serving Size: 6

Amount	Measure	Ingredient – Preparation Method
½	cup	sugar
½	cup	water
1	cup	rice vinegar
2	large	cucumbers – sliced thin
2	large	carrots – grated
1	medium	head of cabbage – shredded
1	medium	green pepper – diced fine

Mix sugar, water and vinegar. Pour over cucumbers, carrots, cabbage and green pepper. Cover and refrigerate one day before serving. I use a plastic bowl with tight fitting cover, so that it can be shaken on occasion to enhance flavors.

Nutritional analysis: Calories 97, Fat 0, Cholesterol 0, Carbohydrate 27, Protein 1, Sodium 19.

SWEET CARROT SALAD

Serving Size: 4

Amount	Measure	Ingredient – Preparation Method
½	cup	plain no-fat yogurt
4	teaspoons	honey
2	cups	carrots, grated
¼	cup	raisins
2	tablespoons	roasted soybeans

In a medium size bowl, mix together the yogurt and honey. Add the remaining ingredients, blend well. Chill before serving.

Nutritional analysis: Calories 105, Fat 1, Protein 4, Carbohydrate 22, Cholesterol 0, Sodium 49.

SWISS GREEN BEAN SALAD

Serving Size: 6

Amount	Measure	Ingredient – Preparation Method
2	cans	green beans – drained
4	slices	Swiss cheese product, fat-free – cubed
1/2	cup	green pepper – chopped
1/2	cup	soybeans, roasted
5	tablespoons	lemon juice
2	large	garlic cloves – crushed
1	envelope	Butter Buds®
1/2	cup	water – hot
1	tablespoon	red wine vinegar
1/2	teaspoon	tarragon
1/2	teaspoon	dill weed
2	teaspoons	Dijon mustard
1/2	cup	parsley – chopped fine
		salt and pepper to taste

Prepare Butter Buds according to package directions, set aside to cool. Combine and mix well, lemon juice, garlic cloves, vinegar, dill weed, mustard, minced parsley, salt and pepper, add Butter Buds when cool. Place green beans, Swiss cheese, and green peppers in a bowl with cover. Pour dressing over bean mixture and marinate 2 to 5 hours (best if overnight). Stir occasionally. Before serving top with roasted soynuts.

Nutritional analysis: Calories 61, Fat 1, Cholesterol 1, Carbohydrate 15.1, Protein 10.6, Sodium 197, Potassium 525, Calcium 125.

TACO SALAD

Serving Size: 6

Amount	Measure	Ingredient – Preparation Method
1	cup	TVP granules
1	cup	boiling water
1/4	cup	vegetable broth
3/4	cup	onion, chopped
1	8 ounce	can tomato sauce
1	16 ounce	can pinto beans, drained
1	tablespoon	chili powder
1	teaspoon	cumin
1/2	teaspoon	oregano
3	cups	lettuce, shredded
		chopped fresh tomatoes
		grated fat-free cheese, optional
		fat-free sour cream, optional

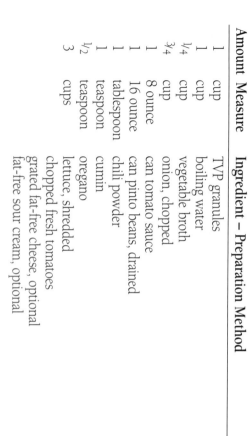

Preheat oven to 350 degrees. On a large cookie sheet place 6 oven-proof soup bowls. Wrap 6 large 10 inch tortillas in damp paper towels and microwave on high 1 minute. Press each tortilla into a bowl, crimping edges as needed to fit. Mist each with no-stick spray. Place tray in oven and bake for 12 to 15 minutes until edges begin to brown. Cool shells. If not using immediately, wrap tightly in a plastic bag.

Mix TVP granules with 1 cup boiling water, set aside for 5 minutes. Place vegetable broth in large saucepan, add onions. Sauté until onions are tender. Stir in tomato sauce, beans, chili powder, cumin, oregano and the TVP. Mix well. Bring to a boil, lower heat and simmer for 20 minutes. Place a tortilla shell on each plate. Into each shell, place 1/2 cup shredded lettuce and 1/6 of the TVP sauce. Garnish each with chopped tomatoes, cheese and sour cream.

Nutritional analysis: Calories 205, Fat 1, Protein 15, Carbohydrate 34.

TANGY THAI PASTA SALAD

Serving Size: 6

Amount	Measure	Ingredient – Preparation Method
12	ounces	corkscrew pasta shells – cooked and drained
20	ounces	pineapple chunks in juice – drained
3/4	cup	green bell pepper – chopped
3/4	cup	red bell pepper – chopped
3/4	cup	carrots – shredded
2	tablespoons	sesame seeds – toasted (optional)
1/2	cup	rice vinegar
2	tablespoons	WONDERSLIM® Fat/Egg Substitute
2	tablespoons	soy sauce, low sodium
1	teaspoon	garlic powder
1/2	teaspoon	ground ginger
1/2	teaspoon	ground pepper
1	teaspoon	cilantro

In large bowl, combine cooked pasta, pineapple, bell peppers, carrot and sesame seeds, set aside. In small bowl, stir together vinegar, fat substitute, soy sauce, garlic powder, ginger, pepper and cilantro until well blended. Pour dressing over salad, toss evenly to coat.

Nutritional analysis: Calories 309, Fat 2.8, Cholesterol 0, Carbohydrate 63.4, Protein 9.3, Sodium 174, Potassium 351, Calcium 38.

TOFU POTATO SALAD

Serving Size: 6

Amount	Measure	Ingredient – Preparation Method
3	medium	potato
5		eggs – boiled
1	stalk	celery (optional) – diced
½	cup	onion – diced
3	ounces	tofu lite firm
2	tablespoons	KRAFT® Miracle Whip Nonfat Dressing
2	tablespoons	fat-free sour cream
1	teaspoon	vinegar
1	tablespoon	mustard
1	clove	garlic
		salt and pepper
		paprika
3	teaspoons	fat-free dry ranch salad dressing mix

To make the salad: in a medium covered saucepan, cook the potatoes in boiling water for 20-25 minutes or until tender. Drain, then peel and cube the potatoes. Transfer to a medium bowl and chill in the refrigerator. Boil the eggs, cool and peel, (DISCARD THE YOLKS.) Chop egg whites, add along with celery and onion to potato mixture.

To make the dressing: In a blender or food processor, puree the tofu on low speed until creamy. Add the miracle whip, sour cream, vinegar, mustard, garlic, dry ranch dressing mix, salt and pepper. Blend or process until smooth.

Add the dressing to the potato mixture. Gently toss until potato mixture is coated. Lightly sprinkle the top with paprika to garnish. Cover and chill in the refrigerator for at least 2 hours to blend flavors.

Nutritional analysis: Calories 60, Fat 0.2, Cholesterol 0, Carbohydrate 12, Protein 2, Sodium 130, Potassium 344.

TOMATO-CUCUMBER SALAD

Serving Size: 4

Amount	Measure	Ingredient – Preparation Method
1 ½	cups	chopped tomatoes
1 ½	cups	peeled, chopped cucumber
½	cup	finely chopped onion
1	clove	garlic, minced
¾	cup	nonfat, plain yogurt
1	tablespoon	honey
		salt and pepper to taste

Combine tomatoes, cucumber and onion in serving bowl. Cover and chill for 1 hour. Combine garlic, yogurt and honey for dressing. Just before serving, drain vegetables of liquid. Pour dressing over vegetables, mixing well.

Nutritional analysis: Calories 70, Fat 0, Cholesterol 0, Protein 1.2.

VEGETABLE-PARMESAN SALAD

Serving Size: 8

Amount	Measure	Ingredient – Preparation Method
2	cups	broccoli flowerets
2	cups	cauliflower flowerets
1	small	red onion – sliced thin
1/4	cup	fat-free parmesan cheese, grated
1/8	cup	sugar
1/4	teaspoon	dried crushed basil
1	cup	KRAFT® Miracle Whip Nonfat Dressing
1/2	large	head of lettuce, torn in bite size pieces
1	cup	fat-free croutons
1	4 ounce	can water chestnuts, drained

Combine broccoli, cauliflower, and onion in a large bowl. In a small bowl, combine the cheese, sugar, basil and Miracle Whip. Mix well and add the cheese mixture to the vegetables. Toss gently, cover and refrigerate overnight. Before serving, add lettuce, croutons and water chestnuts to vegetables. Toss lightly before serving.

Nutritional analysis: Calories 98, Fat 0, Cholesterol 0, Carbohydrate 14, Protein 4, Sodium 313.

WALDORF SALAD

Serving Size: 6

Amount	Measure	Ingredient – Preparation Method
1	medium	green apples – cored/chopped
1	medium	red apples – cored/chopped
4	tablespoons	orange juice
1	tablespoon	lemon juice
1	cup	celery – chopped
1/3	cup	dates – chopped
1/3	cup	raisins
3/4	cup	nonfat plain yogurt
2	tablespoons	honey

Toss apples with 1 tablespoon only of the orange juice and 1 tablespoon of lemon juice, mix well to preserve the color. Add celery, dates and raisins. In a small bowl mix together yogurt, honey and remaining orange juice to make a dressing. Pour over fruit mixture and stir until evenly blended. Cover and chill one hour before serving. Toss again before serving.

Nutritional analysis: Calories 125, Fat 0.3, Cholesterol 0.3, Protein 1.2.

ZORBA SALAD ♥

Serving Size: 6

Amount	Measure	Ingredient – Preparation Method
2	envelopes	Butter Buds®
1/2	cup	water
4	tablespoons	wine vinegar
4	tablespoons	miso
1/2	teaspoon	black pepper
4	cloves	garlic – minced
2	tablespoons	fresh basil – chopped
2	tablespoons	fresh oregano – chopped
1 1/4	cup	tofu lite firm – 1/4 " cubes
1	large bunch	leaf lettuce
2	fresh	tomatoes – cubed
2		cucumbers – cubed
1/2	small	red onion – chopped fine

Dissolve the 2 envelopes of Butter Buds in 1/2 cup warm water. Add the vinegar, miso, black pepper and garlic. Blend well. Stir in the basil and oregano. Pour the dressing over the tofu cubes in a glass bowl, and marinate at least 1 hour or overnight.

Wash and dry the lettuce, and arrange in a in a large salad bowl. Toss all the rest of the ingredients together, arrange over top of lettuce. Pour tofu salad dressing over vegetables right before serving.

Nutritional analysis: Calories 97, Fat 0.6, Cholesterol 0, Carbohydrate 15.4, Protein 5.2, Sodium 505, Potassium 651, Calcium 67.

ARTICHOKES/MUSHROOMS AU GRATIN ♥ ○

Serving Size: 8

Amount	Measure	Ingredient – Preparation Method
2	packages	(9 ounce) frozen artichoke hearts, Birds Eye
1	tablespoon	lemon juice
1	cup	onion – chopped
1/4	cup	vegetable broth
6		mushrooms, fresh – washed/sliced
1	teaspoon	onion salt, black pepper to taste
1/2	teaspoon	dry mustard
1/2	cup	flour
1/2	cup	artichoke liquid (reserved after cooking)
1 1/2	cups	soy milk lite – hot
8	ounces	American or cheddar – grated, fat-free
2	tablespoons	bread crumbs, seasoned

Cook artichoke hearts according to package directions, adding lemon juice to water. Drain and reserve juice. Place artichokes in a sprayed 9 inch baking dish, set aside. Sauté onions and mushrooms in broth until tender. Remove from heat, add salt, pepper, dry mustard and flour. Stir until smooth. Gradually add artichoke juice and hot milk. Return to heat, cook stirring constantly until thickened. Remove from heat, add half of the cheese, stir until cheese has melted. Pour over the artichoke hearts. Top with the other half of cheese and sprinkle with bread crumbs.

Bake in a 350 degree oven for 30 minutes.

Nutritional analysis: Calories 99.6, Fat 0.9, Cholesterol 4, Carbohydrate 13.9, Protein 11.1, Sodium 773, Potassium 120, Calcium 12.

ASPARAGUS DIJON

Serving Size: 4

Amount	Measure	Ingredient – Preparation Method
1	pound	asparagus, cooked
½	cup	skim milk
1	teaspoon	Dijon mustard
1	tablespoon	flour
¼	cup	fat-free sour cream
1	teaspoon	balsamic vinegar
		salt and pepper to taste

Combine the milk, mustard and flour in a small saucepan and blend well. Cook over medium heat, stirring, 3 to 5 minutes or until mixture thickens and is bubbly. Stir in the sour cream, vinegar, salt and pepper. Heat through, and spoon the warm sauce over cooked asparagus.

Nutritional analysis: Calories 54, Fat 0, Cholesterol 0, Carbohydrate 8, Protein 4, Sodium 115.

ASPARAGUS WITH HONEY MUSTARD SAUCE

Serving Size: 8

Amount	Measure	Ingredient – Preparation Method
2 ½	pounds	fresh asparagus spears

SAUCE

3	tablespoons	honey
3	tablespoons	Dijon mustard
3	tablespoons	lemon juice
½	cup	nonfat mayonnaise

Rinse the asparagus with cool water, snap off the tough stem ends. Place the asparagus spears in a microwave or conventional steamer. Cover and cook at high power or over medium-high heat for 4 to 6 minutes, or until the spears are tender. Combine the sauce ingredients in a small saucepan. Over medium heat, cook, stirring constantly until the sauce is heated through. Transfer the asparagus to a serving dish. Drizzle the sauce over the asparagus and serve.

Nutritional analysis: Calories 50, Fat 0.3, Cholesterol 0, Protein 2.5, Sodium 115.

BABY LIMA BEANS WITH SOUR CREAM SAUCE

Serving Size: 4

Amount	Measure	Ingredient – Preparation Method
1	10 ounce	package frozen baby lima beans

SAUCE

¼	cup	fat-free sour cream
3	tablespoons	plain no-fat yogurt
2	tablespoons	minced parsley
1	teaspoon	paprika

Cook lima beans according to package directions. Drain. Combine all of the sauce ingredients in a small saucepan, heating thoroughly. Transfer the lima beans to a serving dish. Pour sauce over the lima beans and serve.

Comment: lima beans can be replaced with green picked soy beans.

Nutritional analysis: Calories 110, Fat 2, Cholesterol 2, Carbohydrate 17, Protein 6, Sodium 87.

BAKED ASPARAGUS

Serving Size: 4

Amount	Measure	Ingredient – Preparation Method
1	pound	asparagus spears
½	cup	water
2	tablespoons	lemon juice
¾	cup	low-fat parmesan cheese, grated, fat-free
		salt and pepper to taste

Spray a 12 x 8 inch baking dish. Arrange the asparagus spears in the dish in rows. Add the water and lemon juice. Season with salt and pepper. Sprinkle with the parmesan cheese. Cover loosely with foil. Bake in a 375 degree oven for 20 to 30 minutes, or until asparagus is tender.

Nutritional analysis: Calories 60, Fat 0.5, Cholesterol 0, Carbohydrate 10, Protein 8, Sodium 200.

BAKED CABBAGE WEDGES

Serving Size: 4

Amount	Measure	Ingredient – Preparation Method
1	large	head of cabbage
1	cup	vegetable broth
¼	cup	dry white wine
¼	teaspoon	black pepper
½	tablespoon	low fat margarine
2	tablespoons	seasoned bread crumbs
2	tablespoons	grated parmesan cheese

Core and cut the cabbage into 8 wedges. Place in a 2-quart casserole with cover. Combine the broth, wine and pepper in a small bowl, pour over the cabbage wedges. Cover the casserole and bake in a 400 degree oven 50 minutes, or until cabbage is fork-tender. In a small nonstick skillet melt the margarine, add the bread crumbs, stirring well, until the crumbs are lightly browned. Remove from heat and set aside. When cabbage is done, remove it from the oven, sprinkle the bread crumbs and cheese over the top. Return to oven uncovered long enough to melt cheese.

Nutritional analysis: Calories 90, Fat 1.5, Cholesterol 2, Carbohydrates 14, Protein 4, Sodium 115.

BRAISED RED CABBAGE

Serving Size: 4

Amount	Measure	Ingredient – Preparation Method
2	tablespoons	tomato paste
¼	cup	water
1	tablespoon	honey
4	cups	red cabbage, chopped
¾	cup	onion, chopped
1	tablespoon	lemon juice
2	tablespoons	nonfat plain yogurt
4	tablespoons	canned water chestnuts, drained and diced
		additional yogurt for garnish

In a large skillet, combine tomato paste with water and honey. Bring to a boil. Add cabbage and onion. Cover and cook over low heat, stirring occasionally, about 15 minutes, or until cabbage is tender. Remove from heat and stir in lemon juice. Then stir in yogurt and water chestnuts. Garnish with additional yogurt if desired after serving.

Nutritional analysis: Calories 60, Fat 0, Cholesterol 0, Sodium 75.

BROCCOLI, CORN AND CHEESE CASSEROLE

Serving Size: 6

Amount	Measure	Ingredient – Preparation Method
2	10 ounce	packages frozen chopped broccoli
1 ½	cups	fat-free cottage cheese
½	cup	fat-free sour cream
2	tablespoons	flour
1	cup	Egg Beaters® (egg substitute)
1	small	onion, chopped
1	teaspoon	garlic powder
		salt and pepper to taste
1	17 ounce	can whole kernel corn, drained
½	cup	parmesan cheese, fat-free

Cook broccoli according to package directions, cutting cooking time in half. Drain very well. Combine the cottage cheese, sour cream, flour, egg substitute, onion and seasonings in a large bowl, mixing well. Carefully fold in the drained broccoli and corn. Pour mixture into a 2-quart microwave-safe casserole. Sprinkle parmesan cheese over top of casserole, cover and cook on medium setting of microwave oven for 10 minutes or until edges of casserole are set. Allow casserole to stand 5 minutes before serving.

Nutritional analysis: Calories 134, Fat 0, Cholesterol 1, Carbohydrate 21, Protein 12, Sodium 369.

BRUSCHETTA WITH VEGGIES

Serving Size: 16

Amount	Measure	Ingredient – Preparation Method
16	slices	French bread, sliced 1/4" thick x 1 1/2" wide
1	medium	onion, chopped coarse
3		plum tomatoes, diced, drain juice
¼	cup	fresh basil, chopped fine
1	tablespoon	balsamic vinegar
		salt and pepper to taste

Preheat oven to 325 degrees. Place the bread in a single layer on a no-stick baking sheet. Spray both sides lightly with low-fat spray. Bake for 20 to 25 minutes, or until golden brown. Cut 1 clove of garlic in half. Rub the cut sides over the top of each toast point. Set toast aside. Spray a large no-stick skillet. Add the onions, cover and cook over medium heat, stirring occasionally, for 4 to 5 minutes or until onions start to soften. Reduce heat, uncover and cook, stirring occasionally for an additional 3 to 5 minutes. Add small amount of water if necessary to keep from sticking. Add the tomatoes. Mince the remaining 2 cloves of garlic and add to onions and tomato mixture. Cook for additional 3 to 4 minutes, or until tomatoes have soften. Remove from heat. Stir in the basil and vinegar. Season with salt and pepper. Place a spoonful of the veggies on each toast point.

Nutritional analysis per slice: Calories 20, Fat 0.3, Cholesterol 0, Carbohydrate 4, Protein 1, Sodium 35.

CARROTS AND ZUCCHINI WITH DIJON SAUCE

Serving Size: 4

Amount	Measure	Ingredient – Preparation Method
2	cups	carrots, sliced thin, 1/4 inch
1/4	cup	vegetable broth
2	cups	zucchini, sliced thin, 1/4 inch
1	tablespoon	apple cider vinegar
1	teaspoon	honey
2	teaspoons	Dijon mustard

Combine carrots and broth in saucepan. Cover and cook over medium heat 10-15 minutes. Add zucchini and cook until vegetables are just tender. Add more broth, if necessary, to keep from burning. Drain if necessary. In small bowl combine vinegar, honey and mustard. Pour over vegetables, stirring until evenly coated.

Nutritional analysis: Calories 55, Fat 0, Cholesterol 0, Carbohydrate 10, Sodium 75.

CARROTS AU GRATIN

♥

Serving Size: 6

Amount	Measure	Ingredient – Preparation Method
2	cups	corn flakes – crushed
1	envelope	Butter Buds®
1/2	cup	water
1	pound	carrots – sliced
1/2	medium	onion – sliced 1/4" thick
1	cup	water
		salt and pepper to taste
1 1/2	cups	EDENSOY® Organic Soy Beverage
1/4	cup	corn starch
3	tablespoons	horseradish
1	cup	nonfat cheddar cheese, shredded

Combine 1 envelope Butter Buds with 1/2 hot water. Place crushed corn flakes in small bowl. Add 3 tablespoons Butter Buds liquid (save the remaining Butter Buds liquid for cheese sauce) to crumbs, mix just until all crumbs have been moistened. Set aside.

Simmer carrots and onion in 1 cup water seasoned with salt and pepper until tender. Drain and place in sprayed 1 quart baking dish.

In medium sauce pan combine remaining Butter Bud liquid, soy milk, salt and pepper to taste. In a small bowl place cornstarch, add just enough water to make a fine paste. After milk has started to heat, add cornstarch, stirring constantly until mixture thickens. Remove from heat add shredded cheese, again stirring until cheese has melted. Add horseradish, blend well. Pour cheese mixture over carrots and onions. Mix well. Top with cornflake crumbs. Bake in 350 degree oven for 30 minutes.

Comment: 1 teaspoon dry dill weed can be used in place of the horseradish for a completely different flavor.

Nutritional analysis: Calories 168, Fat 1.2, Cholesterol 5, Carbohydrate 23, Protein 8.1, Sodium 427, Potassium 402, Calcium 33.

CAULIFLOWER-BROCCOLI FRITTATA

♥

Serving Size: 6

Amount	Measure	Ingredient – Preparation Method
1	10 ounce	package frozen cauliflower – thawed
1	10 ounce	package frozen broccoli – thawed
1	cup	Egg Beaters® (egg substitute)
1	envelope	onion soup mix
3/4	cup	KRAFT® Miracle Whip Nonfat Dressing
1/2	cup	fat-free cracker crumbs

Drain thawed cauliflower and broccoli. Mash vegetables, then mix with egg substitute, onion soup mix and Miracle whip. Lightly spray a 9x13 inch baking dish and sprinkle with part of the cracker crumbs. Pour vegetable mixture in baking dish. top with additional cracker crumbs. Bake in a 350 degree oven for 45 to 50 minutes.

Nutrition analysis: Calories 80, Fat 0, Cholesterol 0, Carbohydrate 13, Protein 5, Sodium 610.

CAULIFLOWER WITH CHEESE SAUCE

Serving Size: 6

Amount	Measure	Ingredient – Preparation Method
1	large head	cauliflower
8	ounces	American or cheddar – grated, fat-free
½	cup	vegetable broth

Wash and remove green leaves from head of cauliflower, place in large saucepan with enough water to steam and cook to desired doneness. While cauliflower is steaming, place cheese and broth in small sauce pan melt slowly over low to medium heat, stirring to keep from burning. When cauliflower has reached desired tenderness, drain well and place in large serving bowl. Pour melted cheese over the top and serve.

Nutritional analysis: Calories 52.3, Fat 0, Cholesterol 0, Carbohydrate 5.2, Protein 11.1, Sodium 631, Potassium 51, Calcium 4.

CAULIFLOWER WITH TOMATOES

Serving Size: 4

Amount	Measure	Ingredient – Preparation Method
1	small	yellow onion, chopped
2	cloves	garlic
½	teaspoon	ground ginger
1	16 ounce	can tomatoes, drained and chopped
¾	teaspoon	ground cumin
¾	teaspoon	ground coriander
¼	teaspoon	ground turmeric
¼	teaspoon	black pepper
⅛	teaspoon	cayenne pepper
½	cup	water
4	cups	cauliflower flowerets
2	teaspoons	lemon juice
2	tablespoons	minced parsley

In a food processor or blender process the onion, garlic and tomatoes, for 15 to 20 seconds. Transfer to a heavy large skillet, add the ginger, cumin, coriander, turmeric peppers and water. Bring to a boil. Adjust the heat so that the mixture bubbles gently and simmer, uncovered for 5 minutes. Stir in the cauliflower, cover and continue to simmer until cauliflower is tender, 12 to 15 minutes. Stir in the lemon juice and parsley before serving.

Nutritional analysis: Calories 38, Fat 0, Cholesterol 0, Carbohydrates 8, Protein 2, Sodium 20.

CHEESE STUFFED CUCUMBERS

Serving Size: 6

Amount	Measure	Ingredient – Preparation Method
3	large	cucumbers
1	cup	cottage cheese, fat-free
1/4	cup	green onions – chopped
1/4	teaspoon	dill weed
1/2	teaspoon	garlic powder
		salt and pepper – to taste

If cucumbers have been waxed, peel them. Cut each one in half, lengthwise. With a teaspoon, scoop out and discard the seeds. Combine remaining ingredients in a small bowl. Mix well. Chill cucumbers and cheese mixture, separately, for several hours or overnight. To serve, blot cucumbers with a towel and fill with cheese.

Per serving: Calories 48, Fat 1, Cholesterol 2, Carbohydrate 6, Protein 6, Sodium 156.

CORN PUDDING

Serving Size: 8

Amount	Measure	Ingredient – Preparation Method
4 1/2	cups	frozen whole kernel corn, thawed
3/4	cup	chopped onion
1 1/2	cups	soy milk lite or skim milk
3/4	cup	fat-free egg substitute
3	tablespoons	flour
		salt and pepper to taste
1/4	teaspoon	ground nutmeg

Place 1 1/2 cups of the corn and all the remaining ingredients in a food processor or blender. Process until mixture is smooth. Place the processed mixture in a large bowl, add the remaining corn kernels, stir to mix well. Spray a 2 1/2 quart casserole with cooking spray. Pour the corn mixture into the dish. Bake in a 350 degree oven for 1 hour and 15 minutes or until a knife inserted in the center comes out clean. Remove from the oven and let sit for 10 minutes before serving.

Nutritional analysis: Calories 95, Fat 1, Cholesterol 0, Protein 3, Sodium 145.

CREAMY CABBAGE

Serving Size: 4

Amount	Measure	Ingredient – Preparation Method
6	cups	shredded cabbage
3	tablespoons	apple cider vinegar
3	tablespoons	honey
1 1/2	teaspoons	Dijon mustard
1/2	cup	nonfat plain yogurt
		paprika

In a large skillet, combine cabbage and vinegar and cook, covered, over medium heat 8-10 minutes or until cabbage is softened. Remove from heat. In a small bowl combine honey, mustard and yogurt. Stir into warm cabbage just before serving. Sprinkle with paprika.

Nutritional analysis: Calories 75, Fat 0, Cholesterol 0, Protein 2.

CREAMY CROCKPOT POTATOES

Serving Size: 6

Amount	Measure	Ingredient – Preparation Method	
2	pounds	small red potatoes – quartered	
8	ounces	cream cheese fat-free	
1	envelope	ranch salad dressing mix	
1	can	Campbell's Healthy Request Cream of	Mushroom Soup
1/2	cup	EDENSOY® Organic Soy Beverage	

Place well scrubbed, quartered potatoes in a 3 1/2 quart crock pot. In a small bowl, combine cream, salad dressing and milk, stir in soup. Pour over potatoes. Cover and cook on low setting 8 hours. Stir to blend before serving.

Nutritional analysis: Calories 171.5, Fat 0.5, Cholesterol 7, Carbohydrate 32.4, Protein 9, Sodium 395, Potassium 840, Calcium 11.

CREAMY SUCCOTASH

Serving Size: 4

Amount	Measure	Ingredient – Preparation Method
1/3	cup	vegetable broth
1	cup	frozen baby lima beans
1	cup	frozen whole-kernel corn
1/2	teaspoon	sugar
1/4	teaspoon	black pepper
1/4	cup	fat-free sour cream

In a medium size saucepan, bring the broth to a boil, add the lima beans and corn, reduce the heat to low. Cover and simmer for 8 to 10 minutes, or until vegetables are tender. Add the sugar and pepper and cook for 3 to 4 minutes and almost all the liquid has evaporated. Stir in the sour cream and transfer to a serving dish.

Nutritional analysis: Calories 100, Fat 0, Cholesterol 0, Carbohydrates 18, Protein 4, Sodium 35.

DILL CORN RELISH

Serving Size: 6

Amount	Measure	Ingredient – Preparation Method
1	can	corn with red and green peppers
1/4	cup	red pepper – chopped fine
1	tablespoon	sugar
1	tablespoon	dill
1	tablespoon	rice vinegar

Combine all ingredients, mix well, chill several hours before serving.

Delicious served over baked tofu slices. Follow directions for baked sticks (cut MORI-NU® Lite SILKEN TOFU, FIRM into 1/4 inch slices instead of sticks). Season and coat the slices with herb style bread crumbs.

Nutritional analysis: Calories 44.6, Fat 0.2, Cholesterol 0, Carbohydrate 9.7, Protein 1.0, Sodium 132, Potassium 85, Calcium 12.

Comment: analysis does not include baked tofu slices.

EASY BAKED SOYBEANS

Serving Size: 8

Amount	Measure	Ingredient – Preparation Method
$\frac{1}{2}$	cup	TVP Granules
$\frac{1}{4}$	cup	water
2	tablespoons	Liquid Barbecue Smoke®
1	cup	onion – chopped
2	cans	Westbrae natural canned soy beans
2	tablespoons	mustard
4	tablespoons	sugar, brown
2	tablespoons	tomato paste

Mix above and bake in 350 degrees 1 hour.

EDAMAME SUCCOTASH
(SWEET GREEN SOYBEANS)

Serving Size: 8

Amount	Measure	Ingredient – Preparation Method
1	pound	edamame – frozen
1	can	corn with red and green peppers
1	tablespoon	lime juice
1	teaspoon	sugar

Mix all of the above ingredients in microwave dish, microwave on high until heated thoroughly. This can also be steamed on stove top.

Nutritional analysis: Calories 63.4, Fat 0.6, Cholesterol 0, Carbohydrate 7.6, Protein 6.9, Sodium 99, Potassium 46, Calcium 2.

ENGLISH PEA CASSEROLE

♥

Serving Size: 8

Amount	Measure	Ingredient – Preparation Method
2	10 oz. pkgs	peas – frozen
1	cup	celery – diced fine
1	cup	onion – diced fine
1	envelope	Butter Buds®
½	cup	water – hot
1	8 ounce	can, water chestnuts – chopped fine
1	can	Campbell's Healthy Request Mushroom Soup
1	2 ounce	jar, pimientos
1	cup	bread crumbs

Cook peas according to package directions; drain well. Prepare Butter Buds according to package directions, set aside. Combine all ingredients, except bread crumbs, and place in a sprayed 9 x 13 glass baking dish. Combine Butter Buds with bread crumbs and top pea mixture. Bake, uncovered, in a 350 degree oven for 40 minutes, until bubbly and brown.

Nutritional analysis: Calories 74.9, Fat 0.8, Cholesterol 2, Carbohydrate 13.2, Protein 3.2, Sodium 218, Potassium 171, Calcium 30.

GARLIC POTATOES

♥

Serving Size: 4

Amount	Measure	Ingredient – Preparation Method
4	medium	potatoes – washed
1	teaspoon	garlic powder
1	teaspoon	garlic salt
½	cup	water – hot
1	envelope	Butter Buds®
		coarse black pepper to taste

Quarter potatoes and place in a sprayed casserole dish. Prepare Butter Buds according to package directions and pour over potatoes. Sprinkle with garlic powder, garlic salt and pepper to taste. Cover and bake in 350 degree oven for 1 hour.

Nutritional analysis: Calories 93.8, Fat 0.2, Cholesterol 1, Protein 2.4, Sodium 55, Potassium 617, Calcium 9.

GLAZED CARROTS

Serving Size: 4

Amount	Measure	Ingredient – Preparation Method
¾	cup	water
8	medium	carrots, peeled and sliced diagonally 1/2 inch thick
1		cinnamon stick
¾	teaspoon	ground cumin
½	teaspoon	ground ginger
¼	teaspoon	ground coriander
⅛	teaspoon	cayenne pepper
2	teaspoons	honey
2	teaspoons	lemon juice

In a heavy large skillet, bring water to a boil, add the carrots, cinnamon stick and four spices. Lower the heat so that the liquid bubbles gently, cover and simmer 12 to 15 minutes. Uncover, add the honey and lemon juice, raise the heat to high and boil until all the liquid has evaporated, stirring gently, for about 4 minutes.

Nutritional analysis: Calories 60, Fat 0, Cholesterol 0, Carbohydrates 14, Protein 1, Sodium 37.

GLAZED SNOW PEAS AND CARROTS

Serving Size: 10

Amount	Measure	Ingredient – Preparation Method
1	teaspoon	crushed fresh garlic
½	teaspoon	ground ginger
1	pound	snow peas
4	large	diagonally sliced carrots
¼	cup	dry sherry or vegetable broth

GLAZE

¼	cup	vegetable broth
2	tablespoons	lemon juice
1	tablespoon	soy sauce, low sodium
2	teaspoons	sugar
2	teaspoons	cornstarch

Combine the glaze ingredients in a small bowl, mixing well. Set aside. Coat a large skillet with nonstick cooking spray, preheat over medium heat. Place the garlic and ginger in the skillet, stir-fry for 30 seconds. Add the peas and carrots to the skillet, pour the sherry or broth over the top. Reduce the heat to medium-low, cover and cook for 8 to 10 minutes, or until the vegetables are tender. Stir occasionally. Add small amount of broth if necessary to keep from sticking. Reduce the heat to low. Stir the glaze mixture and pour over the vegetables. Stirring constantly, cook the vegetable mixture for a minute or 2, until the glaze has thickened. Serve immediately.

Nutritional analysis: Calories 50, Fat, 0, Cholesterol 0, Protein 2, Sodium 90.

GRITS

Serving Size: 1

Amount	Measure	Ingredient – Preparation Method
3	ounces	yellow or white cornmeal
2	cups	water
2	scoops	VEGE FUEL®
5	packets	Equal® sweetener
1	teaspoon	cinnamon
2	teaspoons	vanilla extract
½	teaspoon	salt

Mix the Vege Fuel with the salt and cornmeal in a bowl and blend well. Bring the water to a rolling boil and slowly drizzle in the cornmeal mixture while stirring constantly with a wire whisk. As the mixture thickens, lower the heat and continue to cook until the grits are very thick and bubbles leave craters on the surface. Remove from the heat, cover, and let stand for 10 minutes. Add the remaining ingredients and mix well.

Nutritional analysis: Calories 526, Fat 1, Carbohydrate 75, Protein 51.

HASH BROWN CASSEROLE

Serving Size: 10

Amount	Measure	Ingredient – Preparation Method
2	pounds	frozen hash brown potatoes – thawed
1	cup	onion – diced
1	cup	sour cream, fat-free
1	cup	EDENSOY® Organic Soy Beverage
1	envelope	ranch salad dressing mix
1	can	Campbell's Healthy Request Mushroom Soup
2	cups	nonfat cheddar cheese, shredded
		salt and pepper to taste
½	cup	water – hot
1	envelope	Butter Buds®
2	cups	cornflakes – crushed

In large bowl combine sour cream, milk, ranch dressing mix and soup, after blending add shredded cheese, salt and pepper to taste. Add thawed potatoes and onions. Mix well. Pour mixture into a sprayed 9 x 13 inch baking dish. Prepare Butter Buds according to package directions. In small bowl pour Butter Buds over crushed cornflakes, sprinkle this mixture over the top of potatoes. Bake in a 350 degree oven for 1 hour or until potatoes are tender.

Nutritional analysis: Calories 135.7, Fat 0.5, Cholesterol 7, Carbohydrate 24.4, Protein 8.4, Sodium 660, Potassium 62, Calcium 7.

HEALTHY MEAT MARINADE

Serving Size: 4

Amount	Measure	Ingredient – Preparation Method
½	cup	rice vinegar/balsamic vinegar
1	tablespoon	mustard
1	tablespoon	olive oil
1	tablespoon	lemon juice
1	clove	garlic – minced fine
1	teaspoon	sugar
1	teaspoon	salt

Mix all ingredients together in shallow bowl with cover. Place beef or chicken in marinate turning every 30 minutes for 1-2 hours before grilling. Place meat on grill, discard marinate, do not use to baste meat.

Comment: the rice vinegar works best for the chicken and the balsamic for beef or pork.

HOLIDAY CORN CASSEROLE

Serving Size: 8

Amount	Measure	Ingredient – Preparation Method
1	small	onion – chopped
½	medium	green pepper – chopped
1	can	corn – undrained
1	can	creamed corn
1	box	corn muffin mix
3		Egg Beaters® (egg substitute)
1	cup	sour cream, fat-free
2	cups	nonfat cheddar cheese, shredded

In small microwave bowl with cover, cook onion and green pepper on high for 3 minutes. In large bowl mix both cans of corn, muffin mix and eggs. Add vegetables. Pour into a 9 x 13 inch baking dish. Top with dollops of sour cream and cheese. Bake in a 325 degree oven for 45 to 55 minutes or until browned and set.

Nutritional analysis: Calories 130, Fat 1, Cholesterol 0, Carbohydrate 12.0, Protein 23.4, Sodium 747, Potassium 127, Calcium 39.

HOT SPINACHAPENO CASSEROLE

Serving Size: 8

Amount	Measure	Ingredient – Preparation Method
2	10 oz boxes	chopped frozen spinach
5	tablespoons	vegetable broth
1	cup	onion – chopped
4	tablespoons	soy flour
1	teaspoon	celery seed
1	teaspoon	pepper
1	teaspoon	garlic powder
8	ounces	American or cheddar – grated, fat-free
1	cup	Egg Beaters® (egg substitute)
2	tablespoons	Hot Green Jalapeno Sauce
2	tablespoons	Hot Red Picante Sauce
½	cup	seasoned bread crumbs

Cook spinach as directed on package. Drain very well, set aside.

In large sauce pan sauté onions in broth until tender. Add celery seed, pepper and garlic powder. Make a paste of flour and small amount of water, add to onions. Add cheese, hot sauces and Egg Beaters, continue stirring, fold in the spinach. Blend well.

Pour mixture into a sprayed 9 1/2 x 11 inch casserole dish. Top with seasoned bread crumbs. Bake in a 350 degree oven for 30 minutes.

Nutritional analysis: Calories 94, Fat 0.9, Cholesterol 4, Carbohydrate 11.9, Protein 12.1, Sodium 756, Potassium 165, Calcium 48.

Comment: additional hot sauce can be added if you prefer real hot dish!!!

LO-CAL CREAMY COLESLAW

Serving Size: 8

Amount	Measure	Ingredient – Preparation Method
3	pounds	shredded cabbage
3	small	carrots, grated
2	cups	fat-free sour cream
¾	cup	KRAFT® Miracle Whip Nonfat Dressing
⅓	cup	ketchup
¼	cup	wine vinegar
2	teaspoons	celery seed
2	teaspoons	onion powder
1	teaspoon	sugar
		garlic salt to taste
		pepper to taste

Mix the cabbage and carrots together. Combine the remaining ingredients in separate bowl, mixing well. Pour over the cabbage mixture, tossing to coat evenly. Make a least 5 hours in advance, but much better if made the day before.

Nutritional analysis: Calories 99, Fat 0, Carbohydrate 22, Cholesterol 0, Protein 3, Sodium 315.

MANGO-PAPAYA SALSA

Serving Size: 4

Amount	Measure	Ingredient – Preparation Method
5	slices	mangos – chopped coarse
5	slices	papaya – chopped coarse
1	bunch	green onions – chopped fine
1		lime
		cilantro – chopped fine

Place mangos, papayas and chopped onion in large sauté pan. Sauté over medium heat with the juice of fresh lime. Garnish with cilantro. Terrific served with black bean burger. Makes a very pretty appetizer.

Nutritional analysis: Calories 220, Fat 0, Cholesterol 0, Carbohydrate 43, Protein 1.

MASHED SWEET POTATOES OR YAMS

Serving Size: 12

Amount	Measure	Ingredient – Preparation Method
4	pounds	sweet potatoes or yams – peeled
2	teaspoons	salt
3/4	cup	tofu lite firm
1/4	cup	orange juice
2	tablespoons	brown sugar – firmly packed
1	envelope	Butter Buds®
2	teaspoons	ginger – grated
2	teaspoons	orange peel – grated

Peel sweet potatoes or yams. Place in saucepan, cover with water, add salt. Bring to a boil, lower heat and cover. Simmer until desired doneness for mashing. Remove from heat and drain. While potatoes are cooking, place 3/4 cup tofu, orange juice, brown sugar,Butter Buds and grated ginger, in food processor. Process until creamy consistency. Mash sweet potatoes or yams, add tofu mixture, mixing well. Place in baking dish. Garnish with grated orange peel. Bake in a 350 degree oven for 15 to 20 minutes.

Nutritional analysis: Calories 175, Fat 0.5, Cholesterol 0, Carbohydrate 39, Protein 3, Sodium 393.

MIXED VEGETABLES WITH HONEY MUSTARD SAUCE

Serving Size: 4

Amount	Measure	Ingredient – Preparation Method
1	cup	carrots, sliced thin
2	cups	cauliflower and broccoli flowerets
2	tablespoons	Dijon mustard
2	tablespoons	honey
1	teaspoon	dried dill weed

Steam vegetables until tender. In a small bowl combine mustard with honey and dill to make a smooth sauce. Mix sauce with hot cooked vegetables and stir gently until sauce is evenly distributed.

Nutritional analysis: Calories 60, Fat 0, Cholesterol 0, Sodium 110.

MONTEREY BEANS AND CORN CASSEROLE

Serving Size: 8

Amount	Measure	Ingredient – Preparation Method
1	15 ounce	red kidney beans, canned – drained
12	ounces	American or cheddar – grated, fat-free
1	12 ounce	can, corn – drained
1	4 ounce	can chopped green chiles – drained
1	8 ounce	can, tomato sauce
1	medium	zucchini – sliced 1/8" thick
½	cup	cornmeal
½	cup	soy milk lite
¼	cup	Egg Beaters® (egg substitute)
		dash of Tabasco sauce (optional)

In a 9 inch sprayed glass casserole dish, combine beans, corn, 3/4 cup of the cheese, tomato sauce, chiles and Tabasco; mix well. Top with the zucchini. Combine cornmeal, milk and Egg Beater; mix well. Pour over the vegetable mixture. Bake in a 350 degree oven 35-40 minutes. Sprinkle with remaining 3/4 cup of cheese, continue baking about 2-3 more minutes until cheese melts.

Nutritional analysis: Calories 136, Fat 0.7, Cholesterol 6, Carbohydrate 22, Protein 16.9, Sodium 923, Potassium 315, Calcium 20.

MUSHROOMS WITH SOUR CREAM DILL SAUCE

Serving Size: 4

Amount	Measure	Ingredient – Preparation Method
¾	cup	vegetable broth, divided
1	medium	yellow onion, chopped fine
1	pound	small mushrooms, washed with stems trimmed
¼	cup	dry white wine
3	teaspoons	cornstarch
½	teaspoon	dill weed
½	teaspoon	paprika
¼	cup	fat-free sour cream
2	tablespoons	snipped fresh dill or minced parsley

In a heavy large skillet, pour 1/4 cup of the broth, add the onion and cook uncovered until soft. Add the mushrooms, cover and cook for 3 to 4 minutes. Stir in the wine and cook uncovered 1 minute more. Meanwhile, in a small bowl, combine the remaining broth, cornstarch, dill weed and paprika. Add this mixture to the skillet and simmer, uncovered stirring often for 4 to 5 minutes. Raise the heat, stirring, until the sauce has thickened. Reduce the heat to low, stir in the sour cream and fresh dill or parsley. Do not let the sauce boil or it will curdle.

Nutritional analysis: Calories 70, Fat 0, Cholesterol 0, Carbohydrate 10, Protein 3, Sodium 16.

ONION RELISH

Amount	Measure	Ingredient – Preparation Method
3	small	yellow onions, sliced thin, separate into rings
1	small	red onion, sliced thin, separate into rings
2	tablespoons	sugar
2	tablespoons	balsamic vinegar
2	teaspoons	Dijon mustard
		pepper to taste

Place all the ingredients in a small glass bowl. Mix well to coat evenly. Cover and chill in the refrigerator overnight. Will keep 1 week stored in refrigerator. Makes 2 cups.

Nutritional analysis based on 2 tablespoons: Calories 10, Fat 0, Cholesterol 0, Carbohydrate 2, Protein 0, Sodium 20.

PEPPER RELISH

Amount	Measure	Ingredient – Preparation Method
1	large	green pepper, cored, seeded and chopped
1	large	red pepper, cored, seeded and chopped
1	large	yellow pepper, cored seeded and chopped
1	medium	yellow onion, chopped
1/4	cup	white vinegar
2	tablespoons	sugar
1/2	teaspoon	celery seed
1/4	teaspoon	red pepper flakes

Place all the ingredients in a large saucepan and mix well. Set over moderate heat until the vinegar boils. Stir, reduce the heat to low, cover and simmer for 2 to 3 minutes or until the peppers are tender but still crisp. Remove from heat and let stand, covered at room temperature at least 30 minutes before serving. Or cover and place in the refrigerator overnight to serve cold. Will keep up to 1 week in the refrigerator.

Makes 3 3/4 cups relish.

Nutritional analysis based on 2 tablespoons: Calories 6, Fat 0, Cholesterol 0, Carbohydrates 2, Protein 0, Sodium 0.

SCALLOPED CORN

Serving Size: 6

Amount	Measure	Ingredient – Preparation Method
1	15 oz can	creamed corn
1	cup	cracker crumbs
1/2	cup	green pepper – chopped fine
1/2	cup	red onion – chopped fine
1	cup	soy milk lite
1/2	cup	Egg Beaters® (egg substitute)
		salt and pepper to taste
		cajun seasoning

Combine all ingredients (except cajun seasoning) in medium size mixing bowl. Pour into sprayed 1 1/2 quart casserole, sprinkle with cajun seasoning. Bake in a 350 degree oven about 1 hour.

Nutritional analysis: Calories 114, Fat 1, Cholesterol 0, Carbohydrate 21, Protein 4.9, Sodium 66, Potassium 167, Calcium 21.

SCALLOPED POTATOES

Serving Size: 10

Amount	Measure	Ingredient – Preparation Method
¼	cup	flour, all-purpose
2	teaspoons	dried parsley
		salt and pepper to taste
6	medium	potatoes
2	medium	yellow onions, thinly sliced and separated into rings
½	cup	fat-free grated parmesan cheese
2	cups	EDENSOY® Organic Soy Beverage

Combine the flour, parsley and pepper in a medium bowl, and set aside. Scrub the potatoes and slice very thin, 1/8 inch. You should have 6 cups of potatoes. (Adjust if necessary.) Spray a 8x12 inch baking dish with nonstick cooking spray. Arrange 2 cups of the potatoes in a single layer over the bottom of the dish. Lay half of the onion rings over the potatoes, sprinkle the onions with half of the flour mixture and 2 tablespoons of the parmesan cheese. Repeat these layers and top with the remaining 2 cups of potatoes. Pour the milk over the potatoes, sprinkle with the remaining 1/4 cup of parmesan cheese. Cover the dish with foil and bake in a 350 degree oven for 45 minutes. Remove the foil and bake 15 to 20 minutes or until the potatoes are tender and the top is brown. After removing from oven, let sit for 5 minutes before serving.

Nutritional analysis: Calories 175, Fat 1, Cholesterol 5, Protein 9, Sodium 105.

SIMPLE ARTICHOKE CASSEROLE

Serving Size: 8

Amount	Measure	Ingredient – Preparation Method
2	14 ounce	cans artichoke hearts, drained and halved
1	bunch	green onions, diced including green
12		fat-free saltine crackers, finely crumbled
2	cups	fat-free grated cheddar cheese
1	teaspoon	Pickapeppa Sauce
		salt and pepper to taste
1 ¼	cups	Egg Beaters® (egg substitute)

Preheat oven to 350 degrees. Combine artichokes, onions, saltines, cheddar cheese, Pickapeppa sauce, salt and pepper in a bowl. In separate bowl beat egg substitute until frothy. Fold egg into artichoke mixture and put into a baking dish lightly sprayed with cooking spray. Bake for 30 minutes or until hot and bubbly.

Nutritional analysis: Calories 164, Fat 0, Cholesterol 0, Carbohydrate 16, Protein 22, Sodium, 730.

SKINNY N HOT ZUCCHINI

Serving Size: 6

Amount	Measure	Ingredient – Preparation Method
6	large	zucchini, sliced
2	large	onions, sliced
3	cloves	garlic, chopped
		vegetable broth
½	teaspoon	red pepper flakes, or to taste
3	tablespoons	balsamic vinegar

Spray a large nonstick skillet with cooking spray. Over medium-high heat place, zucchini, onions and garlic into hot skillet, add small amount of vegetable juice as you sauté the vegetables until tender – 10 to 15 minutes. Add pepper flakes and cook 2 minutes longer. Remove from heat, let cool slightly, toss with balsamic vinegar and serve.

Nutritional analysis: Calories 30, Fat 0, Cholesterol 0, Carbohydrate 4, Protein 2, Sodium 4.

SOUTHWEST COLESLAW

Serving Size: 6

Amount	Measure	Ingredient – Preparation Method
4	cups	cabbage – shredded
½	package	MORI-NU® Lite SILKEN TOFU, FIRM
6	slices	mangos
6	slices	papaya
4	tablespoons	nice vinegar or to taste
		salt and pepper to taste

Place tofu, 4 slices mangos, 4 slices papaya and rice vinegar in food processor, process until well blended. Pour mixture over shredded cabbage. Garnish with the 2 additional chopped slices of mangos and papayas.

Nutritional analysis: Calories 268.6, Fat 1.1, Cholesterol 0, Carbohydrate 68.1, Protein 3.6, Sodium 23, Potassium 1,229, Calcium 116.

SPAGHETTI CORN

Serving Size: 8

Amount	Measure	Ingredient – Preparation Method
1	envelope	Butter Buds®
1/2	cup	water – hot
1	can	creamed corn
1	can	corn – do not drain
8	ounces	American or cheddar – grated, fat-free
1 1/2	cups	spaghetti – dry, broken in – small pieces

Prepare Butter Buds according to package directions. Mix all ingredients together. Pour into a sprayed casserole dish, cover and bake in a 350 degree oven for 45 minutes. Uncover and bake 15 minutes longer.

Nutritional analysis: Calories 106.7, Fat 0.4, Cholesterol 4, Carbohydrate 17.4, Protein 10.4, Sodium 425, Potassium 57, Calcium 4.

SUBURBAN STYLE BAKED BEANS

Serving Size: 6

Amount	Measure	Ingredient – Preparation Method
1	cup	onions – chopped fine
2	16 ounce	pinto beans, canned
6	slices	MORNINGSTAR FARMS® Breakfast Strips – cubed
2	tablespoons	mustard
4	tablespoons	brown sugar
1/2	teaspoon	garlic powder
3	tablespoons	tomato paste
3	tablespoons	water
1/4	cup	ketchup

In small microwave bowl with cover, micro wave onions on high 3-4 minutes until tender. In mixing bowl combine beans, cubed breakfast strips, mustard, brown sugar, garlic powder, tomato paste, water and ketchup. Add onions. Blend well. Pour into a sprayed 1 quart casserole, cover and bake in 350 degree oven for 45 minutes.

Hint: when using a small amount of tomato paste, the un-used portion can be put in a small plastic bag and frozen.

Comment: for variety, use 1 can of light red kidney beans and 1 can of pinto beans.

Nutritional analysis: Calories 150, Fat 2.9, Cholesterol 0, Carbohydrate 25.4, Protein 5.6, Sodium 731, Potassium 432

SUMMER VEGETABLES

Serving Size: 6

Amount	Measure	Ingredient – Preparation Method
1	pound	zucchini, thinly sliced
1	medium	onion, thinly sliced
1		yellow pepper, diced
2		cloves garlic, minced
1	cup	tomatoes, chopped
1	tablespoon	fresh basil, chopped
1	tablespoon	balsamic vinegar, or to taste
		salt and pepper to taste

Spray a large no-stick skillet. Add the zucchini, onions, yellow pepper and garlic. Cover and cook over medium heat, stirring occasionally, 5 to 6 minutes, or until the vegetables soften and start to brown. Add small amount of water if necessary to keep from sticking. Add the chopped tomatoes. Uncover and cook over medium heat, stirring occasionally, for 6 to 8 minutes, or until the vegetables are tender. Stir in the basil and vinegar. Season to taste with the salt and pepper.

Nutritional analysis: Calories 36, Fat 0, Cholesterol 0, Carbohydrate 8, Protein 2, Sodium 70.

SWEET AND SOUR BEANS AND CABBAGE

Serving Size: 6

Amount	Measure	Ingredient – Preparation Method
6	cups	shredded cabbage
1	cup	tomato sauce
1	tablespoon	lemon juice
2	teaspoons	apple cider vinegar
1	tablespoon	frozen apple juice concentrate
2	tablespoons	honey
2	teaspoons	Dijon mustard
2	cloves	garlic, minced
1/4	teaspoon	celery seed
1	teaspoon	onion powder
		pepper to taste
2	15.8 ounce	cans, great northern beans, drained

In a large saucepan, combine all ingredients except beans. Bring cabbage mixture to a boil while stirring. Cover and simmer until cabbage is tender. Add beans to cabbage and cook 5-10 minutes to heat through.

Nutritional analysis: Calories 200, Fat 1, Cholesterol 0, Carbohydrates 9, Protein 2, Sodium 65.

SWEET AND SOUR BEETS

Serving Size: 4

Amount	Measure	Ingredient – Preparation Method
1 1/2	cups	water
6	medium	beets, scrubbed with tops trimmed
1/4	cup	cider vinegar
2	teaspoons	sugar
2	teaspoons	cornstarch
1/8	teaspoon	ground cloves
		pepper to taste

In a heavy saucepan, bring the water to a boil, add the beets and cook, covered over moderate heat until beets are tender. Drain, reserving 1 cup of the cooking water. When beets are cool enough to handle, peel and cut them into 1/4 inch thick slices. Place the reserved cooking water and the vinegar in a saucepan. In a small bowl combine the sugar and cornstarch, blend this into the saucepan liquid. Add the cloves and pepper. Heat the liquid over moderate to low heat, stirring until the mixture thickens slightly and turns clear. Return the beets to the saucepan and heat through. Transfer to serving dish to serve.

Nutritional analysis: Calories 65, Fat 0, Cholesterol 0, Carbohydrates 4, Protein 2, Sodium 80.

TANGY HORSERADISH MASHED POTATOES

Serving Size: 4

Amount	Measure	Ingredient – Preparation Method
4	medium	russet potatoes
		water
1/2	cup	silken tofu
1-2	teaspoons	horseradish or to taste

Peel potatoes, quarter and place in large saucepan. Cover with water. Bring to a boil over high heat, cover, reduce heat, simmer until potatoes are tender. Drain. While potatoes are cooking, place tofu and horseradish in a small food processor, process until smooth. After draining potatoes, add tofu mixture and mash. Serve hot.

Nutritional analysis: Calories 130, Fat 1, Cholesterol 0, Carbohydrate 22, Protein 4.

TWO BEAN BAKED BEANS

Serving Size: 8

Amount	Measure	Ingredient – Preparation Method
½	cup	TVP Granules
¼	cup	water
2	tablespoons	Liquid Barbecue Smoke®
1	cup	onion – chopped fine
1	can	soybeans
1	can	vegetarian baked beans
2	tablespoons	mustard
4	tablespoons	sugar, brown

Rehydrate TVP with 1/4 cup hot water to which you have added 2 tablespoons Liquid Barbecue Smoke, let set for 15 to 30 minutes. Mix all ingredients together well, place in sprayed casserole dish. Bake for 30 to 45 minutes, in 350 degree oven.

Nutritional analysis: Calories 163, Fat 5.0, Cholesterol 0, Carbohydrate 17.5, Protein 16.6, Sodium 136, Potassium 461, Calcium 81.

VEGGIE FUEL BAKED CORNMEAL

Serving Size: 1

Amount	Measure	Ingredient – Preparation Method
3	ounces	cornmeal
2	cups	vegetable broth
2	scoops	VEGE FUEL®
½	cup	peeled whole tomatoes
2	cloves	garlic, finely minced
2	tablespoons	fresh basil, chopped
½	cup	onion, finely chopped
½	teaspoon	nutmeg
2	teaspoons	salt
½	teaspoon	pepper
		cooking spray

Preheat the oven to 350 degrees. Mix the cornmeal, 1/2 teaspoon salt, and Vege Fuel in a small bowl. Bring the vegetable broth to a rolling boil and slowly drizzle in the cornmeal mixture while stirring constantly with a wire whisk. Continue to cook the cornmeal for about 5 minutes, until it thickens. Immediately pour the cooked cornmeal into a lightly sprayed baking dish. Spread it evenly across the bottom of the dish, set aside. Coat a sauté pan with cooking spray. Sauté the garlic with the onion and the remaining salt until the liquid has evaporated and the onion begins to brown. Add the remaining ingredients and let the sauce simmer over medium heat for about 10 minutes, or until thickened. Pour the sauce over the corn mixture and bake for 30 minutes. Remove from oven and let cool before serving.

Nutritional analysis: Calories 601, Fat 1, Carbohydrate 95, Protein 54.

VEGGIE FUEL MASHED POTATOES

Serving Size: 4

Amount	Measure	Ingredient – Preparation Method
2	medium	potatoes, peeled and cubed
1	cup	non-fat milk
2	teaspoons	Butter Buds®
1	teaspoon	salt
½	teaspoon	ground black pepper
1	scoop	VEGE FUEL®

Cut the potatoes into small cubes and boil in 1 quart lightly salted water for about 15 minutes, or until very soft. Drain well and return to the pot. Combine the Vege Fuel, milk, salt, pepper and Butter Buds in a blender. Pulse the blender several times to break up any lumps. Add the milk mixture to the potatoes. Using a hand beater, whip the potatoes until light and fluffy. Adjust the seasonings and serve.

Optional: 1-2 teaspoons of minced horseradish or minced roasted garlic may be added for a different flavor.

Nutritional analysis: Calories 159, Fat 0, Carbohydrate 29, Protein 10.

VEGGIE FUEL RICE

Serving Size: 1

Amount	Measure	Ingredient – Preparation Method
⅓	cup	white rice, uncooked
1	cup	vegetable broth
1	teaspoon	salt
2	scoops	VEGE FUEL®

Preheat oven to 350 degrees. Using a blender, dissolve the Vege Fuel in the vegetable broth. fill an oven-safe saucepan with the rice, then pour the Vege Fuel mixture over it. Slowly bring the mixture to a boil, cover, and place in the oven. Bake for 30 minutes, until all the liquid has been absorbed and the rice is tender.

Nutritional analysis: Calories 285, Fat 0, Carbohydrate 21, Protein 50.

Vege Fuel rice makes a nicely textured vehicle for a variety of flavors. Virtually any cooked vegetable or fresh herb can be added during the final stages of cooking. After the rice has been in the oven for 10 minutes, stir in 1/2 cup to a cup of any cooked vegetable or 1-2 teaspoons of any fresh or dried herb. Mix well, cover and continue to cook for another 15-20 minutes, until all of the liquid has been absorbed and the rice is tender.

VEGGIE RELISH

Serving Size: 1

Amount	Measure	Ingredient – Preparation Method
1	large	tomato, cored, seeded and chopped fine
2	tablespoons	sweet pickle relish
1/4	cup	yellow onion, minced
1/4	cup	red pepper, minced
1	clove	garlic minced
3	tablespoons	rice vinegar
1	teaspoon	sugar
1/2	teaspoon	celery seed
1	teaspoon	Dijon mustard

Place yellow onion, red pepper and garlic clove in small food processor to mince. After processing, place all ingredients in a medium size glass bowl and mix well. Cover and chill overnight in the refrigerator. This relish will keep up to 1 week in the refrigerator. Makes 1 1/2 cups.

Nutritional analysis based on 1 tablespoon: Calories 5, Fat 0, Cholesterol 0, Carbohydrate 1, Protein 0, Sodium 15.

ZIPPY CREAMED CARROTS

Serving Size: 4

Amount	Measure	Ingredient – Preparation Method
1	pound	carrots
1	small	onion – sliced thin
1	cup	KRAFT® Miracle Whip Nonfat Dressing
3	tablespoons	grated horseradish
1/3	cup	liquid reserved from boiled carrots
1/4	cup	seasoned bread crumbs
		parsley flakes
		paprika

Peel and slice carrots. In medium saucepan cook carrots and onion until tender, drain, reserving 1/3 cup liquid. Place carrots and onion in sprayed baking dish. In a small bowl mix together Miracle Whip, horseradish and liquid reserved from carrots. Spread over carrots and onion layer. Sprinkle with bread crumbs, parsley and paprika. Bake in a 350 degree oven 30 minutes.

Nutritional analysis: Calories 138.8, Fat 0.5, Cholesterol 0, Carbohydrate 29.4, Protein 2.6, Sodium 819, Potassium 428, Calcium 55.

CHEESE SAUCE

Serving Size: 4

Amount	Measure	Ingredient – Preparation Method
1	cup	skim milk
1	tablespoon	flour
1	teaspoon	Dijon mustard
1	teaspoon	Worcestershire sauce
3	drops	Tabasco sauce
1	cup	fat-free shredded cheddar cheese

Combine the milk, mustard, Worcestershire sauce and Tabasco sauce in a saucepan over moderately low heat until the mixture bubbles gently. Let the mixture simmer for 4 minutes, stirring constantly. Stir in the cheese, a little at a time, and cook sauce over moderately low heat for 4 minutes or until it is smooth. (Do not let the mixture boil.) Serve this over toast or steamed vegetables.

Nutritional analysis: Calories 137, Fat 0, Carbohydrate 20, Cholesterol 1, Protein 13, Sodium 530.

CRANBERRY-ONION-ORANGE SAUCE

Serving Size: 6

Amount	Measure	Ingredient – Preparation Method
2	large	onions
1	can	wholeberry cranberry sauce
1/4	cup	orange juice
1	teaspoon	orange zest

With a fork, pierce top of each unpeeled onion. Place in small microwave dish. Microwave on high 5-6 minutes. Remove from microwave. Peel onions and chop coarsely. Place in a medium size sauté pan, using a small amount of the orange juice slowly brown the onions, add the cranberry sauce, remaining orange juice and orange zest. Add salt and pepper to taste. Continue to sauté on low heat until thoroughly heated.

Nutritional analysis: Calories 124, Fat 0, Cholesterol 0, Carbohydrate 32, Protein 0.5, Sodium 218.

Comment: excellent with yams or squash.

CREAMY TOMATO BASIL SAUCE

Serving Size: 4

Amount	Measure	Ingredient – Preparation Method
1	6 ounce	can, tomato paste
2	tablespoons	Dijon mustard
1	tablespoon	honey
¾	cup	EDENSOY® Organic Soy Beverage
1	tablespoon	basil
1	teaspoon	soy sauce, low sodium
		pepper to taste

Combine above ingredients in mixing bowl, mixing until all ingredients are well blended. Refrigerate any unused portion.

Excellent served over grilled tofu cut in rounds, coated with your favorite coating and baked.

Nutritional analysis: Calories 78, Fat 1.1, Cholesterol 0, Carbohydrate 13.8, Protein 3.3, Sodium 82, Potassium 430, Calcium 36.

DIJON LIME SAUCE

Serving Size: 4

Amount	Measure	Ingredient – Preparation Method
2	tablespoons	Dijon mustard
1	tablespoon	fresh cilantro, chopped
2	teaspoons	low sodium soy sauce
1	clove	garlic, minced
		juice of two limes

Combine all of the ingredients in a small bowl. Mix well with a wire whisk. Serve over poached salmon or Easy Oven Baked Tofu Sticks. (See recipe under Appetizers.)

Nutritional analysis: Calories 13, Fat 0, Carbohydrate 1, Protein 0.

HEAVEN AND EARTH SAUCE

Serving Size: 6

Amount	Measure	Ingredient – Preparation Method
2	large	sweet onions – sliced and chopped
2	medium	plums – chopped
1	small	jalapeno pepper – chopped fine
2	tablespoons	balsamic vinegar
1	tablespoon	water
		apple juice, frozen concentrate

Sauté onions and jalapeno pepper in apple juice until desired doneness, (add apple juice slowly to get onions nicely caramelized), add plums stirring and heating thoroughly. Season with salt and pepper to taste. Add balsamic vinegar and water, sauté a few minutes longer to get flavors to blend.

Serve over grilled sliced tofu, grilled portabella mushrooms or sliced grilled sweet potatoes.

Nutritional analysis: Calories 55, Fat .03, Cholesterol 0, Carbohydrate 17, Protein 1.3, Sodium 14.

Comment: nutritional analysis does not include tofu, portabella mushrooms or sweet potatoes.

THREE FLAVORED SEAFOOD SAUCE

Serving Size: 4

Amount	Measure	Ingredient – Preparation Method
½	cup	KRAFT® Miracle Whip Nonfat Dressing
1 ½	teaspoons	dry dill weed
1	teaspoon	anisette

Combine all ingredients, chill 1-2 hours prior to serving.

Nutritional analysis: Calories 33.4, Fat 0, Cholesterol 0, Protein 0.1, Sodium 223, Potassium 13, Calcium 7

Comment: additional dill weed and anisette may be added according to taste.

NOTES:

DESSERTS

Apple or Rhubarb Crisp, page 191

APPLE OR RHUBARB CRISP

Serving Size: 12

Amount	Measure	Ingredient – Preparation Method
CRUST		
1	cup	oatmeal
1	cup	sugar, brown
1/8	teaspoon	salt
1/4	cup	soy flour
3/4	cup	flour, all-purpose
1/2	cup	Butter Buds®
FILLING		
5	cups	apples – chopped
1	cup	sugar
2	tablespoons	cornstarch

Crust: mix together dry ingredients, set aside. Dissolve 1 envelope Butter Buds in 1/2 cup hot water. Pour over dry ingredients, cut in to make crumbly mixture. Spray a 9x13 inch baking pan, pour 3/4 of the crumb mixture over bottom, set remaining crumbs aside.

Filling: in large bowl pour 5 cups of apples, cut in 1/2 inch pieces. Pour sugar and cornstarch over rhubarb, mix to coat fruit. Pour over bottom crust, top with remaining crumbs. Bake in 350 degree oven 35 minutes.

Comment: you may substitute fresh chopped rhubarb in place of the apples.

Nutritional analysis: Calories 193.5, Fat 2.1, Cholesterol 3, Carbohydrate 38.8, Protein 4, Sodium 268, Potassium 394, Calcium 108.

APPLE- CINNAMON-RAISIN BAGEL PUDDING

Serving Size: 6

Amount	Measure	Ingredient – Preparation Method
4		raisin bagels, cubed
1 1/2	cups	Egg Beaters® (99% egg substitute)
1/2	cup	brown sugar
1	teaspoon	ground cinnamon
2	cups	skim milk
1	teaspoon	vanilla
1		apple, finely chopped
1	cup	raisins

Preheat oven to 350 degrees. Lightly spray a 2-quart casserole with cooking spray. In a medium size mixing bowl, pour egg substitute, cinnamon, milk and vanilla, mix well. Arrange ingredients in casserole dish, starting with half the bagels, half the apples, half the raisins and half the egg mixture. Repeat the layers. Cover with lid. Set the casserole in oven in large pan filled halfway with boiling water. Bake for 1 1/2 hours.

Nutritional analysis: Calories 187, Fat 0.4, Cholesterol 1, Carbohydrate 50, Protein 15.

APPLE- CINNAMON-RAISIN BREAD PUDDING

Serving Size: 4

Amount	Measure	Ingredient – Preparation Method
8	slices	fat-free wheat bread
1	cup	Egg Beaters® (egg substitute)
1/4	cup	brown sugar
1	teaspoon	ground cinnamon
2	cups	skim milk
1/2	teaspoon	vanilla
1	cup	finely chopped apple
1/3	cup	raisins

Preheat oven to 350 degrees. Lightly spray a 2-quart casserole dish with cooking spray. Beat egg substitute, brown sugar, cinnamon, milk and vanilla in a bowl. Arrange ingredients, starting with half the bread, 1/2 the chopped apples, 1/2 the raisins, and 1/2 the egg mixture. Repeat the layers, ending with half the egg mixture. Set casserole in oven in a large pan filled halfway with boiling water. Bake in preheated oven for 1 hour and 15 minutes.

Nutritional analysis: Calories 251, Fat 0, Cholesterol 2, Carbohydrate 50, Protein 15, Sodium 369.

APPLE HONEY CAKE

Serving Size: 12

Amount	Measure	Ingredient – Preparation Method
2	cups	honey
3/4	cup	WONDERSLIM® Fat/Egg Substitute
1 1/3	cups	sugar
2	cups	chunky natural applesauce
4	cups	flour, all-purpose
1	teaspoon	baking soda
1	teaspoon	cinnamon
1	teaspoon	ginger

Preheat oven to 350 degrees. Combine honey and egg substitute in a large bowl. Add sugar, applesauce, flour, baking soda, cinnamon and ginger. Lightly spray 2 loaf pans with cooking spray and divide honey cake batter between the two pans. Bake in preheated oven for 50 minutes, or until toothpick comes out clean when inserted in the center of the cake.

Nutritional analysis: Calories 185, Fat 0, Cholesterol 0, Carbohydrate 44, Protein 3, Sodium 49.

APPLE PIE

Serving Size: 6

Amount	Measure	Ingredient – Preparation Method
6		tart pie apples, quartered and sliced
¾	cup	sugar
3	tablespoons	lemon juice
¼	cup	quick-cooking tapioca
1	teaspoon	cinnamon
¼	teaspoon	ground allspice
1		egg white
1 ½	cups	fat-free cinnamon-and-honey cookie crumbs

Spray a 9" pie plate with no-stick cooking spray. In a large bowl, combine the apples, sugar, lemon juice, tapioca, cinnamon and all-spice. Mix well. Cover and let stand stirring occasionally, for 15 to 20 minutes. Place the egg white in a medium size bowl and beat lightly. Add the cookie crumbs and mix well. Press into the bottom and up the sides of the pie plate. Mist and crust with no-stick spray. Spoon the apple mixture into the crust. Bake in a 350 degree oven for 45 to 60 minutes, or until the filling bubbles and the apples are tender.

Nutritional analysis: Calories 350, Fat 0.4, Cholesterol 0, Carbohydrate 86, Protein 2, Sodium 198.

APRICOT BARS

Serving Size: 18

Amount	Measure	Ingredient – Preparation Method
½	cup	soy flour
1	cup	flour, all-purpose
1	teaspoon	baking powder
¼	teaspoon	salt
1 ½	cups	oatmeal – quick cooking
1	cup	sugar, brown
¾	cup	Butter Buds®
1	cup	apricot preserves
½	cup	soy nuts, roasted – chopped fine

Sift together flours, baking powder and salt. Stir in roasted soy nuts that have been processed in food processor until finely chopped, rolled oats and sugar. Mix in Butter Buds that have been dissolved according to package directions. Spread mixture over the bottom of sprayed 9x11 inch baking dish. Spread preserves evenly over the bottom layer. Bake in a 350 degree oven for 25 to 30 minutes. Cool and cut into bars.

Nutritional analysis: Calories 146, Fat 1.1, Cholesterol 3, Carbohydrate 30, Protein 3, Sodium 299, Potassium 135, Calcium 74.

BAKED FRUIT COMPOTE

Serving Size: 8

Amount	Measure	Ingredient – Preparation Method
1	can	light cherry pie filling
3/4	cup	white wine
1	can	mandarin oranges – drained
1	can	pineapple chunks in juice
1/2	cup	dried prunes
1/2	cup	dried apricots

Preheat oven to 350 degrees. Mix all the ingredients together in a 2 quart casserole lightly sprayed with cooking spray. Bake for 45 minutes.

Nutritional analysis: Calories 140, Fat 0, Cholesterol 0, Carbohydrate 34, Protein 1, Sodium 8.

BAKED PUMPKIN CUSTARD

Serving Size: 8

Amount	Measure	Ingredient – Preparation Method
1 1/2	cups	canned pumpkin
1	12 ounce	can evaporated skim milk
1 3/4	cups	Egg Beaters® (egg substitute)
1/3	cup	orange juice
1 1/2	teaspoons	vanilla extract
1/2	cup	light brown sugar
1 1/2	teaspoons	pumpkin pie spice

Place all of the ingredients in a blender or food processor, and process until smooth. Spray a 2-quart souffle' dish with cooking spray. Pour the mixture into the dish, and place the dish in a pan filled with 1 inch of hot water. Bake in a 350 degree oven for about 1 hour and 15 minutes, or until a knife inserted in the center of the custard comes out clean. Chill for at least 8 hours before serving.

Nutritional analysis: Calories 131, Fat 0.3, Cholesterol 0, Protein 8, Sodium 130.

BLUEBERRY COBBLER

Serving Size: 8

Amount	Measure	Ingredient – Preparation Method
6	cups	frozen blueberries, thawed
3	tablespoons	cornstarch
1/3	cup	sugar
1	tablespoon	frozen orange juice concentrate – thawed

TOPPING

1/3	cup	oat bran
2/3	cup	flour
1/2	cup	nonfat buttermilk or soy milk
1	quart	nonfat vanilla ice cream

Spray a 2 1/2 quart casserole dish. Combine the blueberries, cornstarch, sugar and orange juice in a medium size bowl, and set aside for 15 minutes to allow the juices to develop. Then stir gently to mix well, then transfer to the prepared dish. Combine all of the topping ingredients except for the buttermilk or soy milk in a medium size bowl, stir to mix well. Add the milk and stir just until the dry ingredients are moistened. Drop heaping tablespoons of the batter onto the blueberry mixture to make 8 biscuits. Bake in a 375 degree oven for about 45 minutes, or until the filling is bubbly and the topping is brown. If the topping starts to brown too quickly, cover the dish loosely with foil during the last 10 minutes of baking. Remove from the oven and let sit for 10 minutes. Serve warm, topping each serving with a scoop of the ice cream.

Nutritional analysis: Calories, Fat 1, Cholesterol 2, Protein 5, Sodium 137.

CAPPUCCINO CHEESECAKE

Serving Size: 10

Amount	Measure	Ingredient – Preparation Method
7	large	fat-free graham crackers
2	tablespoons	chocolate syrup

FILLING

15	ounces	no fat ricotta cheese
1	cup	nonfat cream cheese
		1/4 cup plus 1 tablespoon flour
3/4	cup	sugar
1/2	cup	Egg Beaters® (egg substitute)
3	tablespoons	coffee liqueur
1	teaspoon	vanilla extract

TOPPING

1 1/2	cups	fresh strawberry slices

To make the crust, place the crackers in a food processor or blender. Process into fine crumbs, you should have 1 cup. Place the crumbs in small bowl, add the chocolate syrup. Stir until crumbs are moist and crumbly. Spray a 9-inch springform pan with cooking spray. Use a spoon to pat the crust mixture over the bottom and 1/4 inch up the sides. Bake in a 350 degree oven for 8 minutes. Remove from oven and set aside to cool. To make the filling place all of the ingredients in a food processor or blender and process until smooth. Pour the filling into the crust. Bake in a 350 degree oven for 40 to 50 minutes, or until center feels firm when lightly touched. Turn the oven off, and let the cake cool in the oven with the door ajar for 1 hour. Remove from oven and refrigerate for 6 hours. Release the sides of the pan, place the cheesecake on serving plate. Arrange the strawberries slices on top. Cut into wedges and serve.

Nutritional analysis: Calories 208, Fat, 0.3, Cholesterol 4, Protein 13, Sodium 270.

CARROT CAKE

Serving Size: 16

Amount	Measure	Ingredient – Preparation Method
1 ½	cups	nonfat margarine (Promise Ultra)
1	cup	sugar
1	cup	brown sugar
1	cup	Egg Beaters® (egg substitute)
3	cups	self-rising flour
2	teaspoons	cinnamon
½	teaspoon	nutmeg
¼	teaspoon	ground cloves
1	8 ounce	crushed pineapple – undrained
2	teaspoons	vanilla
3	cups	carrots – grated
1	cup	raisins
1	cup	Grape-Nuts®

In a large mixing bowl, cream together margarine, sugars, Egg Beaters, pineapple, and vanilla. Add raisins and Grape-Nut cereal. Mix well. Add the flour and spices. Mix well. Fold in the grated carrots. Pour into a bundt pan sprayed with non-fat spray. Bake in a 350 degree oven for 45 to 60 minutes. Remove from oven and cool cake upright on baking rack for 5 minutes. Remove from pan. Let cake cool completely before frosting with your favorite nonfat cream cheese frosting.

Comment: Be sure to use self-rising flour.

Nutritional analysis: Calories 244, Fat 0.5, Cholesterol 0, Carbohydrate 57, Protein 4, Sodium 385.

CHERRY CHEESECAKE

Serving Size: 12

Amount	Measure	Ingredient – Preparation Method
1 ¼	cups	fat-free graham cracker crumbs
2	tablespoons	sugar
2	tablespoons	Egg Beaters® (egg substitute)

FILLING

Amount	Measure	Ingredient – Preparation Method
15	ounces	no fat ricotta cheese
12	ounces	nonfat cream cheese
½	cup	Egg Beaters® (egg substitute)
⅓	cup	all-purpose flour
¾	cup	sugar
2	teaspoons	vanilla extract
1	tablespoon	lemon juice

TOPPING

Amount	Measure	Ingredient – Preparation Method
1 ½	cups	canned light cherry pie filling

Place the cracker crumbs, sugar and egg substitute in mixing bowl, blend until mixture is moist and crumbly. Coat a 9-inch springform pan with nonstick cooking spray. Use the back of a spoon to press the crumbs over the bottom of the pan and 1/2 inch up the sides. Dip the spoon in sugar to prevent sticking. Bake the crust in a 350 degree oven for 8 to 10 minutes. Cool the crust to room temperature. Place all of the filling ingredients in a food processor, and process until smooth. Pour the filling into the crust, and bake in a 325 degree oven for 55 to 60 minutes, or until the center feels firm when lightly touched. Turn the oven off, and let the cake cool in the oven with the door ajar for 1 hour. Remove from oven and cool another hour at room temperature. Remove from pan to serving plate. Spread the cherry filling over the top of the cooled cake. Refrigerate for 6 hours or overnight. Cut into wedges and serve.

Nutritional analysis: Calories 205, Fat 0.4, Cholesterol 10, Protein 12.6, Sodium 300.

CHOCOLATE MOUSSE

Serving Size: 6

Amount	Measure	Ingredient – Preparation Method
1 1/4	cups	MORI-NU® Lite SILKEN TOFU, FIRM
1/4	teaspoon	vanilla
1	cup	WONDERSLIM® Raspberry/Chocolate Spread
		fresh mint
		fresh raspberries

Place tofu and vanilla in food processor and blend very well. Add raspberry/ chocolate sauce and process until well blended.

Place in dessert dishes and chill overnight. Prior to serving garnish each dish with a sprig of fresh mint and fresh raspberry.

Comment: the mousse can also be chilled overnight in large bowl, next day place in pastry bag. Take low fat vanilla wafers and decorate with chocolate mousse stars. Children love these, but adults adore them!

Nutritional analysis does not include comment: Calories139.9, Fat 0, Cholesterol 0, Carbohydrate 33.5, Protein 0.2, Sodium 31.

CHOCOLATE PIE

♥

Serving Size: 8

Amount	Measure	Ingredient – Preparation Method
3		egg whites, room temperature
¼	teaspoon	cream of tartar
⅔	cup	sugar
1	tablespoon	cornstarch

CHOCOLATE FILLING

Amount	Measure	Ingredient – Preparation Method
¼	cup	cold water
1	envelope	1/4 ounce unflavored gelatin
1	can	14 ounce fat-free sweetened condensed milk
¼	cup	cocoa powder
1	teaspoon	vanilla
2	cups	fat-free sour cream
½	cup	fat-free vanilla yogurt
2	cups	fat-free whipped topping

Preheat oven to 275 degrees. Coat a 10-inch pie plate with no-stick spray. Dust with flour, shaking out the excess. Place the egg whites and cream of tartar in a large bowl. Beat with an electric mixer until foamy. In a small bowl, combine the sugar and cornstarch. Add to the egg whites, 1 tablespoon at a time, beating until stiff peaks form and the sugar dissolves. Spread the meringue carefully into the bottom and up the sides of the pie plate. Bake for 1 hour. Turn the oven off and leave the meringue in the oven until completely cooled, 2 to 3 hours. To make the filling, place the water in a cup, sprinkle with the gelatin and set aside for 5 minutes to soften. In a medium saucepan, combine the condensed milk and cocoa. Over low heat, whisk for 2 to 3 minutes, or until the cocoa is completely blended with the milk. Add the vanilla. Remove from the heat and stir in the gelatin mixture until dissolved. Cool to room temperature. Add the sour cream and yogurt, mix until well blended. Pour into the meringue shell. Chill for 2 to 3 hours, or until firm. Before serving, top with whipped topping.

Nutritional analysis: Calories 344, Fat 0.5, Cholesterol 5, Carbohydrate 74, Protein 10, Sodium 150.

CRANBERRY APPLE CRISP

Serving Size: 8

Amount	Measure	Ingredient – Preparation Method
8	cups	thinly sliced peeled apples
½	cup	fresh or frozen cranberries – coarsely chopped
⅓	cup	brown sugar
¼	cup	raisins
1	tablespoon	cornstarch
1	tablespoon	apple juice concentrate, thawed

TOPPING

²/₃	cup	quick-cooking oatmeal
3	tablespoons	soy flour (defatted)
¼	cup	brown sugar
½	teaspoon	ground cinnamon
2	tablespoons	frozen apple juice concentrate, thawed

To make the topping, combine the oatmeal, flour, sugar and cinnamon in a small bowl. Mix well. Add the apple juice and stir until moist and crumbly. Set aside. In a large bowl, combine the apples, cranberries, brown sugar, raisins, cornstarch and apple juice. Toss to mix well. Spray a 2 1/2 quart casserole dish with nonstick cooking spray. Place the filling mixture in the dish, and sprinkle with the topping. Bake in a 375 degree oven for 30 minutes. Cover the side loosely with foil and bake for 15 minutes more, or until filling is bubbly and the topping is brown. Serve warm.

Nutrition analysis: Calories 175, Fat 0.8, Cholesterol 0, Protein 1.5, Sodium 7.

CREAM CHEESE FROSTING

Serving Size: 16

Amount	Measure	Ingredient – Preparation Method
1	cup	cream cheese fat-free
1 ½	cups	ricotta cheese fat-free
½	cup	sugar
1	tablespoon	lemon juice
1 ½	teaspoons	vanilla
2	tablespoons	instant vanilla pudding mix

Place all of the ingredients, except the pudding mix in the bowl of a food processor, and process until smooth. Add the pudding mix, and process just until the frosting is well mixed. Spread the frosting over the cooled cake. Serve immediately or refrigerate.

Nutritional analysis: Calories 55, Fat 0, Cholesterol 0, Carbohydrate 8, Protein 5, Sodium 148.

CREAMY BAKED CUSTARD

Serving Size: 6

Amount	Measure	Ingredient – Preparation Method
2	cups	skim milk
1	cup	evaporated skim milk
1	cup	Egg Beaters® (egg substitute)
½	cup	sugar
2	teaspoons	vanilla extract
		ground nutmeg

Place all of the ingredients except the nutmeg in the bowl of a food processor or blender, process for 30-45 seconds to mix well. Spray a 1 1/2 quart baking dish. Pour the custard mixture into the dish. Sprinkle with nutmeg. Place the dish in a pan filled with 1 inch of hot water. Bake uncovered at 350 degrees for 1 hour and 20 minutes, or until set. When set, a sharp knife inserted in the center of the custard should come out clean. Chill for several hours or overnight before serving.

Nutritional analysis: Calories 214, Fat 0.3, Cholesterol 4, Protein 12, Sodium 220.

CRÈME BRULÉE

Serving Size: 4

Amount	Measure	Ingredient – Preparation Method
1	12.3 ounce	tofu lite, firm
1	cup	lemon curd
1	teaspoon	vanilla extract
3	teaspoons	powdered sugar
10		strawberries – sliced
		raw sugar (garnish)

Place tofu in food processor, process until smooth. Add lemon curd, vanilla and powdered sugar. Process until well blended and smooth.

Pour into mixing bowl, blend in sliced strawberries. Place in four oven-proof ramekins. Chill for 3-4 hours. Cover top with raw sugar. Place under broiler of oven until sugar has caramelized. Remove from oven and serve.

Nutritional analysis: Calories 179, Fat 2.5, Cholesterol 0, Carbohydrate 28.2, Protein 2.6.

CUSTARDS LAST STAND

Serving Size: 4

Amount	Measure	Ingredient – Preparation Method
2 ½	cups	soy milk lite
1	cup	Egg Beaters® (egg substitute)
3	tablespoons	sugar
1	teaspoon	vanilla
4	tablespoons	sugar
4	tablespoons	water

Custard Mixture:
Place 3 tablespoons sugar in mixing bowl, whisk in egg beaters. Add soy milk and vanilla. Set aside.

Carmel Sauce:
Place 4 tablespoons sugar and 4 tablespoons water in small sauce pan. Stir and heat mixture to boiling, continue boiling until mixture has caramelized. Pour into 4 ramekins. Pour custard mixture over the carmel sauce in ramekins. Place ramekins in glass baking dish in which you have added about 1/4 inch of water. Bake in 350 degree oven for 30 minutes.

Best if chilled overnight.

Nutritional analysis: Calories 160, Fat 2.9, Saturated Fat 0.3, Cholesterol 0, Carbohydrates 27.2, Protein 7.6, Sodium 104, Potassium 302, Calcium 47.

DE-LIGHTFUL LEMON CAKE

Serving Size: 12

Amount	Measure	Ingredient – Preparation Method
1		angel food cake (1 pound)
2 ¼	cups	canned lemon pie filling

TOPPING

¾	cup	nonfat lemon yogurt
1 ½	cups	nonfat whipped topping

Just before assembling the cake, make the topping by gently folding the yogurt into the whipped topping. Set aside. To assemble the cake, use a bread knife to cut the cake into 3 layers. Place the bottom cake layer on a serving platter, and spread with half of the lemon pudding. Repeat with the second layer. Top with the third cake layer, spread the topping over the top and sides of the cake. Chill the cake for 2 hours, slice and serve.

Nutritional analysis: Calories 165, Fat 0.5, Cholesterol 0, Protein 4, Sodium 238.

FROZEN FRUITY POPS

Serving Size: 8

Amount	Measure	Ingredient – Preparation Method
1		banana, cut in quarters
1	cup	crushed pineapple in juice, drained
2	cups	strawberries, hulled and sliced
1	cup	nonfat vanilla yogurt
1/4	cup	honey
8		6 ounce paper cups
8		wooden sticks

Combine banana, pineapple, strawberries, yogurt and honey in food processor or blender, and blend until very smooth. Fill paper cups with fruit mixture, place a wooden stick in the center of each, and freeze.

Nutritional analysis: Calories 101, Fat 0, Cholesterol 0, Carbohydrate 25, Protein 2, Sodium 21.

FROZEN YOGURT MELON RING DESSERT

Serving Size: 4

Amount	Measure	Ingredient – Preparation Method
4	slices	cantaloupe, cut into rings
1	cup	fresh strawberries, chopped
2		kiwi fruit, peeled, chopped
1	tablespoon	honey
2	cups	lemon or pineapple fat-free frozen yogurt

Place cantaloupe rings on individual plates. In a small bowl, combine strawberries, kiwi fruit and honey and toss lightly. Place 1/2 cup yogurt in center of each melon ring and spoon strawberry mixture over yogurt and melon.

Nutritional analysis: Calories 152, Fat 0, Cholesterol 0, Carbohydrate 40, Protein 5, Sodium 66.

FRUIT WITH CARAMEL SAUCE

Serving Size: 6

Amount	Measure	Ingredient – Preparation Method
3	medium	peaches
2		kiwi fruit – peeled and sliced
2	cups	strawberries – halved
1	cup	blueberries
2/3	cup	fat-free caramel ice cream topping
1/4	teaspoon	rum extract

Peel and cut peaches into wedges. Arrange the fruit on 6 individual dessert plates. In a small saucepan, heat topping and rum extract over medium heat until warm, stirring occasionally. Drizzle topping mixture by tablespoon over each serving.

Nutritional analysis: Calories 125, Fat 0, Cholesterol 0, Carbohydrate 32, Protein 1, Sodium 127.

KEY LIME CHEESECAKE

Serving Size: 10

Amount	Measure	Ingredient – Preparation Method
CRUST		
30		low-fat gingersnaps or graham crackers
2 1/2	tablespoons	sugar
1		egg white
CHEESECAKE		
2	tablespoons	cold water
1	teaspoon	unflavored gelatin
2	8 ounce	packages fat-free cream cheese, room temperature
1	14 ounce	can sweetened condensed milk
1/2	cup	key lime or plain lime juice
2		egg whites
2	tablespoons	cornstarch
2	teaspoons	lime rind, grated
KIWIFRUIT TOPPING		
3		kiwifruit
1 1/2	tablespoons	confectioner's sugar

Preheat the oven to 350 degrees. Coat a 9 inch springform pan with no-stick spray. Break the gingersnaps or graham crackers and place in a food processor. Process until the gingersnaps or crackers are fine crumbs (there should be 1 1/2 cups of crumbs). Add the sugar and egg white; process until blended and slightly moist. Press into the bottom and 1/2 inch up the sides of the springform pan. Back for 10 minutes, or until the crust is lightly browned. Set aside. To make the cheesecake, place the water in a cup, sprinkle with the gelatin and set aside for 5 minutes to soften. Place the cream cheese, condensed milk, lime juice, egg whites, cornstarch and lime rind in the food processor and process until smooth. Add the gelatin mixture and process until well blended. Pour into the warm crust. Bake in a 350 degree oven until a knife inserted in the center comes out clean. Cool on a wire rack, then chill for 2-3 hours. Before serving, peel and thinly slice the kiwifruit. Remove the outer ring from the springform pan and gently remove cheesecake from bottom onto a serving plate. Arrange the kiwifruit in a spiral pattern on top of the cheesecake. Dust with confectioners' sugar and serve.

Nutritional analysis: Calories 235, Fat 0.8, Cholesterol 8, Carbohydrate 45, Protein 12, Sodium 353.

LEMON BARS

Serving Size: 16

Amount	Measure	Ingredient – Preparation Method
CRUST		
24		low-fat vanilla wafers
1/3	cup	confectioner's sugar
1 1/2	teaspoons	lemon rind, grated
3	tablespoons	unsweetened applesauce
LEMON FILLING		
3/4	cup	sugar
2		egg whites
1/4	cup	Egg Beaters® (egg substitute)
3/4	cup	fat-free lemon yogurt
3 1/2	tablespoons	flour, all purpose
2	tablespoons	fresh lemon juice
1 1/2	teaspoons	lemon rind, grated
1/2	teaspoon	baking powder
		confectioner's sugar

Preheat oven to 350 degrees. Spray an 8 x 8 inch baking dish. Break the wafers into pieces and place in a food processor. Process to make crumbs. Add the confectioner's sugar, lemon rind and applesauce; process to make dough. Flour your fingers, then press the dough into the prepared baking dish. Bake for 15 to 20 minutes, or until the crust feels firm and is lightly browned. Set aside. In a medium size bowl, place the sugar, egg whites and Egg Beaters. Beat with an electric mixer until thick and smooth. Add the yogurt, flour, lemon juice, lemon rind and baking powder. Mix until smooth. Spread over the baked cookie crust. Bake in a 350 degree oven for 25 to 30 minutes or until set and lightly browned. Cool on a wire rack. Place in the freezer 1 hour before cutting into 16 bars. Keep refrigerated if not serving right away. Sprinkle with confectioner's sugar before serving.

Nutritional analysis: Calories 92, Fat 0, Cholesterol 0, Protein 1, Sodium 55.

LEMON CHEESECAKE WITH STRAWBERRY TOPPING

Serving Size: 12

Amount	Measure	Ingredient – Preparation Method
3/4	cup	fat-free granola
2	cups	cottage cheese, (fat-free)
8	ounces	cream cheese fat-free
1/4	cup	flour, all purpose plus
1/2	tablespoon	flour, all-purpose
1 1/4	cups	sugar
4		egg whites – beaten
1	tablespoon	lemon juice
1	tablespoon	lemon rind – grated
2	cups	strawberries – sliced

Preheat oven to 325 degrees. Place granola in food processor or blender, and blend until slightly ground. Lightly spray a 8 inch springform pan with cooking spray and place ground granola in pan. Combine cottage cheese and cream cheese in food processor or blender; process until smooth. Add flour, sugar egg whites, lemon juice and lemon rind to cheese mixture. Pour into prepared pan and bake in preheated oven for 50 minutes. Turn oven off and let cheesecake remain in oven for another hour, with the door slightly open. Remove pan from oven and allow cheesecake to cool completely before removing sides of pan. Top cheesecake with sliced strawberries. Or if you prefer use blueberries or raspberries.

Nutritional analysis: Calories 155, Fat 0, Cholesterol, 5, Carbohydrate 29, Protein 9, Sodium 228.

LEMON DESSERT ROLL

Serving Size: 8

Amount	Measure	Ingredient – Preparation Method
3/4	cup	granulated sugar
2/3	cup	cake flour, sifted
6	large	egg whites
3/4	teaspoon	vanilla extract
1/4	teaspoon	cream of tartar
2	tablespoons	confectioner's sugar
1/4	cup	granulated sugar
2	tablespoons	cornstarch
1 1/4	cups	evaporated skim milk
3	tablespoons	lemon juice
1	tablespoon	lemon rind, grated

Preheat the oven to 300 degrees. Lightly spray a 15"x10"x1" jelly roll pan, spray again, and set aside. Sift 6 tablespoons of the granulated sugar with the flour onto a piece of wax paper and set aside. In a large bowl with an electric mixer, beat the egg whites, vanilla extract, and cream of tartar at moderate speed until foamy, then beat in the remaining granulated sugar, 1 tablespoon at a time. Increase the speed to moderately high and beat the whites until they hold very soft peaks. (Do not overbeat the whites or the cake will be tough.) Sift 1/4 of the flour mixture over the egg whites and, with a rubber spatula, fold in gently but thoroughly, repeat until all the flour is incorporated. With the spatula, spread the batter evenly in the pan and bake for 20 to 25 minutes or until the cake is pale tan and the top springs back when touched. With a thin bladed metal spatula, loosen the cake around the edges and invert immediately onto a clean dish towel that has been sprinkled with 1 tablespoon of the confectioners sugar. Peel off the wax paper and trim off any crisp edges. Sprinkle the cake with the remaining confectioners sugar and, starting at the narrow end, roll it up in the towel, cool seam side down for 1 hour on a wire rack.

Continued on following page.

MINT BROWNIE PIE A' LA MODE

Serving Size: 10

Amount	Measure	Ingredient – Preparation Method
1/2	cup	plus 2 tablespoons flour
1/2	cup	quick-cooking oatmeal
1	cup	sugar
1/2	cup	cocoa powder
1/4	cup	plus 2 tablespoons plain nonfat yogurt
2	tablespoons	water
4		egg whites
1	teaspoon	vanilla extract
5	cups	nonfat vanilla or mint ice cream
1/2	cup	confectioner's sugar
2	drops	peppermint extract
1	drop	green food coloring
2	teaspoons	skim milk

In a medium-sized bowl, combine the flour, oatmeal, sugar, cocoa and baking powder. Stir to mix well. Stir in the yogurt, water, egg whites and vanilla. coat a 9-inch round pan with cooking spray.

Nutritional analysis: Calories 187, Fat 0.2, Cholesterol 1, Carbohydrate 41, Protein 6, Sodium 85.

VARIATION: Strawberry Dessert Roll. Prepare the cake as directed. For the filling, in a food processor or blender, process 1/2 cup fresh strawberries for 30 seconds or until smooth. In a small heavy saucepan, combine 3 tablespoons sugar and 2 tablespoons cornstarch. Blend in 3/4 cup evaporated skim milk, the pureed strawberries, and 1 1/4 teaspoons lemon juice. Set over moderate heat and cook, stirring for 3 minutes or until thickened and clear. Remove from the heat, stir in 1/2 cup thinly sliced strawberries, cover, and cool to room temperature. fill, roll and serve dessert as directed above.

Meanwhile, prepare the filling. In a small heavy saucepan, combine the granulated sugar and cornstarch. Blend in the milk and lemon juice, set over moderate heat, and cook, stirring, for 3 minutes or until thickened and clear. Remove from heat and stir in the lemon rind. cover and cool to room temperature, whisking occasionally. To fill the cake, unroll the cooled cake and remove the towel. Whisk the filling until smooth, then spread it evenly over the cake, leaving 1/2 inch margins all around. Reroll the cake, place it seam side down on an oblong platter, and sift the remaining confectioners sugar over it. Using a sharp serrated knife in a gentle seesaw motion, cut the roll slightly on the bias into 1-inch slices.

Spread the batter evenly in the pan. Bake in a 325 degree oven about 25 minutes, or just until edges are firm and the center is almost set. Be careful not to overbake. Cool to room temperature. To make the glaze, combine the confectioner's sugar, peppermint extract, food coloring and milk in a small saucepan. Heat on low heat until runny. Drizzle the glaze back and forth over the cooled pie, set aside for a few minutes to allow the glaze to set. Cut the pie into wedges. Transfer the wedges to serving dishes, top each with 1/2 cup of nonfat ice cream.

Nutritional analysis: Calories 246, Fat 0.8, Carbohydrate 0, Protein 8, Sodium 132.

OATMEAL RAISIN COOKIES

Serving Size: 24

Amount	Measure	Ingredient – Preparation Method
1	cup	flour, all-purpose
1	teaspoon	baking powder
½	teaspoon	baking soda
½	teaspoon	salt
1	teaspoon	ground cinnamon
1	cup	brown sugar, packed
¼	cup	unsweetened applesauce
3	tablespoons	Egg Beaters® (egg substitute)
2	teaspoons	water
1	tablespoon	WONDERSLIM® Fat/Egg Substitute
1	teaspoon	vanilla
1 ⅓	cups	quick-cooking oatmeal
1	cup	raisins

In a small bowl, combine the flour, baking powder, soda, salt and cinnamon. Mix well. In a large bowl, combine the brown sugar, applesauce, Egg Beaters, water Wonderslim egg and fat substitute and vanilla. Mix well. Stir in the flour mixture. Add the oatmeal and raisins, mix well. Drop by rounded teaspoonfuls, onto a sprayed cookie sheet. Bake in a 375 degree oven for 10 to 12 minutes, or until lightly browned. Remove the cookies from the baking sheet and let cool on a wire rack.

Nutritional analysis: Calories 55, Fat 0, Cholesterol 0, Carbohydrate 12, Protein 0.5, Sodium 55.

OLD-FASHIONED CHOCOLATE CAKE

Serving Size: 18

Amount	Measure	Ingredient – Preparation Method
1 ¾	cups	flour, all-purpose
½	cup	soy flour
1 ¾	cups	sugar
⅔	cup	cocoa
1 ¼	teaspoons	baking soda
1 ½	teaspoons	baking powder
1	teaspoon	salt
½	cup	MORI-NU Lite SILKEN TOFU , FIRM
1 ½	cups	water
1	teaspoon	vanilla
½	cup	applesauce, unsweetened

Preheat oven to 350 degrees. Lightly spray and flour a 13x9x 2 inch baking pan (or 2-8 inch round cake pans.) In large bowl, sift together flour, sugar, cocoa, baking powder, baking soda, and salt. Set aside. In a food processor, puree tofu with 1/2 cup of the water. Add remaining water and vanilla and process until mixture is smooth. Add the dry ingredients and process on high until mixed. Add applesauce and process on high until completely mixed. Spread batter into pan or pans and bake for 35 to 40 minutes (30 to 35 minutes for round pans), or until a toothpick inserted in the center comes out clean. Remove cake(s) from oven and let cool completely before frosting.

Nutritional analysis: Calories 151, Fat 1.3, Cholesterol 0, Carbohydrate 31.3, Protein 3, Sodium 240.

PEACH-BANANA BREAD PUDDING

Serving Size: 8

Amount	Measure	Ingredient – Preparation Method
8	slices	fat-free bread, cut into 1 inch cubes
1 ½	cups	evaporated skim milk
4		egg whites, lightly beaten
½	cup	frozen apple juice concentrate – thawed
1	16 ounce	can juice packed peaches, drained chopped
2		bananas – sliced
1	teaspoon	lemon juice
1 ¼	teaspoons	cinnamon
¼	teaspoon	ground nutmeg
⅓	cup	lite maple syrup
1	teaspoon	vanilla

Preheat oven to 325 degrees. In a large bowl combine all of the ingredients. Mix well. Pour mixture into a 8x11 inch baking dish lightly sprayed with cooking spray. Bake 60 to 65 minutes, or until toothpick inserted in the center comes out clean. Cool slightly. Can also be served cold.

Nutritional analysis: Calories 199, Fat 0, Cholesterol 2, Carbohydrate 33, Protein 8, Sodium 199.

PINEAPPLE CHEESECAKE

Serving Size: 12

Amount	Measure	Ingredient – Preparation Method
¾	cup	fat-free granola
2	cups	cottage cheese, fat-free
8	ounces	cream cheese fat-free
¼	cup	flour, all-purpose, plus
2	tablespoons	flour, all-purpose
1 ¼	cups	sugar
4		egg whites – beaten
1	teaspoon	vanilla
1	cup	pineapple – drained

Preheat oven to 325 degrees. Place granola in food processor and process until ground. Lightly spray an 8 inch springform pan with cooking spray and place ground granola in pan. Combine cottage cheese and cream cheese in food processor or blender, and blend until smooth. Add flour, sugar, egg white and vanilla and blend well. Stir pineapple into cheese mixture, then pour into prepared pan. Bake cheesecake in preheated oven 1 hour. Turn oven off and let the cake remain in the oven for another hour, with the door slightly open. Remove from oven and allow cake to cool completely before removing sides of pan.

Nutritional analysis: Calories 158, Fat 0, Cholesterol 5, Carbohydrate 32, Sodium 228.

PINEAPPLE UPSIDE-DOWN CAKE

Serving Size: 8

Amount	Measure	Ingredient – Preparation Method
½	cup	brown sugar, packed
¼	cup	fat-free prepared caramel topping
6	slices	canned pineapple, reserve juice
6	large	cherries, pitted
2		egg whites, room temperature
¼	teaspoon	salt
1	teaspoon	vanilla
½	cup	sugar
¾	cup	flour, all-purpose
¾	teaspoon	baking powder

Preheat oven to 350 degrees. Coat a 9 inch round cake with no-stick spray. Spread the brown sugar evenly over the bottom of the pan, drizzle evenly with the caramel topping. Top with the pineapple in a decorative pattern. Place a cherry in the center of each pineapple slice. Sprinkle with 2 tablespoons of reserved pineapple juice. Set aside. Place the egg whites and salt in a large mixing bowl. Beat with an electric mixer until soft peaks form. Beat in the vanilla. Gradually beat in the sugar until the whites are stiff. In a small bowl, sift together the flour and baking powder. Stir half the flour mixture over the egg whites. Gently fold in with a large spatula. Fold 1/4 cup of the reserved pineapple juice into the egg-white mixture. Sift the remaining flour mixture over the egg-white mixture and fold in. Spread the batter evenly over the pineapple mixture. Bake for 30 to 35 minutes, or until a toothpick inserted in the center comes out clean. Cool in the pan 2 to 3 minutes, invert onto a serving plate. Cool for 1 to 2 hours before serving.

Nutritional analysis: Calories 220, Fat 0.2, Cholesterol 0, Carbohydrate 54, Protein 2.5, Sodium 170.

QUICK PUDDING PARFAITS

Serving Size: 6

Amount	Measure	Ingredient – Preparation Method
1	cup	skim milk
1	8 ounce	container nonfat lemon yogurt
½	teaspoon	lemon peel – grated
1	small	package instant vanilla pudding
3	cups	fresh fruit of your choice, sliced in bite size pieces

Combine milk, lemon peel and pudding mix in a small bowl. Beat pudding mixture 2 minutes a low speed or until mixture has slightly thickened. In 6 parfait glasses, make two alternate layers beginning with the fruit. Chill until serving time. Garnish with sliced fruit.

Nutritional analysis: Calories 125, Fat 0, Cholesterol 1, Carbohydrate 28, Protein 3, Sodium 142.

RHUBARB SAUCE

Serving Size: 4

Amount	Measure	Ingredient – Preparation Method
1	pound	fresh rhubarb, cut into 1" lengths or 1 pound frozen rhubarb pieces
1/4	cup	fresh squeezed orange juice
2	tablespoons	lemon juice
1 1/2	teaspoons	orange rind, grated
1/2	teaspoon	ground cinnamon
1	cup	sugar

In a large saucepan, combine the rhubarb, orange juice, lemon juice, orange rind, cinnamon and sugar. Stir well to combine. Bring to a boil over medium-high heat. Reduce the heat to low, cover and simmer, stirring occasionally, for 25 to 30 minutes, or until rhubarb is tender. Serve warm or cold. Excellent served over fat-free vanilla ice cream or frozen yogurt.

Nutritional analysis: Calories 175, Fat 0, Cholesterol 0, Carbohydrate 45, Protein 1, Sodium 5.

RICE PUDDING WITH PEACHES

Serving Size: 8

Amount	Measure	Ingredient – Preparation Method
2	cups	water
3/4	cup	long grain white rice
1	14 oz can	fat-free sweetened condensed milk
2		egg whites
1	teaspoon	ground cinnamon
3		peaches, sliced

In a no-stick medium size saucepan over medium -high heat, bring 1 3/4 cups of the water to a boil. Add the rice. Return to a boil, reduce the heat to low, cover, and simmer for 15 to 20 minutes, or until the rice is tender and the water is absorbed. While the rice is simmering, in a large saucepan, combine well the condensed milk, egg whites, cinnamon and the remaining 1/4 cup water. Cook over medium heat, stirring constantly, for 10 to 15 minutes, or until slightly thicken. Remove from the heat, stir in the rice. Refrigerate for 1 to 2 hours. Spoon the pudding into 8 dessert dishes and top with sliced peaches before serving.

Nutritional analysis: Calories 240, Fat 0, Cholesterol 4, Carbohydrate 52, Protein 6, Sodium 68.

SOY BRITTLE

Serving Size: 4

Amount	Measure	Ingredient – Preparation Method
½	cup	roasted soy nuts
2	tablespoons	sugar

Place soy nuts and sugar in small saute pan, heat over medium high heat stirring constantly until sugar has crystallized. Pour mixture onto wax paper, cool. Break into bite size pieces to serve.

Nutritional analysis: Calories 138.1, Fat 5.7, Carbohydrate 13.8, Cholesterol 0, Protein 7.9, Sodium 0.

Comment: dehulled split, non salted soynuts work the best.

STRAWBERRY - BANANA SORBET

Serving Size: 6

Amount	Measure	Ingredient – Preparation Method
⅓	cup	sugar
⅔	cup	water
2	tablespoons	light corn syrup
1		banana – sliced
2	cups	strawberries

Combine the sugar, water and corn syrup in a small saucepan and mix well. Bring mixture to a boil and boil 1 minute. Cool slightly and refrigerate 30 to 45 minutes or until chilled. Place banana and strawberries in a food processor or blender, and process until blended. Gradually add chilled sugar mixture and continue blending until smooth. Pour mixture into baking dish, cover and freeze until firm, about 3 to 4 hours. Stir mixture once during freezing time.

Nutritional analysis: Calories 92, Fat 0, Cholesterol 0, Carbohydrate 24, Protein 0.5, Sodium 10.

STRAWBERRY-RASPBERRY-ORANGE SHORTCAKE

Serving Size: 8

Amount	Measure	Ingredient – Preparation Method
2	8 ounce	containers nonfat vanilla yogurt
2	tablespoons	frozen orange juice concentrate – thawed
2	cups	fresh strawberries – sliced
1	10 ounce	package frozen raspberries – thawed
1		package fat-free pound cake, cut into 8 slices

Combine the yogurt and orange juice in a mixing bowl and blend well. In a separate bowl, combine strawberries and raspberries and mix lightly. To serve, place cake slices on individual dessert plates. Spoon 1/3 cup fruit mixture over each slice and top each with 3 tablespoons yogurt mixture.

Nutritional analysis: Calories 269, Fat 0, Cholesterol 1, Carbohydrate 60, Protein 7, Sodium 275.

STRAWBERRY TART ♥

Serving Size: 8

Amount	Measure	Ingredient – Preparation Method
TART		
3		egg whites, room temperature
1/2	teaspoon	cream of tartar
		pinch of salt
1/2	teaspoon	vanilla
3/4	cup	sugar
3/4	cup	flour, all purpose
TOPPING		
2	cups	fresh strawberries, sliced
1/3	cup	red currant jelly
1	cup	fat-free whipped topping

Preheat oven to 375 degrees. Coat a 10 inch pie pan with no-stick spray. Dust with flour, shaking out the excess. Place the egg whites, cream of tartar and the salt in a large mixing bowl. Beat with an electric mixer until soft peaks form. Beat in the vanilla. Gradually beat in 1/4 cup of the sugar until the whites are stiff, but not dry. In a medium bowl, sift together the flour and the remaining 1/2 cup of sugar. Sift over the egg whites. Gently fold in with a spatula. Spread the batter in the pie plate. Bake for 20 to 25 minutes, or until a toothpick inserted in the center comes out clean. Cool on a wire rack. With a sharp knife, gently loosen the edges of the tart and place on a serving plate. Arrange the strawberries over the top of the tart. Place the jelly in a small saucepan. Heat over low heat until liquid. Spoon over the berries. Top with the whipped topping just before serving.

Nutritional analysis: Calories 175, Fat 0.3, Cholesterol 0, Carbohydrate 40, Protein 2.8, Sodium 35.

VEGE FUEL RICE PUDDING

Serving Size: 8

Amount	Measure	Ingredient – Preparation Method
1	cup	white rice
4	scoops	VEGE FUEL® (TWINLAB® protein powder)
1	quart	non-fat milk
12	packets	Equal® sweetner
2	teaspoons	cinnamon
1	teaspoon	nutmeg
2	tablespoons	vanilla extract

Using a blender, dissolve the Vege Fuel in the milk. Combine this mixture with the rice in a 2-quart saucepan. Slowly bring the mixture to a boil, stirring constantly. As the mixture begins to boil, reduce the heat to low. Cover and cook for 20 to 30 minutes, until the rice is very tender and the liquid has thickened. Remove from the heat and stir in the cinnamon, nutmeg, sweetener, and vanilla. Pour the mixture into a 9 x 13 inch baking dish and sprinkle the top with more cinnamon. Cover with plastic wrap and refrigerate overnight.

Nutritional analysis: Calories 131, Fat 0, Carbohydrate 14, Protein 17.

VEGE FUEL STRAWBERRY FROZEN YOGURT

Serving Size: 4

Amount	Measure	Ingredient – Preparation Method
32	ounces	non-fat plain yogurt
2	scoops	VEGE FUEL® (TWINLAB® protein powder)
10	packets	Equal® sweetner
6	ounces	(1/2 jar) Smucker's light sugar-free strawberry fruit spread

Divide the yogurt in half and place each half into a fine strainer suspended over a bowl. Cover with plastic wrap and refrigerate for 24 hours. The only way to fortify the yogurt with Vege Fuel is to separate the liquid (the whey), mix the Vege Fuel with the whey, and then add the whey back to the solids. Be sure to mix vigorously with a wire whisk.

Add the strawberry fruit spread and the sweetener to the fortified yogurt, cover and refrigerate for at least 2 hours. Process the yogurt according to your ice cream maker's directions. Divide the finished product into 4 separate containers and store in the freezer.

Nutritional analysis: Calories 274, Fat 0, Carbohydrate 45, Protein 23.

VEGE FUEL VANILLA CUSTARD

Serving Size: 4

Amount	Measure	Ingredient – Preparation Method
6		egg whites
1	cup	non-fat milk
2	scoops	VEGE FUEL® (TWINLAB® protein powder)
6	packets	Sweet'n Low® sweetener
2	tablespoons	vanilla extract
¼	teaspoon	ground nutmeg

Preheat the oven to 325 degrees. Combine the ingredients in a blender and pulse just enough to dissolve any lumps. Pour the mixture into a small aluminum loaf pan. Bake the custard in a water bath. (Place 1 inch boiling water in a 9 x 13 inch baking pan.) Place the loaf pan in center. Bake for 1 hour and 15 minutes or until firm. Let cool, then refrigerate. Serve cold.

Nutritional analysis: Calories 111, Fat 0, Carbohydrate 5, Protein 19.

DEVANSOY FARMS, INC.
P.O. Box 885
Carroll, IA 51401
Contact: Bev Tierney
Phone: 712-792-9665
Fax: 712-792-2712
Soy Products: Soy Flour, Soymilk Drinks, Soymilk Powders, Tofu Powder
Product Names: Solait, Enzact, Soy Roast
Distribution: National, Supermarkets, Health/Natural Food Stores
To Locate Product: Contact company
Classification: Manufacturer

DIXIE USA
P.O. Box 55549
Houston, TX 77255
Contact: Bob Beeley
Phone: 800-233-3668
Fax: 713-688-4881
Email: info@dixieusa.com
Soy Products: Meat Alternatives (Meat Analogs), Soynut Butter, Tofu Powder
Product Names: Beef Not, Chicken Not, Fat Not, Fat Not Creme It (tofu powder), Fat Not® ShakeMate, Nutlettes soy breakfast cereal, Beanut Butter
Distribution: National, Direct Mail/Catalogs
To Locate Product: Contact company
Classification: Direct Mail/Catalog

EDEN FOODS, INC.
701 Tecumseh Road
Clinton, MI 49236
Contact: Sally Trombley, Sales Manager
Phone: 517-456-7424
Fax: 517-456-7025
Email: edeninfo@eden-foods.com
Soy Products: Miso, Organically Grown Soybeans, Soy Sauce & Soy Sauce Products, Soymilk Drinks, Tamari & Tamari Products, Tofu & Tofu Products, Whole Soybeans
Product Names: Edensoy Soy Beverages, Edensoy Extra Soy Beverages, Eden Blend (soy/rice) Beverage, Eden Misos, Eden Shoyu Soy Sauce & Tamari, Eden Dried Tofu
Distribution: International, Supermarkets, Health/Natural Food Stores
To Locate Product: Call company at 1-800-248-0320
Classification: Manufacturer, Distributor

MIRAGE FINE FOODS
PASTO "Pasta for the next Millennium"
see page XIII
3625 Del Amo Boulevard, Suite 390
Torrance, CA 90503
Contact: Tom McReynolds
Phone: 800-405-9214
Fax: 310-793-1622
Available Flavors: Regular, herb-garlic, spinach, tomato-basil, lemon-pepper, beet, garlic-parsley, artichoke, sesame, whole wheat, jalapeño, chili rojo
Available Forms: Rotelli, noodle (four sizes), stars, rigatoni, yolanda, hearts, large/small elbow, ziti, ABC, ditalini, corkscrews, large/small shells, rosmarino or angel hair

MORINAGA NUTRITIONAL FOODS, INC.
2050 West 190th Street, Suite 110
Torrance, CA 90504
Contact: Tom McReynolds
Phone: 310-787-0200
Fax: 310-787-2727
Soy Products: Tofu & Tofu Products
Product Names: Mori-Nu Silken Tofu,
Mori-Nu Silken "Lite" Tofu, Tofu Magic
Cookbook, Tofu Magic Cooking Video,
Tofu and You (weight loss/healthy eating
guide), Tofu Times Newsletter
Distribution: National, Supermarkets,
Asian Food Stores, Health/Natural Food Stores
To Locate Product: Look in health or Asian
food stores and major supermarkets or call
1-800-NOW-TOFU
Classification: Distributor

TWINLAB
150 Motor Parkway
Hauppauge, NY 11788
Contact: Customer Service Department
Phone: 516-467-3140 EXT. 8185
Fax: 516-630-3486
Soy Products: Vege Fuel®, a highly digestible
protein powder that contains Supro®, a 100%
pure isolated Soy (all-vegetable) protein. A
complete protein source fat free, lactose free
with no sugar or artificial sweeteners. Use it in
cooking to create low fat, high protein dishes or
in shakes for a nutritious drink. Vege Fuel is
available unflavored and in Chocolate,
Strawberry-banana and Chocolate Peanut
flavors.

Other TWINLAB Soy products or products
containing soy isoflavone concentrate or soy
phytoestrogen concentrate are:
Maxi Life® DHEA Anti-oxidant Formula
Maxi Life® DHEA Women's Formula
Maxi Life® Women's Bone Protector
Maxi Life® Women's Phytoestrogen Protector
Maxi Life® Women's Skin Protector
Maxi Life® Men's Protector
Maxi Life® Prostate Protector
Maxi Life® Phytonutrient Protector
Maxi Life® Soy Cocktail
Maxi Life® Mega Soy
Distribution: Health/Natural Food Stores
including GNC and Vitamin World
(for selected products).

WORTHINGTON FOODS, INC.
900 Proprietors Road
Worthington, OH 43085-3194
Contact: David Maxwell
Phone: 614-885-9511
Fax: 614-885-2594
Soy Products: Meat Alternatives (Meat
Analogs), Okara, Soymilk Drinks, Soynut
Butter, Tofu & Tofu Products
Product Names: Morningstar Farms
products (Prime Patties, Vege-Patties, Chik
Patties, Deli Franks, Breakfast Links, Patties
and Strips, Grillers) also look for Worthington
Food products and Loma Linda products and
Natural Touch Okara Frozen Patties
Distribution: International, Supermarkets,
Health/Natural Food Stores
To Locate Product: Check Seventh Day
Adventist book centers or contact company
Classification: Manufacturer

APPENDIX A

PLANT PROTEIN SUBSTITUTION

Food Ingredient	Soyfood Substitution	Serving Size	Fat Grams Saved	Cholesterol Milligrams Saved	Calories Saved
Ground Beef (85% lean)	1/2 cup textured vegetable protein granules (plain or beef flavord), reconstituted	3 ounce portion, cooked	14	71	99
Egg (as a leavening agent in baking)	1/4 cup silken "Lite" firm tofu, mashed	equivalent to 1 egg	4.5	213	53
Cheddar Cheese	soy-based cheddar cheese	per ounce	4	30	36
Dairy Whole Milk	regular soymilk or regular reconstituted instant soymilk	8 ounces	4	33	10
Dairy 2% Milk	soymilk – lite or reduced fat or reduced fat reconstituted instant soymilk	8 ounces	3	18	20
Chicken Breast (without skin, small chunks)	textured vegetable protein small chunks (chicken flavored) 1/2 cup rehydrated	3 ounce portion, cooked	3	77	58
Sour Cream	tofu sour cream	1 tablespoon	2.5	5	19
Egg (as a leavening agent in baking)	1/4 cup soft tofu, mashed	equivalent to 1 egg	2.5	213	33
Ricotta Cheese (part skim)	tofu, firm, mashed to ricotta consistency	1 tablespoon	no difference	5	no difference

Sources: USDA Human Nutrition Service, Agriculture Handbook, #18-16, Composition of Food, Legumes and Legume Products; and product information.

APPENDIX B

TRICKS ON CONVERTING RECIPES TO HEALTHY DISHES
No need to give up what you like just change your recipe.

In place of:	Substitute
butter, margarine, oils, or shortening	defatted broth, butter substitutes, nonfat yogurt, pureed fruits, nonfat or lowfat buttermilk, nonstick vegetable sprays, applesauce, dealcholized wine or beer
whole eggs	two beaten egg whites, egg substitutes
whole milk or other dairy products	nonfat varieties of milk, cheese, yogurt, etc.
cream cheese	yogurt cheese, nonfat cream cheese
cream	evaporated skim milk
mayonnaise	whipped nonfat cottage cheese
nuts and seeds	grapenuts cereal, fat free granola
broths	unsalted homemade vegetable broth
marinades	fruit juices, vinegars, fat free dressings
salt	lemon, herbs, spices
white flour	blended oats, whole grain flours
sugar or honey	fructose, dried fruit, fruit concentrate, pureed fruit, blackstrap molasses
dough or crumb crusts	filo dough, grapenuts cereal crumb crust
chocolate	cocoa powder combined with mixed fruit concentrate
meringue	egg whites combined with vanilla and fructose

ADDITIONAL RECOMMENDATIONS

- Green Giant "Harvest Burgers for Recipes" can be substituted for Morningstar Farms Ground Meatless.

- Use Worcestershire Sauce without Anchovies instead of regular Worcestershire Sauce.

- Use Cream of Mushroom Soup Recipe, page 55, instead of Healthy Choice Cream of Mushroom Soup.

- Use EDEN "EXTRA" ORGANIC SOY BEVERAGE instead of regular EDEN ORGANIC SOY BEVERAGE for extra fortified nutrients.

ADVANCED RESEARCH PRESS PUBLICATIONS
(To Order Call 1-888-841-8007)

The Cooking Cardiologist (Video - 50 Minutes) - Dr. Richard Collins, a cardiologist and leading researcher on reversing heart disease discusses and demonstrates how to cook delicious healthy meals that can lessen the risk of cardiovascular disease and improve one's overall health - 50 minute video. $19.95

The Cooking Cardiologist by Dr. Richard Collins - over 350 luscious recipes to lower cholesterol reduce the risk of heart disease, lower weight and improve health through the addition of plant proteins, fiber, and foods high in 3-omega fatty acids to your favorite recipes. Hard cover, 224 pages. $21.95

The Consumer's Guide To Herbal Medicine by Dr. Steven B. Karch, M.D. - a professional medical review of 65 of the most widely used herbs, their use, benefits and effectiveness; safety considerations, drug interactions, including German Government Commission E recommendations of which every user of herbs should be aware. Hard cover, 240 pages. $29.95

Tomato Power by James F Scheer with Forward by James F Balch, M.D. - discusses the benefits of a super-antioxidant, lycopene, that can slow aging and reduce heart disease and cancer risks. Soft cover, 116 pages. $12.95

Sex Pills A-Z, from Androstenedione to Zinc. What Works and What doesn't by Dr. Carlon M. Colker, M.D. - examines a plethora of sex enhancing substances for added pleasure, better sex, longer sex, restoring sex drive, reversing sexual dysfunction and improving sexual powers. Soft cover, 140 pages. $14.95

Optimum Sports Nutrition, Your Competitive Edge, by Dr. Michael Colgan - a complete guide to the nutritional requirements of athletes. Soft cover, 562 pages. $24.95

Muscular Development magazine - brings its readers the very best and latest scientific information on strength training, physique development, nutrition, health and fitness in an entertaining and contemporary format. 12 issues. ($2.50/copy - 50% off cover price). $19.95

Living Longer In The Boomer Age by Dr. John L. Zenk M.D. - discusses integrating alternative and conventional medicine. He describes the benefits of a new miracle anti-aging miracle supplement, 7-Keto DHEA for improving the immune system, losing fat and enhancing memory. Soft cover, 160 pages. $9.95

Periodization Breakthrough! The Ultimate Training System by Drs. Fleck and Kraemer. A straightforward explanation of periodized training. An essential system for successful strength training. Hard cover, 182 pages. $19.95

Muscle Meals by John Romano - a cookbook for bodybuilders and all athletes featuring a delicious array of easy-to-prepare energy-packed low-fat meals. Written by culinary expert, TV chef on ESPN's American Muscle Meals. Hard cover, 221 pages. $19.95

Mike Mentzer (New Advanced) High Intensity Training Program - a series of 4 audio-taped lectures, each approximately 50 minutes, by Mike Mentzer, Mr. Universe Champion, student and master of the art of bodybuilding. Included with these tapes is a 40 page High Intensity Training Program Guide; all attractively packaged. $39.95

These items can also be ordered via the internet - www.advancedresearchpress.com, click on the product mall to view.

NOTES: